Buddhism as/in Performance

Emerging Perceptions in Buddhist Studies
(ISSN 0971-9512)

Emerging Perceptions in Buddhist Studies, no. 11

Buddhism
as/in
Performance

Analysis of Meditation and Theatrical Practice

by
David E. R. George

D.K.Printworld(P)Ltd.
NEW DELHI - 110 015

Cataloging in Publication Data — DK

George, David E. R., 1939 –
    Buddhism as/in Performance.
    (Emerging perceptions in Buddhist studies; no. 11).
    Includes bibliographical references (p.   ).
    Includes index.

    1. Knowledge, Theory of (Buddhism). 2. Hinayana
Buddhism.   3. Tantric Buddhism. 4. Mahayana Buddhism.
I. Title.   II. Series: Emerging perceptions in Buddhist
studies; no. 11.

ISBN 81-246-0123-2

First Published in India in 1999

Published and printed by:
D.K. Printworld (P) Ltd.
Regd. office : *'Sri Kunj'*, F-52, Bali Nagar
New Delhi - 110 015
Phones : (011) 545-3975, 546-6019; *Fax* : (011) 546-5926
E-mail: dkprint@4mis.com

Preface

PERFORMANCE and Buddhism are both contemporary intellectual growth-industries in the West, even — some would argue — the foundations of a new paradigm, a new cognitive model with its own and very different Epistemology and Ontology, its own radically new ways to look at Time, Person, Experience. . . .

So it seems obvious that one should want to bring them together.

At the same time, studies of the performing arts from a philosophical viewpoint — let alone as a philosophical paradigm — are not very common — about as much so as studies of Buddhism as a performing art.

The reason and legitimacy for bringing the two together will be argued in detail in the pages which follow but their genesis lies in a personal history. I came to Buddhism after twenty years studying and writing about Hinduism. Hindu performing arts attracted me as a radical challenge, alternative and inspiration for Western theatre, one which I then discovered went far beyond and deeper than practice. If Hindu theatre is radically different from Western the reason lies in Indian culture and, beneath that, in the philosophical paradigms underlying it — in its basic epistemology, its conceptions of Time, Space, Person. . .

That resulted in a number of articles, some productions and two books[1] after which I turned to Buddhism — with the obvious

---

1. Cf. the articles: "Ritual Drama — a theoretical Essay", *Asian Theater Journal*, Vol. 4, no. 2. University of Hawaii, 1987, pp. 127-65; "On Ambiguity", *Theatre Research International*, Glasgow, 1988, pp. 71-85; "The Tempest in Bali — a Director's Log", *Performing Arts*

→

question: if Hindu theatre reflects and presents the experience of a cosmology and a psychology radically different from the West, did Buddhism also produce one too? Is there Buddhist theatre and, if so, does it present a similar challenge to Western philosophy as much as to Western theatrical practice?

At the same time as this intellectual journey, my own interests in theatre — like those of so many others — had also shifted — from Theatre to Performance. Performance began to appear as a 'third reality', one separate from Text and form Theatre, one we are only just beginning to take seriously in its own right — as a primary reality, or rather primary event which precedes all others. That already generates a radical questioning of Western philosophy, predominantly its historical reluctance to take Events seriously as possible fundamental components of universes. In our century, some Western philosophers have begun to investigate Events as necessary complements of the Objects and Substances it has traditionally preferred[2] but nowhere near to the same extent as Buddhists had done over two thousand years ago. Because the real excitement began when I discovered that the two interests — in Buddhist philosophical paradigms and cultural history on the one hand, and Performance as a 'third reality' on the other — not only met but mutually fed one another — a process I illustrate and argue at length in Part One of what follows. There I have attempted to present:

1. first the case for Performance as an Epistemology, one which perhaps reflects and expresses contemporary needs better than any other, to the extent that it can be proposed as a new cultural paradigm.

→   *Journal*, New York, Special Interculturalism Issue, 1989, pp. 84-107; "Performance as Paradigm: the Example of Bali", *Modern Drama*, 35, 1992, pp. 1-9; "Performance Epistemology", *Performance Research*, (Journal of the Centre for Performance Research), 1996, pp. 16-25.

    Books: *India: Three Ritual Dance-Dramas*, Chadwyck-Healey, Cambridge, 1986 (Theatre in Focus Series); *Balinese Ritual Drama*, Chadwyck-Healey, Cambridge, 1990 (Theatre in Focus Series).

2.   For a recent and very useful collection of Western philosophical opinions on Events, see *Events*, ed. by Roberto Casati and Achille C. Varzi, The International Research Library of Philosophy, 15, Darmouth, 1996.

2. This reality, I argue, is characterised by eight basic theses which define this 'world' as one of primary experiences — unique, singular, particular, immediate, direct and temporary encounters with a primordial reality.

3. Both the concept of Experience, and that of Event or Process, I then argue, are fundamental to Buddhist philosophy too—as are all the other defining characteristics of such a world-view — with the result that Buddhist philosophy and Performance Epistemology are seen as mutually illustrating and defining each other.

Establishing Performance as a valid philosophical stance is as revolutionary to Western philosophical thinking as arguing Buddhism as a performing art is in the Asian context. Does not Buddhism despise the performing arts? Is not one of the ten abstinences for monks that from dancing and music—as bad as sex, murder, drunkenness? Do not the Precepts (*śīla*) include "I observe the precept of refraining from dance, vocal and instrumental music . . ."? Did not Buddha himself in his own lifetime establish dancers as representative of everything that attaches a person to the endless cycle of desire, suffering, and rebirth? Was it not the sight of his dancing girls asleep in unseemly and disgusting attitudes which immediately preceded his own decision to leave home? And was it not through illusion and then dance that Mara tried to tempt him away from the *bodhi* tree meditation which opened his eyes to enlightenment? Is not Mara the spirit of *māyā*, and *māyā* the source of Evil? Is not theatre therefore, dangerous not only for its sensuality —which can be relatively easily transcended—but, most significantly, for its temptation to believe in the reality and truth of illusion?

But the point has already been made: theatre is not performance. Buddha himself had also established that truth is something which must be rediscovered by each searcher experientially, and that Enlightenment must generate a form of praxis. The history of Buddhism from the Hīnayāna to the Mahāyāna and beyond is an increasing emphasis on praxis, on 'performing' the truth: the crucial difference between a Hīnayāna Arhat and a Mahāyāna Bodhisattva is the translation of personal enlightenment into a mode of being and behaving in the world.

So that it is perhaps not so surprising after all that there is nevertheless theatre in all Buddhist cultures. Part Two examines each of the three main divisions of Buddhism — the Theravāda, Mahāyāna and Vajrayāna — and offers detailed analyses of its performing arts, the Hīnayāna practising 'Karma Drama', the Vajrayāna a 'Bodhisattva Theatre of Compassion', the Mahāyāna 'Boddhi-drama . . .'

That has, traditionally, been explained away as a survival of pre-Buddhist practices, merely an expedient adoption by Buddhists of existing means of persuasion for their own purposes. Both that explanation and that rationale are re-examined in the Second Part of this present study. Buddhist theatre — once it is analysed in its *performative* aspect — is argued instead to provide the opportunity for some of the most basic cognitive experiences a Buddhist can have — immediate apprehensions of the truths of *karma*, the *trikāya*, *śūnyatā*, even *satori*. Such cognitive experiences are normally reserved for meditation but, I attempt to argue, are fundamental experiences of performance too, which thus emerges as a *meditation* on *karma*, *śūnyatā*, *tathatā*, and the *trikāya*. Because each time it can, I suggest, be shown that the fundamental psychology involved in negotiating the world of performance is parallel to meditation practices in the same culture. Whatever the historical truth may be that Buddhist theatre represents a survival and co-option of pre-Buddhist animistic (or Tāntric, or Shinto, or Bon) practices employed to preach to the illiterate, the analyses undertaken in Part Two reveal that Buddhist cultures do not so much separate 'folk theatre' from 'true Buddhism' but rather provide cognitive transformations inherent in Buddhist itself — which performance can facilitate and in fact is based on.

Reality in Buddhism 'perfoms' and it is through Performance that it can best be apprehended in its real form.

It is therefore, with performance that we must and now will begin. . . .

New York,   **David E.R. George**
January 1999

Contents

Part I

The Theory
Buddhism as Performance

The Epistemology of Performance

*Train yourself in such a way that there is only seeing in
what is seen, there is only hearing in what is heard, there is
only sensing in what is sensed, there is only cognising in
what is cognised. . . . That will be the end of suffering.*[1]

We are such stuff as dreams are made on. . . .[2]

The term 'performance' has two—related but distinct—meanings:

(i)   a 'carrying out' or 'execution' (and hence implicit service to
and dependence on a predetermined task, set of orders,
text. . .),

(ii)   a 'presentation'.

The first use of the term in its first sense was in Shakespeare's
The Tempest where Ariel — Prospero's 'stage-manager' — puts on
little plays to deceive (and reform) the other characters. Since then,
performances have tended to be seen as the execution of someone
else's orders — authors, directors. . . . It was also in *The Tempest*
that Shakespeare, at the end of his life, faced the problematic
implications of performance as 'presentation' too, namely the
ephemerality and insubstantiality of the worlds it constructs:

---

1.   Lily de Silva's translation of the celebrated passage from the *Bodhi-
vagga* of the Udana — from "Sense Experience of the Liberated Being
as reflected in early Buddhism," *Buddhist Philosophy and Culture,* ed.
by Kalupahana, D.J., and Weeraratne, W.G., Colombo, 1987, p 17.

2.   Shakespeare, *The Tempest.*

Our revels now are ended. These our actors,
As I foretold you, were all spirits, and
Are melted into air, thin air:
And, like the baseless fabric of this vision,
The cloud-capp'd towers, the gorgeous palaces,
The solemn temples, the great globe itself,
Yea, all which it inherit, shall dissolve,
And, like this insubstantial pageant faded,
Leave not a rack behind. . . .

Prospero tells Ferdinand not to regret this evanescence — 'be cheerful sir', he says — but the strange and disturbing 'reality' of the world of performance continues to elude as much as to haunt us — especially today when the term is enjoying such a contemporary explosion of usage and meanings. Already in 1981, Bonnie Marranca could write:

> The concept of 'performance' increasingly dominates American culture as a way of viewing everyday activity. It is, for example, encouraged as a therapeutic technique, and used to describe sexual activity, the operation of a car, a politician's form, business management style. . . .[3]

Since then, adoption of the term has grown in popularity and at a rate and extent which signal some deeply-felt contemporary affinity with the concept and its implications. Schechner especially has mapped out its terrain, extending performance from play, dance, concerts, TV, circus and carnival to include press conferences, political terrorism, rituals, sport, and concluding:

> Performance is no longer easy to define or locate: the concept and structure has spread all over the place.[4]

---

3.   Marranca, Bonnie, *Theatrewritings,* Performing Arts Journal Publications, New York, 1984, p. 135.

4.   General Introduction to the Performance Studies Series: cf. *The End of Humanism* (New York, 1984); *Performance Theory* (New York, 1988); *By Means of Performance* (Cambridge, 1990), *The Future of Ritual* (London and New York, 1993).

The term is now regularly used

- as a criterion of evaluation;
- as a category of contemporary research and post-modern 'theatre' and, even more profoundly,
- as a discourse, an emerging paradigm.

There remain, however, three critical but crucial problems:

(i) The term is *still* often confused with 'theatre'. To cite but one example: Julian Hilton's *Performance* [MacMillan, 1987], though it seeks to emancipate theatre from text, fails to distinguish between performance and theatrical realization. At the same time, what has come to be called 'task-based performance' and, beyond that, a great deal of actionism and performance art has not only broken ranks with 'theatre' but works without any prior text, locating performance not in the execution of some other construct but as a reality in its own right.

That reality needs exploring — in its own right. . . .

(ii) The methodology for its investigation is, however, to date, suspect. Schechner's attempts to identify the lowest common denominators of a wide range of phenomena from sports to rituals to sex shows, Grotowski's attempts in the Theatre of Sources to locate the basic rhythms and patterns of liturgies, Barba's cross-cultural attempts to identify the worldwide roots of performance techniques — all of these in their different ways adopt the same methodology. It is largely inductive-reductive, a form of positivism which extrapolates laws and common features from a range of cited phenomena. Typically, research into Performance bases itself on lists of purportedly related phenomena followed by an attempt to identify their common denominators.

As a methodology — in *any* discipline — this is, however, suspect:

(a) because it assumes that the list of phenomena is both comprehensive and internally coherent, and

(b) because it is, therefore, trapped in a classic 'hermeneutic circle'. Because some — at least glimmering — definition has already been used to identify the items to be analyzed, the list of which was, however, meant to provide the definition — with which it actually started. . . . No 'set' can be filled except on the basis of a definition; no inductive definition is, however, possible without a pre-existent set of items. . . . Any list of items purporting to be 'performances' has been based in its selection on some implicit, latent definition of what Performance is; but that very definition has been derived from that list. . . .

There is, however, a — now also classical — solution and alternative to this: a Phenomenological epoche. Husserl's "Origin of Geometry"[5] remains the foundational statement of this alternative method, one which seeks not to deduce a list of phenomena from a definition or induce a definition from a list but rather to 'step back' from both, to 'bracket' the phenomenon and ask after its presuppositions.

Phenomenology is especially useful to this present inquiry both because of its affinities with Buddhism and because of its recognition of the way we all construct and live in a variety of different realities, each one defined by certain conventions, certain specific cognitive operations and assumptions. As we step from one reality (the academic or professional world, for example) into others (reading, listening to music, watching or engaging in a play) we reformat our consciousness in the sense of altering radically our expectations of the kinds of experiences and knowledges we are turning from and to. As Husserl argued, the continuity of any cultural phenomenon, the praxis of any

---

5.   Originally written in 1936 and published in 1939 (*Revue internationale de philosophie*, Vol. 1, No. 2.).

body of knowledge involves not a string of people simply learning a set of axioms which someone invented in the past but — in order to do that — necessarily themselves repeating the cognitive breakthrough of its 'inventor': actually reinventing the institution itself each time. Geometry (Performance, any such phenomenon) can be understood and practised only when each new member repeats the original cognitive leap. Any geometrician must repeat Euclid's leap if their consciousness is to be able to understand what Euclid found out; any spectator at any performance does the same: reconfigures their expectations of the kinds of experience and knowledge this special reality can supply. But we do this largely unconsciously, and what Phenomenology proposes is that we 'step back' — simultaneously engage in each reality but at the same time observe ourselves doing so. Luckmann, therefore, describes the phenomenological method as: "attending to experiences precisely as they present themselves";[6] Natanson writes at more length:

Such reconstruction includes a precising of the elements of meaning necessary for the possibility of the phenomenon. . . the ego turns toward its awareness — of what is given, moves towards its having awareness in being able to reflect on its own procedures. . . .[7]

If we are to know what Performances are we must somehow dredge up the sedimented cognitive operations we perform when we encounter and participate in them. We have all learned how to do this but that knowledge has become buried, instinctive, intuitive. As we walk into a performance, we all make massive adjustments to fundamental cognitive assumptions; we know that the time, the place, the persons

6. Luckmann, Thomas, *Phenomenology and Sociology*, Penguin, 1978, p. 8.

7. Natanson, Maurice, "Phenomenology as a Rigorous Science", in *Phenomenology and Sociology, op. cit.*, p. 185.

we will encounter will be radically different — in kind —
from time, place and person in other — social — realities.
. . . It is not only our bodies which enter the world of
performance; it is even more significantly, our minds which
step from one set of assumptions about one kind of reality
through a threshold into another. Those realities consist of
both implicit epistemologies — cognitive operations and
assumptions — and their ontological implications — the
kind of reality they posit.

Such a phenomenological reduction is attempted below;
what it produces will also begin to resolve the third gap in
current research, namely:

(iii)   Performance has, as yet, no developed theory as an
epistemology/ontology in its own right. What kind of a
reality performance is; what kind of *knowledge,* what sorts
of *truths* it provides: that remains to be fully analyzed and
clearly stated. Some epistemology and ontology are implicit,
but inquiry into their being remains dispersed. Because
there have, of course, been statements about Performance
Time, about its Objects, its Inhabitants . . . ; its Liminality,
Contingency, Ephemerality, etc., have all been noted but
not — comprehensively — as a system, as an epistemological
'map'. But that is what is needed: an attempt to identify
how, for example, the unique time of Performance relates
to its unique objects, people, etc., how they form an internal
system, constructing a unique kind of reality and providing
a unique form of experience.

Such an epistemology is implicit, and what this present chapter
seeks is to bring it out: to inquire into what Performance may be —
as an actual way of knowing and, therefore, as a, very different,
"Existenz" of Time/Space/Person.

Performance today looms as a possible philosophical paradigm,
a radical alternative to the Modernist Text-paradigm: Nick Kaye,
for example, writes that "Performance may be thought of as a

primary postmodern mode."[8] Performance is enabling Post-modern theorists to find an alternative to Text — in Process, Event:

> the theatrical is taken up by theorists of the postmodern as a positive refusal of the frozen abstraction of the idea of the work-in-itself in favour of the idea of the work-as-process.[9]

Natalie Crohn Schmidt extends the significance:

> In science it has come to be understood that the event is the basic unit of all things real — that energy, not matter, is the basic datum. In the increasingly widespread perception of reality as endless process, performance, not the art object, becomes primary... performance makes clear its nature as event rather than object.[10]

This focus on event, on process has already found creative expression in New Performance but its significance is deeper, more philosophical, paradigmatic: Performance suggests other ways to look at Time, at Space, at Person, at Knowledge, at Experience; ways which may be closer to both contemporary scientific research (Quantum Theory, Chaos, Complexity) and contemporary philosophcal inquiry (Cognitive Science, Process Philosophy). It is time to probe those parallels more deeply too, but if Performance is to be more than a derivative of other fields of inquiry, someone has to stake a claim for Performance as itself a philosophical system — not parasitically, not by leaning on other systems, but in its own right.

To identify what that may mean, it is necessary to begin by removing first the major historical stumbling-block and lingering categorical confusion:

8. Kaye, N., *Postmodernism and Performance*, MacMillan, London, 1994, p. 22. and cf. Harvey, D., *The Condition of Postmodernity: An Enquiry into the Origins of Cultural Change*, Oxford, 1989, p. 97; Calinescu, Matei and Douwe Fokkema, *Exploring Postmodernism*, Amsterdam and Philadelphia, 1987, pp. 9, 13.

9. Connor, Steven, *Postmodern Culture: An Introduction to Theories of the Contemporary*, Oxford, 1989, p. 134.

10. Schmidt, Natalie Crohn, "Theorizing about Performance: Why Now?", *National Theater Quarterly*, 7, no. 23, 1990, p. 231.

Theatre and Performance

Ariel, thy charge
Exactly is performed: but there's more work.

As I have written in another — analogous — context, it is today an urgent task to draw the line between the ongoing study of theatre and the new theory of performance. [11]

Conventionally: theatre is the translation of a written text — a drama — into representation in space and time. Performance is a one-off version of that transformation: a drama is 'performed' in and by the theatre.

Conventionally, that makes a performance, by definition, a twice-removed, twice-adulterated, doubled 'betrayal' of the original text, the drama. Aristotle already didn't like it. [12]

That conventional flow-chart is, however, a reversal of both the historical and the experiential facts. In both historical fact [for all but a few hundred years] and in ongoing reception, the Drama, the written text was — and is — far from occupying the primary place. The priority of text over performance represents in fact only a very brief phase in the history of Western drama — a couple of hundred years — and has never presumed such a place in Asia. The Greeks, the medieval playwrights, Shakespeare, Molière all wrote what Zeami and Kuan Han-ching wrote: scenarios — performance texts — not works of literature, wrote only to formulate, to provide learnable scripts for actors, and supply records for future possible performances. It was really only for a couple of hundred years that Drama texts supplanted theatrical performances in the West as the primary mode of being of the art form.

It is no accident that that same period is the one we now designate as the reign of Modernity — the reign of the [Meta]narrative.

---

11.   George, D.E.R., "Performance as Paradigm: The Example of Bali", *Modern Drama*, 35, 1992, p. 2.

12.   Aristotle's indifference, and even antipathy to the theatre is overt and explicit in the *Poetics* (cf. *On The Art of Poetry*, tr. by Bywater, I., O.U.P., 1920, p. 39) — probably because of the state of decadence it had entered by his time.

That Modernist reversal of the priority of performance and its replacement by text represents more than just a logocentric bias; it is also a typical example of one of the most compulsive tendencies in Western philosophy, namely the propensity to deduce from primary experiences a putative, prior source on the one hand and a *post facto* effect on the other, and then rewrite the whole sequence as if the cause had really preceded the effect when experientially it is always the other way round (as Nietzsche writes "the prick causes the pin . . .").

That reconstruction of causality was as endemic in Modernism as its Logocentrism, and it is no accident, therefore, that Performance Theory has emerged strongly only during the last twenty or so years,[13] for it is only the Postmodern debunking of all Modernist hierarchies which has enabled performance to claim its place not only as a legitimate field of inquiry in its own right but as a primary phenomenon, enabling us now to reverse the old flow chart: in place of DRAMA → THEATRE → PERFORMANCE, we now have PERFORMANCE as the primary ontology — and the one to be re-examined and theorized.

This reversal has many implications:

- Far from theatrical performance being a betrayal of some 'objective reality', that reality itself is re-cognised as the primary 'fiction', the secondary construct.

- Far from theatre being a second-hand version of some primary reality, that reality itself is exposed as a mere representation — of a metaphysical belief system.

Robert Corrigan writes:

As distinctions break down and patterns dissolve, our 'makers' of theatre seem to have a diminished sense of confidence that there is a world *out there* or one *in here* that can be represented.[14]

---

13. Cf. George, *op. cit.*(1992), p.1.
14. Corrigan, R.W.,"The Search for New Endings: The Theatre in Search of a Fix, Part III", *Theatre Journal,*vol. 36, no.2, 1984, p. 160.

- Far from performances being falsifications, they are
  recognised as the primary data.

This primacy of performance creates, however, serious problems for
the theorist: texts are re-readable, have, for all their possibilities of
reinterpretation, a certain ontological fixity and stability denied to
performance, which is fundamentally ephemeral and cannot be
recorded or documented without betraying it — to the text — again.

Performance was and is primary: the text was always only an
approximation — a derivative — of the potential performance
which writers imagine in-the-head and which is the real *a priori*
metatext which precedes verbal transcription and transformation.
Drama texts were only ever hypotheses of future possible realizations
and re-transformations: they never were nor could be performed *as
they are*, and the theatre was and is only the medium through which
they pass. So it was before Aristotle: before there were texts, before
there was writing, before there was theatre, there were surely
performances.

They are, however, very hard to theorize: their temporality,
ephemerality, their ambiguity, their specificity, their restless
improvisation, their haunting by shadowy options: all of this makes
them events or at best processes. One can understand why it was
far easier to focus attention on texts, on the dramas. Marco de
Marinis whose *Semiotics of Performance* (Indiana UP, 1993) sets as
its agenda to conceptualize theatre as "an autonomous primary
phenomenon"[15] writes:

> The written text, when its exists, is generally the only
> component of the performance which is *present* and
> *persistent* . . . the only part available to the analyst. The
> other components disappear, as we know, with the end of
> the performance, because their presence is *ephemeral* and
> *non-persistent*. . . .

He concludes,

---

15.   Marco de Marinis, *The Semiotics of Performance,* Indiana UP, 1993,
      p. 1.

> This state of things, has undoubtedly favored the 'promotion' of the dramatic text from the status of a single component that happens to be present and lasting to the status of a unique, significant component, a prioritized element, totally representative of all other components.[16]

Dramatic texts were written to be realized in performance but, in between the writing and the performing, there was the Theatre — an institution — with rules, regulations, disciplines, conventions [even, some theorists argued, some ethical usefulness]. Any lingering confusion between theatre and performance is removed when one realizes that the one is an institution, the other an event. It is only now, when events and processes are being recognized — scientifically as much as philosophically — as the fundamental data of experience, and experience as the foundation of knowledge that serious attempts are being made to analyze performance as the primary reality.

That 'reality' needs exploring and defining: mapping. . . .

Performance: Eight Epistemological Theses

"The fringed curtains of thine eye advance,
And say what thou seest yond"

```
                        Temporality
Singularity              R    F           Particularity
                   E                O
Liminality                                Doubling
                 P                    R
Experience       E                    M   Othering
               C
                 N          A
                     Speculation
```

---

16. Marco de Marinis, *The Semiotics of Performance*, Indiana UP, 1993, p. 16.

The ontology of performance is accessible through at least eight epistemological gates, each of them suggesting a radical reappraisal of the nature of this — and other — 'realities'. . . .

1. TEMPORALITY

1.1. A performance exists only and ever in time. It is therefore always about "presence, presentness and presenting".[17]

1.2. That time cannot be frozen, suspended or repeated: it is a flux.

> There is neither past nor future, but only a continuous present — that of the immediacy of things, of an action taking place.[18]

> Performance's only life is in the present. Performance cannot be saved, recorded, documented, or otherwise participate in the circulation of representations *of* representations: once it does so, it becomes something other than performance. . . .[19]

1.3. That unrepeatable, unique flux is not at all like the simple linear time of Modernism or of its preferred linguistic art form — the narrative. The overlap of 'history' and 'story' betrays the ambition of the Modernist enterprise: narrative time is past time, past tense. "To this extent," as I have written elsewhere,

> A Text-culture lives in its past or rather by it, for the historical orientation contains both the implicit assumption

17.   Corrigan, R.W., *The World of the Theatre,* Glenview, Illinois, 1979, p. 24.

18.   Feral, J., "Performance and Theatricality: The Subject Demystified", *Modern Drama,* vol. XXV, no. 1, 1982, p.173, and cf. Pontbriand, C., "The eye finds no fixed point on which to rest . . .", *Modern Drama,* vol. 25, no. 1. 1982, p. 155; Bell, S., *Reading, Writing, and Rewriting the Prostitute Body,* Indiana UP, 1994, p. 139; Connor, *op. cit.,* 1989, p. 134; Pavis, P., "The Classical Heritage of Modern Drama: The Case of Postmodern Theatre", *Modern Drama,* vol. XXIX, no. 1,1986, p. 16.

19.   Phelan, P., *Unmarked. The Politics of Performance,* Routledge, London and New York, 1993, p. 146.

and the imposed duty of 'reading' the past, deducing its inscribed causality. A Text-culture is a culture of readers whose lives consist in deciphering the causal, rational purpose, design, scheme written into history by its implied Author.[20]

1.4. Past time, linear time are (or can be made to seem) rational, causal, teleological: time made safe for philosophy. By contrast, Performance time is not only ephemeral, transient, it is also fundamentally *doubled* [a present which is somehow parallel to another present] and *ambiguous:* a now which is not-now but also not-not-now. 'Neither now nor not-now', performance time provides none of the security of past time; an eternal present whose past lies in the future. But that, of course, is where all experiential pasts in fact reside: it is only *after* it has occurred that a past is held to lie somehow *before.* . . .

1.5. This transient, ambiguous, unique presence of performance creates a radical shift in cognitive presumptions, for whereas the past can be analyzed, the present can only be experienced.

Peggy Phelan writes:

Performance is the art form which most fully understands the generative possibilities of disappearance. Poised forever at the threshold of the present, performance enacts the productive appeal of the nonreproductive.[21]

Marco de Marinis writes — similarly — that the discrete and specific aspect is "that every theatrical performance (every *single* theatrical performance) constitutes an *unrepeatable, unique event*".[22]

The corollary of temporality is singularity.

2. SINGULARITY

2.1. No performance is ever the same as any other. Performances

20. George, *op. cit.*, (1992), p. 3.
21. Phelan, *op. cit.*, p.17.
22. Marco de Marinis, *op. cit.*, p. 51.

are singular events, characterized by improvisation [the word means, literally, 'unforeseen'.]

Again theory appears stymied, for theory depends always on the reiterability of the phenomena it analyzes: an experiment must be repeatable if it is to yield 'scientifically' valid results. Performances can do that only in the broadest terms; its secrets lie elsewhere — in the unrepeatable. A performance mode such as Noh uses this very fact as the basis of its aesthetic ambitions: 'hana' — the moment when the 'flower blooms', the moment when a performer startles, surprises an audience by an unexpected variation on a fixed form — that is held to be the secret of the whole art form.[23] Nor is this unique to Noh: many a Western director and theorist has discovered the same — Stanislavski, for example:

> Actors achieve the pinnacle of their art when they have that quality of the unexpected which startles, overwhelms, stuns me. Something that lifts the spectator off the ground, sets him in a land where he has never walked, but which he recognises easily through a sense of foreboding or conjecture. He does, however, see this unexpected thing face to face, and for the first time. It shakes, enthrals, and engulfs him.[24]

2.2. Such descriptions, such theories rest on a basic contrast — between a fixed form and an improvised variation: it is only because the Noh actor performs a gesture which every spectator has already seen dozens of times *as if* it had never been performed that way before; it is only because the Western actor intones a word or phrase, discovers a new rhythm in a known passage that the

---

23.   Cf. *On the Art of the No Drama: The Major Treatises of Zeami*, ed. by Rimer, Thomas and Masakuza, Yamazaki Princeton U.P., 1984; Colbath, A., *The Japanese Noh Drama and its Relation to Zen*, Ph.D. thesis, Western Reserve University, 1962; Covell, J.E.H.C., *Zen Gleanings*, Idyllwild, Cal., 1973; Ku, Hung-ting, *The Influence of Zen on Noh Plays in Japan,* Singapore, 1976.

24.   Stanislavski, K., *Building a Character*, Methuen, London, 1979, p. 298. Cf. Brook, Peter in *Actors on Acting*, ed. by Cole, T. and Chinoy, H.K., 1949, p. 424.

surprise and hence the aesthetic shock occurs. This, it might be argued therefore, is all still theatre, since all of this is shadowed by a prior 'Text' — be that a script or a performance tradition. Where performance theory goes further is in erasing that shadow.

2.3. Theatre has always been shadowed by the text and therefore by the author [or the director, herself shadowed by authorial privilege and precedence]. Performances are shadowed at most only by other performers, that itself, however, only one exemplification of a more general and radically different epistemological paradigm, namely that Performances are shadowed only by their own other possibilities. These unfold simultaneously with their creation: in performance there is no prior — and therefore no prioritized — other world which is somehow re-presented or reflected.

Performances are exercises in restless semiosis, in which all meaning is derived from interdependent relations and not by ascription to some objective referent.

2.4. To that extent, the critics of Theatre were right to be so suspicious of it: Plato was right to see in the classical theatre a double betrayal of the Truth — but only because Plato believed the Truth lay in *a priori*, absolute Ideas — of which *any* representation must therefore, *ipso facto*, be a form of falsification. "Theatricality," as Matei Calinescu writes,

> has a way of dramatising the old philosophical distinction between appearance and essence, between surface phenomena and profound — 'really real' — processes . . . to get to the truth one must unmask or demystify the deceptions of naive realism, one must tear up the veil of illusory appearances and courageously identify the hidden actual causes of what one perceives.[25]

Remove that 'essence', however, remove that metaphysical presumption, remove that transcendental absolute and one removes also the [pejorative notion of] appearance too, one removes the

---

25. Calinescu, M. and Fokkema, D., *Exploring Postmodernism*, Amsterdam and Philadelphia, 1987, p. 9.

whole false dualism: performance is never a re-presentation of anything, except itself.

2.5. The primary lie of language has always compounded the primary deception of metaphysics: Logocentrism and Absolutist Metaphysics go hand in hand [as Nietzsche wrote: "I am afraid we are not rid of God because we still have faith in grammar."[26]] Language constructs generalizations out of particulars, abstractions out of concrete phenomena, substances out of attributes, ideas out of appearances.... Performance always reverses that process: since nothing can be repeated or re-presented, everything in a performance is personalized, individualized, concretized, particularized.

If the corollary of temporality is singularity, then the corollary of singularity is particularity.

3. PARTICULARITY

3.1. Already in the theatre, no-one ever saw Hamlet, only a Hamlet; no-one ever heard Tosca, only a Tosca sing. Performances reverse what language has done to the world: they restore the specificity of experienced phenomena and to that extent every performance is a betrayal of every text — but only because every text is already a betrayal of the primary experience of reality.

In performance, things — and characters — are given back their discrete uniqueness.

3.2. Hume had already anticipated the philosophical implications of this:

I may venture to affirm of the rest of mankind, that they are nothing but a bundle or collection of different perceptions, which succeed each other with an inconceivable rapidity and are in a perpetual flux and movement. Our eyes cannot turn in their sockets without varying our perceptions. Our thought is still more variable than our sight; and all our other senses and faculties contribute to this change; nor is there

---

26.   *The Portable Nietzsche*, ed. by Kaufmann, Walter, Penguin Books, 1976, p. 483.

any single power of the soul, which remains unalterably the same, perhaps for one moment. The mind is a kind of theatre, where several perceptions successively make their appearance; pass, repass, glide away, and mingle in an infinite variety of postures and situations.[27]

Hume already understood that all experiences — in the theatre and elsewhere — are contingent; as particular, relational and dependent as they are temporal. Paradoxically, that, however, is the source of the fourth and most intriguing characteristic of performance: the way that it always creates its own doubles, its own shadows.

Just as presence creates absence, so too the corollary of *actual* singularity and particularity is *potential* doubling, hypothetical shadowing.

4. DOUBLING

4.1. One of the major challenges of performance research is to explain how spectators make judgements about the quality of what they are witnessing. In some performance modes, the apparent answer lies in the fact that spectators are often aficionados, technical experts. The finite range of classical operas, ballets, concertos, Noh plays means that most spectators have seen other performers perform the 'same' part differently. Such performances are shadowed by their own ghosts. But one could argue that a very similar thing applies also to performances we are seeing for the first time. When a spectator witnesses a performance she has not seen before, even as one watches what a performer does, one sees simultaneously what they do not do — what they omit. This becomes itself the criterion of evaluating what they do. Peggy Phelan writes therefore about the "supplemental excess" of performance which generates "multiple and resistent readings".[28]

De Marinis writes at more length about the way that a theatrical text can only ever be "directive" not "prescriptive":

27. Hume, David, *A Treatise on Human Nature*, ed. by Selby-Bigge, L.A., Oxford, 1888, p. 252.

28. Phelan, *op. cit.*, p. 2.

> The theatrical text contains *directives* (orders, advice,
> suggestions, etc., depending on the situation) about the
> way, or ways, in which it *may* be staged. Yet it never
> *prescribes* nor can it prescribe a *single* solution for how it
> should be performed.... Rather it suggests a range of *more
> or less* equally appropriate possibilities.[29]

It is these innate, supplemental, other possibilities which shadow
any performance and provide the basis for comparison and
evaluation. Who has not been to a performance and not said: that
speech could (should) have been delivered differently, that blocking
was not the best; they should not have moved on that sentence?
Performance excess creates shadows, so that performances always
create their own alternatives. Performers stand in a certain way,
speak in a certain tone, move in a certain direction, make a certain
gesture: in doing so they create one version of that scene but
simultaneously other possible ways in which it could have been
done. Those other possibilities remain latent — they do not occur on
the stage but they live on in the spectators' minds and are indeed
compared to what the performers do do.

In other words: the very fact of actual particularization is what
creates hypothetical options. Options create comparisons;
comparisons prevent closure.

Performances are created 'in between'. ...

5. LIMINALITY

5.1. What applies to and derives from time applies also to space:
temporariness, singularity, particularity, doubling. A performance
is 'present' in a spatial sense too: it is happening here. That 'here'
is, however, similarly doubled and ambiguous: it is a here which is
not-here but also not-not-here. We shall need to examine the role of
the spectator in all this very soon but one implication is already
clear: spanning at least two different space - times, performances
occur always and only in a liminal field. Performances do not occur

---

29.   Marco de Marinis, *op. cit.*, p. 45.

on stage nor in the auditorium but in between the two; they are, in effect, exercises in the creation and occupation of thresholds.

5.2. Realistic theatre sought to overcome this by merging the two 'realities', constructing the one 'here' as a mirror image of the other, reducing the binary to one preferred choice. Either the theatre 'disappeared' — into a quasi-realism — or the realism disappeared — into a pan-theatricality. It never did work very well: putting real furniture, real trees, real taps which drip real water on a theatrical set does not create the illusion of another reality; it merely exposes the unreality of the theatrical world even more. It was always an act of bad faith, one which failed to recognize the secret triplicity of all apparent binaries. Because binaries necessitate always a third factor: a relational axis, and:

> though all binaries establish simultaneously both the identity and the difference of the two terms, the third element — the relational axis itself — can either collapse the two into identity or create out of difference a third state of pure potentiality. . . .[30]

Traditionally, we either project a world (subjectivism) or recover it (objectivism); performance, by denying the distinction between appearance and essence, presentation and re-presentation, reminds us that 'the real' is neither the one nor the other, neither here nor there but always in between. Performances occur on and enable spectators to sit on thresholds — ambiguous Time-spaces in-between, the 'Middle Way' between Identity and Difference, Reality and Illusion, Emptiness and Form: the Time-spaces of experience.

Metaphysics has always extrapolated from such experiences the classical binary of Object-World/Subject-Self but these were only ever extrapolations and hence betrayals of primary experience. Performance retains the liminal quality of all experience, and performance theory has to take these ambiguous Space-times seriously, for they are inhabited by peculiar creatures, creatures who are similarly *other* than themselves.

---

30. George, D.E.R.., "On Ambiguity", *Theatre Research International,* vol. 14, No. 1, p. 79.

6. OTHERINGS

6.1. Schechner pointed the way: "Olivier is not Hamlet but also he is not not Hamlet; his performance is in between a denial of being another (= I am me) and a denial of not being another (= I am Hamlet).... Performing," he goes on, "is a paradigm of liminality ... the essence of in-betweenness."[31]

6.2. In the classical, naturalistic theatre, actors work very hard to erase that ambiguity, in theory disappearing into the character. At least that is what 'The Method' is supposed to mean, although its founder knew better:

"As I was taking my bath," writes Stanislavski in *Building a Character,*

> I recalled the fact that while I was playing the part of the Critic I still did not lose the sense of being myself. The reason, I concluded, was that while I was acting I felt exceptionally pleased as I followed my own transformation. Actually I was my own observer at the same time that another part of me was being a fault-finding, critical creature.

> Yet can I say that creature is not a part of me? I derived him from my own nature. I divided myself, as it were, into two possibilities. . . .

Strangely enough," he concluded,

> this duality did not impede, it actually promoted my creative work.[32]

Where and what, in such a description, is the 'self'? What role in such a description of the performing psyche, could a 'self' play? Whatever may have been achieved by realistic theatre in terms of creating a total illusion, a total fusion of actor and character in the

---

31. *Between Theater and Anthropology,* University of Pennsylvania Press, 1985, p. 4.

32. Stanislavski, *op. cit.,* p. 21.

audience's mind, no *theatre artist* ever abandoned their innate schizophrenia, the paradox of their being: it was and is the secret of their craft, for this doubling and ambiguity are the ground of that elusive 'presence' of performers. . . .

6.3. The psychology of *theatre* already splinters the 'self' into its roles on the one hand and an observing subject on the other. *Performance* goes further: denying the necessity of character, it transports both of its participants — those who perform on stage and those who perform as spectators — into a territory where the self is apprehended only in its activities, and where there is no possibility of reduction to a single unitary monad.

This plural fragmentation of the 'self' had been anticipated by George Herbert Mead as early as 1934 with his notion of the world of the mind as a 'monodrama' in which one is simultaneously playwright, director, actor, cast, audience and critic. Lyman and Scott extend and explicate his metaphor:

> As *playwright,* the 'self' exploits its capacities and needs to determine how best to achieve its desires and also endows other selves with character, motivation, and various capacities to establish the 'plot' of the next 'scene'. As *director,* the 'self' 'stages' the 'scene' in the 'theater of the mind', which is to the theatre of reality what New Haven is to New York City, that is, the 'place' where the drama is perfected before the performance that really counts. As *actor,* the 'self' imaginatively performs in the scene, which has been prefigured, and interacts with the other 'performers' who are part of that scene. As *cast* of players, the 'self' imaginatively acts out the roles of all the other players in the scene. As *audience,* the 'self' watches the entire scene it has written, directed, and in which it acts as a performer of a requisite role. As *critic,* the 'self' evaluates the scene, decides on its efficacy, morality, and potential, and when satisfied, sends it out to perform in the theatre of reality.[33]

33. Lyman, S.M. and Scott, M.B., *The Drama of Social Reality,* Oxford UP, 1975, p. 104.

But it is only recently that such a decentred self has become more than a fanciful, extended metaphor and taken its rightful place in the radical deconstruction of Western metaphysical *a prioris*. Schechner writes:

> To see 'I' at the center of the world is modern feeling. For the self to see itself and become involved with that reflection or doubling as if it were another is a postmodern experience. To become conscious of this doubling — to posit a third self aware of the mutuality of the other two selves, this geometrically progressive 'reflexivity' is postmodern.[34]

Spalding Gray writes,

> Look at me, I am one who sees himself seeing himself.[35]

Performance deconstructs the body and consciousness into what Peters calls "multiple centers and discrete modes of thought and perception"[36] — a description which already and clearly anticipates connection with Buddhist skandha theory when Peters goes on to talk about the performer becoming dispersed into a "stratified field of codes, centers of energy, physical signs, tones of voice, strips of behavior, and impulses".[37]

Vanden Heuvel summarizes:

> processual in nature, refusing to be anchored within a stable system of referents, the performative self exists in an indeterminate and pluralistic state, joyously transforming and diffusing itself into 'ludic diffractions of the self' (Hassan, 1987:65).[38]

---

34. Schechner, *op. cit*, (1982), p. 99.
35. Gray, S., "About Three Places in Rhode Island", *TDR, The Drama Review*, vol. 23, no. 1, 1979, p. 35.
36. Peters, S.J., "Modern to Postmodern Acting and Directing: An Historical Perspective", Ph.D. Diss., Texas Tech, 1986, p. 217.
37. *Ibid.*, p. 233.
38. Vanden Heuvel, Michael, *Performing Drama / Dramatizing Performance. Alternative Theater and the Dramatic Text*, University of Michigan Press, Ann Arbor, 1991, p. 6.

6.4. The psychological model which emerges from Performance goes then far beyond the theatrical binary of person and role, performer and character — and the paranoia which that juxtaposition of authenticity and hypocrisy encouraged. The Self in performance is not some frightened little homunculus hiding behind roles in fear of being misled, deceived, betrayed — the model which Goffman derived from The Theatre. The self in performance, living in a world of permanent change, living in a world of singular events and particular objects, living through doubling and in a state of extended liminality, is 'itself' a whole world of ever changing experiences, and ever new patterns, unable to freeze or stop because acutely aware that it is unstable, dispersed, empty. . . .

In performance we create who we are, and it is always another. . . .

To summarize for now: what distinguishes Performance as an ontological-epistemological system is a set of characteristics and experiences which systematically reverse the generalizing and immobilizing metaphysics of language in favour of a re-temporalization and re-particularization of experience, and a strategic deconstruction — of time, space and person. . . .

To illustrate:

- a set in a *theatre* may be seen as representing a place described in a text [which may itself reproduce some 'real' antecedent];

- in contradistinction: an object in a *performance* is no more or less than what it generates as possibilities of signification. Not a representation of any thing, it is a collection of properties, qualities; a condensed mode of semiosis.

- Likewise, a *character* in a play may be seen as re-enacting the behaviour prescribed in a text [which may itself be shadowed by some real, historical or mythical metanarrative and personage];

- a performer, on the other hand, need not even be a person; only ever a bundle of temporary and ever changing attributes. . . .

From which we can now *conclude:*

'Theatre' and 'Performance' are not different events; they are different perspectives on the event — now seen as the theatrical realization of prior text, now experienced as performance. The 'same' event, in other words, can be seen as re-presenting characters on quasi-real sets enacting authored scripts OR as performers generating multiple, particular significations in ambiguous time and space.

The difference lies in where one starts: one can begin with the act — the performance — or (and this has been the traditional approach) one can begin with the assumption that it is only the end of a process, in which case one begins with its ghosts. . . .

Performance is not a new art form so much as a new paradigm: it offers not so much a new phenomenon as a new way of looking at 'known' existing phenomena, different ways of responding to them, experiencing them, thinking about them.

Performance is less a new mode of artistic expression than a new way of seeing and thinking. It is important to emphasize this because there have been attempts recently to establish some kind of historical demarcation line between Performance and Theatre, and to some extent that can be done: a Post-modern Installation is radically different from a Cherry Orchard at the Moscow Arts Theatre. But that historical development from Theatre to Performance Art, that change in creative expression is, I would argue, itself only one reflection of a more fundamental paradigm shift in perspective [and Post-modernism is a paradigm shift, a shift in perspective]. The new Performance Art reflects the new epistemology, for if Performance Art does anything it refocuses attention on the artist and the process rather than the artwork, exploding the falsely static quality of the 'product', its self-denying fixation out-of-time. It does more than that: if the history of realistic theatre is a history of [failed] attempts to reduce differences in performances, to use intensive rehearsal, dictatorial direction, discipline, ideology and a work ethic to erase the particular, the different, then one of the historical achievements of Performance

Art is that it joyfully accepts that difference is ineradicable and therefore better to be courted, explored, foregrounded. Performance Art reintroduces improvisation into performance itself, letting it out of the closet of the rehearsal room and the workshop process and reinstating it in performance itself. But that is where it actually always belonged. Indeed, to that extent, one can now even revisit The Cherry Orchard — as a performance; indeed, if one had no prior knowledge of the play or of the theatre, if one simply fell in there, one would receive it as a performance.

It is, however, true that that primary experience would soon itself construct a cognitive doubling: one cannot for long see an Actor representing a Character and not do this, and to that extent Post-modern Performance Art is a new development in resisting *that* doubling, and substituting its own.

What it cannot resist is the other doubling, the doubling of its own unfolding with its latent possibilities of otherness. That operation — and all the rest of the epistemological operations outlined above — are performed by the Spectator.

7. SPECULATION

7.1. The spectator as much as the performer is the originator of theatre which did not begin when someone decided to pretend to be someone else but did so in the presence of other people. Traditionally the end-point, the destination of the process, the spectator in fact stands at the very beginning of it — not only historically but praxiologically: all along the way towards a performance, the practitioners have been speculating on the spectator.

7.2. This was already the case with theory: ever since Aristotle responded to Plato's condemnation of the supposed effect of theatre on its spectators with his alternative hypothesis of response, theorists have based their analyses of drama and theatre on teleological models. Masquerading as descriptions of how spectators must respond, they were, however, all really prescriptive. Only recently has any real work been done on what epistemological operations spectators actually perform. And yet speculation on their responses pervades not only the theory, it pervades the praxis too: directors have always defined and legitimized their function as being both the voice of the Author and the 'first spectator': that is the only reason actors have put up with them for so long.

Performance is spectator-orientated behaviour: it is the Spectator who sits in the limen, steps into the threshold to perform their strange exercise in 'othering'.

7.3. The concentration which this requires has deceived some observers into accusing them of passivity. Those physically inert bodies are, however, only the necessary precondition of a cognitive and emotional intensity, an exercise in virtual experience.

The term *experience* is crucial: for all too long spectators have been equated with readers as decipherers of meaning. Classically, a spectator is supposed to 'read' a director's meanings which are themselves readings of the author's meanings which are themselves readings of the world's meanings. . . . That may have some validity in the context of a given text; it has no validity in the context of a performance which is not an exercise in linguistics or in hermeneutics but one in semiosis. Performances create significations as they unfold but they do more than that: they create their own shadows, their own alternatives too. Or rather spectators do that: speculate on possible alternatives. The 'passive spectator' is as much a fiction as the prediction that they will obediently follow the narrative's path towards closure. Even in the traditional theatre-of-narrative-and-character, the spectator never was the passive sponge directors may wish them to be. As I have written elsewhere:

> As a play unfolds, each spectator beigns to build up hypotheses of how they think the plot **might** unfold. Simultaneously, they watch the actor and hypothesize how **they** might enact this. It's a game — a tension — between opening up multiple hypotheses and their closing down as authors and actors make choices. The plot and the characters close down other options as they go along: they enact only a few of the many hypothetical possibilities open at any moment in a play, but what's done and said also amplifies

what is not done, not said. . . .

I think spectators get a lot of their pleasure from listening attentively, from agreeing and disagreeing with the choices being made. To that extent the role of narrative and character enactment in theatre is similiar to that of formal structure in dance and music. In all three cases, there is a conjuncture of openings and closings. A pulsational rhythm.[39]

Every performance generates a bewilderingly rapid succession of puzzles: why that colour with that shape, why that movement with that speech, why that gesture after that word. . . . ? As the new signs accumulate and cross-reference each other, the puzzle is resolved, meaning is ascribed, but closure is never definitive: even as a performer selects one option, the others remain open; there remain other ways to speak any sentence, other gestures to accompany it. Spectators create such options even as they experience what the performers have chosen, and those 'others' continue to haunt them.

In contemporary performance, the spectator may be deprived of narrative and hence of narrative hypotheses, they may be deprived of characters too; they may have only the performer to follow: 'how does one make sense of it?' people ask, assuming that 'making sense' is what they are trying to do. Perhaps they aren't: there are better places than the theatre to make sense of the world but very few which offer such unique experiences.

Those experiences are both cognitive operations and forms of emotion.

8. EXPERIENCE

8.1. The word derives etymologically from the French and means 'to put to the test'.

Experience is an experiment. For all too long, theatre has been

---

39. "Listening to Images: David George in conversation with David Willams", to be published in *Writings on Dance,* Melbourne.

categorized as a form of representation when it was really always an experiment in creating alternatives, a vision of otherness. For all too long the ambition of Western theatre was to 'close that gap' — a futile operation when performances are always doubling themselves, opening gaps. In this sense, realistic theatre opposed the very essence of theatre in attempting to transform one reality into another when the theatre was always creating its own others. Performance today has liberated itself from that sterile exercise in mimesis, in the process exposing all meanings as interpretations, all facts as fictions, all truths as constructs. Performers and spectators are returned instead to the primacy of experience in its first sense — that of experimenting with other ways worlds might be thought of, and made, and acted in.

8.2. 'Experience' means, however, more than experimentation; it is also a form of knowledge — gained first-hand, knowledge gained from praxis.[40] Before producing — becoming — knowledge, experience is simply the direct, immediate, particular, singular apprehension of a contact — between an 'object' and a 'subject'. Experiences thus postulate and even construct objects and subjects as their two assumed, necessary poles but, until they do that, while they remain pure experiences, while they sit on the threshold, they are nothing but an axis, nothing but a connection, a relationship. Recapitulating what was already claimed above: the real secret of the notorious binaries is that they were and are always secretly triads in the sense that any binary necessitates a relational axis. That axis both joins and simultaneously separates: it is upon that 'third axiom' that spectators sit and swing, and experience.

There is, however, in any act and process of experiencing, an inevitable tendency to vacate this seat, to move from the act and process of relat*ing* to the postulate of a relation*ship* and from there to the deduction of the poles — which are then reified, hypostatised into objects and subjects. . . . This process happens very fast and compulsively: we are forever turning primary experiences into

---

40.   Cf. Stevenson, Leslie, *The Metaphysics of Experience,* Oxford, 1982, p.1.

'knowledge', forever constructing metaphysical binaries out of thresholds. What performances do is retard — suspend — this process: retain spectators on the axis, in the threshold. Performance, because of its constant unfolding, because of its ephemerality, because of its restless creation of difference, helps to keep it all pure process.

8.3. That has traditionally been devalued: experiences are there to be learned from, but Tennyson understood:

> all experience is an arch wherethrough
> Gleams that untravelled world, whose margin fades
> For ever and for ever when I move.
> How dull it is to pause, to make an end
> To rust unburnished, not to shine in use. . . .[41]

Performance has this special gift for its spectators that it resists that 'pause', suspends that transformation of experience into mere learning. As Vaden Heuvel writes, performance — because of its "immanence of a continuous present" — is always "experienced firsthand, unmediated by any preconditioned scheme of meaning."[42]

In cognitive terms, then, performance returns all its practitioners to the unique, singular, personal, immediate, direct and temporary encounters on which we construct our 'truths'. All too soon such moments pass as we construct from experiences both objective worlds and subjects cognizing them. Experiences are always accompanied by an awareness of a 'self' having that experience and hence very rapidly shift from direct cognition to self-consciousness, from immediate apprehension to construction of a dualism of subject and object. These are, however, increasingly today recognized as falsifications against which performance stands as a constant reminder.

8.4. Those *cognitive* operations performed by spectators are paralleled by *emotional* operations. Here Western theory has been simplistic and even crude, invariably failing to make any distinction

---

41. *Ulysses,* I, 6.
42. Vaden Heuvel, *op. cit.,* p. 51.

between our emotional responses to a performance and those towards 'real life'. Western theorists have tended more often to be angry that spectators have not responded morally, ethically to theatrical stimuli than to recognize that those stimuli never were activating. It took Sanskrit theory to follow a more profitable path, recognizing that the primary factor which distinguishes an emotion from an aesthetic feeling is that it is not motivational. . . .

This is no place to engage in a detailed account of *rasa* theory;[43] its main arguments may, however, be briefly summarized:

- what distinguishes aesthetic sentiments from social emotions is that the former are always vicarious;

- that in turn means that, whereas an emotion is always accompanied by an urge to act, is always in some way motivational, aesthetic feeling is truncated at the point;

- aesthetic sentiments — *rasas* — are therefore desireless emotions; sensual impressions which do not generate want.

The value of this for a Buddhist is already transparent; what it means for any spectator of any performance is that it halts our emotions this side of being transformed into something else. Just as the seamless temporal flux of performance inhibits the normal transition from experience to knowledge, so too the same flux inhibits the normal transformation of sensation and sentiment into release through action. Emotions can be savoured, even rediscovered in all their purity, all their uncontaminated joy: desire without longing, passion with equanimity. . . .

Summarizing

> *my ending is despair,*
> *Unless I be reliev'd by prayer*

---

43. Cf. George, D.E.R., *India: Three Ritual Dance-Dramas,* Cambridge, 1986; Mishra, Hari Ram, *The Theory of Rasa in Sanskrit Drama,* Bhopal, 1964; Nandi, T., *The Origin and Development of the Theory of Rasa and Dhvani in Sanskrit Poetics,* Ahmedabad, 1973; *Indian Poetics and Western Thought,* ed. by Kushwaha, M.S., Lucknow, 1988; Masson, J.L., and Patwardhan, M.V., *Santarasa and Abhinavagupta's Philosophy of Aesthetics,* Poona, 1969.

We are all familiar now with the tyranny of language, the translation of experience into reason, causality, plot, order. Conceiving of life in terms of the book has always involved conceiving of life as something which already has meaning, already has purpose, logic, narrative — built into it by the author, be that author God, society or some other authority.

The only alternative appeared to be chaos, ambiguity, insecurity.

That alternative is represented today by performance — but no longer negatively, no longer as a symbol of metaphysical illusion; rather as a model of existential reality.

Performance stands today as the best potential alternative to the old paradigm of the world as text.

The implications of that for the *theatre* are already revolutionary. Theatre was once unambiguously understandable as the translation of a text (a Drama) into an enactment. Performance was simply the completion of that process.

Today, that whole hierarchy stands reversed: theatre is only one of the phenomena which are grouped under the new general category of Performance — along with rituals, film, video, pop, music, ballet, opera, sport, politics, law, education [even cooking, sex. . . .].[44] Whereas, in the past, performance was seen as one example of the theatrical realization of a text, today theatre is seen as one example of the category Performance.

Some theorists have attempted to glean from this ever widening spectrum of performance certain common denominators and hence some base model. That inductive method has proved to be unexpectedly difficult. What is offered above is an alternative method, one derived from Phenomenology, namely a series of reflections on the preconditions of the phenomenon, deductions of its epistemology from its ontology and vice versa.

As an ontology, performance may now be summarized as:

- temporal, transient, ephemeral;

---

44. Schechner, R., *Performance Theory*, London, Routledge, 1988, p. xiii.

- particular, singular;
- doubled;
- ambiguous;
- speculative.

As an epistemology, performance offers:

- a rediscovery of the now; relocation in the here;
- return to the primacy of experience, of the event;
- rediscovery that facts are relations; that all knowledge exists on the threshold and in the interaction between subject and object [which are themselves only hypostatisations. . .];
- a rediscovery of ambiguity, of contradiction, of difference;
- . a reassertion that things — and people — are what they do. . . .

Plessner and others write about the Phenomenological method as a 'making strange', a process of 'defamiliarization'.[45] But Performance is a strange world, a strange reality: its space, its time, its persons are all radically different from those we experience in other realities. Until recently, those other realities have been ascribed some greater degree of truth; the theatre has suffered from that, especially in the West whose culture always had problems with it, worried about the deceptive, illusory quality of theatre, worried that it represented some alternative and therefore, by definition, blasphemous act of alternative creativity.[46]

Theatre in the West was always haunted by the Drama, by the Word, by the Idea and thus by the metaphysical assumption that any representation must be a distortion of a transcendent truth. Only the wholesale jettisoning of that metaphysics could possibly emancipate the theatre from entrapment in its own metaphor.

---

45.   Cf. Luckmann, *op. cit.,* pp. 30ff.
46.   Cf. Barish, Jonas A., *The Antitheatrical Prejudice,* Berkeley, University of California Press, 1981.

Disguised as theatre, performance has had to wait a long time for its contemporary emancipation, but one can conjecture that theatre-people must have always found their marginalization puzzling. Non-theatre-people kept accusing them of practising deception, not understanding how one can live with the creation of artifacts that have no continuous material base; theatre-people shrug: we live in a world of elusive temporality; isn't that what the world is actually like? They always knew that their worlds were 'unreal', the product of their wills, consciousness, perceptions, sensations, desires, that they had no substance, had no 'self', existed only in time. . . . Paradoxically, it was theatre-people who never made the cognitive and emotional mistakes which Buddhists spend their lives refuting. No-one needed to tell them about dependent arising, impermanence, temporality, insubstantiality, no-thing-ness. . . . Because any Buddhist will have already anticipated the connections in what has been mapped out above; any reader with some prior knowledge of Buddhist philosophy will already have realized how the epistemology of performance as described above is replete with Buddhist insights — into time, perception, insubstantiality, the [no-] self. . . .

Quite how close the two epistemologies are must now be examined.

2

Buddhist Epistemology
The World as Performance

*My first attraction to Buddhism was that it had a better
vocabulary than mine. It had more tools for teaching what
I had been trying to teach, it had more ways of undercutting
things that I had been trying to undercut, and so I liked it.
So I would say that Buddhism can help to spread the gospel
of theatre.* — Lee Worley, "Interview: on Acting[1]

Buddhists have always had problems with ontology[2] and with the
metaphysics which supports it. Buddhism is a philosophy of direct
experience, one which — long before our Postmodern revisionists
began to question some of the most basic assumptions of Western
metaphysics — already raised profound doubts about the tendency
towards reification and hypostatization inherent in all Text-cultures
— such as the Hinduism against which early Buddhism defined
itself. In Buddhism, we have a philosophical system which, early
on, exposed the distorting mediation of language and argued for re-
establishment of the primacy of experience — the personal, direct,
immediate act of knowing.[3] More than any other factor, it is language

1.   *Performing Arts Journal,* III/1, 1978, p. 60.
2.   Ontology is a thorny topic, sometimes defined as the philosophy of
     'Essents' or Being, sometimes as the realm of Existence: it is with the
     former that Buddhism disputes, not the latter. . . .
3.   Cf. Conze, Edward, *The Perfection of Wisdom in 8000 Lines,* Bolinas,
     California, 1973, p. 274; Gudmunsen, Chris, *Wittgenstein and
     Buddhism,* MacMillan, London, 1977, p. 37; Mookerjee, Satkari, *The*
     →

which the early Buddhists recognized as the key to the way that the experiential primacy of process and event cedes to the metaphysics of object and substance.

Buddhism's solution was, from the start, to adopt and encourage a posture which is fundamentally empirical, unwilling to accept anything which has not been personally and directly experienced. Buddha himself spent many years studying the major metaphysical systems of his times and found them all wanting; after his enlightenment, he resisted his own canonization as an authority, as a source of revelations, offering instead only a method — a praxis — whereby his followers could themselves pursue the truth.

Though he did eventually speak, though he knew that he had to bow to both compassionate and transmissive necessity and attempt to formulate his experiences in words, the Buddha already realized that it was not praxis which betrays some 'original' text but texts which betray original experiences. As Douglas Daye writes:

> The Buddhists suggest that language and the coordinated relationships presupposed by language and its constant cultural reinforcement through years of preadult development constitutes a framework or grid of reified static epistemic components projected (and reprojected) on both an ever-changing inner (first person) environment and a simultaneous outer (third person) environment.[4]

Of all the world religions it is Buddhism which has most resolutely resisted the falsifying tendencies of the Word; every serious Buddhist soon learns that words can help only as signposts, as indications, as fingers which point towards the primary necessity of direct experience.

Buddhists also, early on, recognized the problem: the way that

---

→   *Buddhist Philosophy of Universal Flux,* Motilal Banarsidass, New Delhi, 1975, p. 102.

4.   Daye, D.D., "Major Schools of the Mahayana", *Buddhism. A Modern Perspective,* ed. by Charles S. Prebish, Penn State University, 1975, p. 79.

experiences themselves project and construct Subjects and Objects. They devised sophisticated methods to subvert this process, to return the seeker to the point of experience by re-cognizing those Subjects and Objects as mere categories, as 'empty', as transcendental extrapolations from primary experience. Though there is some dispute over this, there are — among Buddhists and among their interpreters (notably Conze and Guenther)[5] — many who see in 'immediate apprehension' the purest kind of knowledge that can be achieved.

That 'immediate apprehension' is termed *pratyakṣa*: the primary contact preceding actual perception and conception (sometimes called 'disturbance by an object')[6]. Placed at the very bottom of the congnitive scale by Hegel, this first contact remains very important in some sects of Buddhism, treasured as a kind of uncontaminated, direct, immediate and true cognition. As Conze writes in *Buddhist Thought in India:*

> On this level the world of things as they are ultimately by themselves, i.e. as momentary flashes of energy, each one unique in its concrete being which is shared by nothing else, impinge on the mind; only to be lost sight of very soon by the superimposition of imaginary and arbitrary thought-constructions. The series of indivisible point-instants which is disclosed here is the only thing in the universe which is not a fictitious construction.[7]

Those instants of sensory contact are, however, very fleeting (though some later schools evolved meditational practices to hold onto them); almost at the very moment we experience something we begin to add to that experience other cognitive processes — identification, interpretation, comparison, feeling, memory.... We

---

5. Cf. notably Conze, Edward, *Buddhist Thought in India,* University of Michigan Press, Ann Arbor, 1973 and Guenther, Herbert V., *Buddhist Philosophy in Theory and Practice,* Penguin Books, London, 1971.

6. Cf. Jayasuriya, W.J., *The Psychology and Philosophy of Buddhism. An Introduction to the Abhidhamma,* Colombo, 1963.

7. Conze, *op. cit.* (1973), p. 267.

perceive a chair, almost immediately we supply a word for it, a function for it, a comparison with other chairs, a feeling about it. ... (The great Theravāda Buddhist, Buddhaghosa, once calculated that a mental event occurs sixteen times as fast as a natural event, later it was calculated to last 0.0˙48 seconds.)[8] The early Buddhists worked out very complex and elaborate lists of the stages between sensory contact and actual thought: *pratyakṣa*, they decided, is almost immediately followed by sensation itself — as a sense-datum is followed by a sense-reception; this is in turn followed by sense investigation, sense decision. ... Sensation itself is, in turn, followed by perception, and perception is analyzed down into nine phases: one notes, recognizes, determines, discriminates, classifies, hypostatises, attaches oneself to. ... So fleeting is that first contact that some later schools passed over into pure idealism, denying the separate reality of the 'objective trigger' completely. Other Buddhists, however, have attempted not to do this in the sense of actually denying the reality of world-out-there. They hold on to the conviction that that fleeting, immediate, personal and direct apprehension prior to conceptualization, prior to understanding, prior to judgement is primal and valuable knowledge, more valuable than 'higher' cognitions which are characterized by a built-in tendency towards conceptualization and hence create reified fictions. It is mental cognition, Buddhism argues, which **creates** ontologies, which constructs categories, which creates absolutes, so that one can either conclude, along with the Yogācāryas, that reality itself is only mind, or look around for some form of cognition which does not have such built-in fictionality.[9]

---

8.   Buddhaghosa's calculation was not so hard: in Buddhism, every mental event occurs because of the existence of four factors — an object, a sense to cognise the object, the particular consciousness peculiar to that sense, and the cognition of that consciousness. Since every moment of time is also in four parts — the arising, the coming into being, the being and the ceasing, we get sixteen.

9.   As Saṅgharakṣita writes "one can never be really free so long as ideas, even the most highly refined and spiritualised are treated as corresponding to ultimately real objects instead of as operative concepts". *The Three Jewels. An Introduction to Buddhism*, London, 1967, p. 91.

Pratyakṣa is the main candidate for such a form of cognition —
one which it would not be hard to label as 'aesthetic' apprehension.

Guenther writes:

> Philosophy which once was a comprehensive science
> involving sensation and imagination, feeling and thinking,
> has been relegated and restricted to semantic and logical
> activity. The result is that many of us have lost the capacity
> of understanding that, apart from an intellectual
> apprehension of the world, there is another one which
> yields truths just as valuable and valid. This is the aesthetic
> apprehension or intrinsic perception by the artist, the poet,
> and the seer, whose words are a commentary on a vision
> rather than a futile attempt to establish a system of
> supposedly universal truths. . . . Aesthetic experience
> belongs to the core of man's Being; it is more fundamental
> than any intellectual experience. Being basic to man's
> striving, it is the *terminus a quo,* enlightenment being the
> *terminus a quem* which is nevertheless permanently
> grounded in aesthetic experience.[10]

Guenther also makes the connection between this and *pratyakṣa*:

> To perceive anything as it is in its intrinsic uniqueness is
> to perceive it aesthetically.[11]

Buddhism is sometimes described as an anti-sensual religion, but
Buddha and his followers knew that renunciation does not by itself
extinguish desire, that hating the body leaves one just as attached
to it as indulging in it.[12] Buddha himself practised and then rejected

---

10.   Guenther, *op. cit.,* pp. 160-61.
11.   *Ibid.,* p. 181.
12.   One must be especially careful about the term *duḥkha.* There is a
       popular perception of Buddhists as obsessed with suffering: this is a
       misconception. Buddhists are not obsessed with suffering in any
       physical sense nor do they court it like some Hindu sects: Buddha
       himself found the Hindu yogic practices of physical mortification
       unsatisfactory and many later schools of Buddhism, notably the

→

the ascetic paths of bodily mortification, and remained in his body for decades after his own enlightenment. Buddhism preaches enlightenment in the body — the Middle Path which neither denies that a world of forms exists nor affirms that it has essence: that, it is argued, could be called an aesthetic attitude.

Beyond that, every other kind of knowledge is suspect to a Buddhist, especially any metaphysical grand narratives. It was in order to prevent the mind's tendency to fabricate such fictions that Buddha devised and taught the Middle Way, a method designed to prevent his followers from straying over into either nihilism at one end or substantialism at the other. Formulated already by Gautama Buddha, this was then turned into a rigorous philosophical system by Nāgārjuna in whose works we find the double negatives which have teased us already in the context of Performance theory.

Nāgārjuna tests any proposition by applying four formulae:

- does x equal y?

- does x not equal y?

- does x both equal and not equal y?

- until he comes to the fourth — the double negative: is x neither y nor not y?

Application of these four syllogisms to any proposition was — and is — a fundamental practice in ambiguous thinking, in training the mind to retain simultaneously two contradictory possibilities without collapsing one into the other, no more or less than continual praxis in living on a cognitive threshold.

→   Tibetans and other Tāntric schools, have a great deal of respect for the human body, and do not share the belief that we should torment it for the sake of our souls. *Duḥkha* is not about physical suffering; it is about mental suffering — the sheer unsatisfactory nature of all human experience, unsatisfactory because all experiences are so impermanent, an impermanence which in turn proves their lack of substance. *Duḥkha* is probably best translated as unsatisfactory; it is a response to *aniccā* — impermanence — which demonstrates in turn *anatta* — no substance.

It was also, for Nāgārjuna, a way to stretch the mind so as to prepare it for meditation. Because the purpose of Buddhist philosophy is soteriological, directed at escaping or at least improving *karma* and achieving enlightenment. Enlightenment is, of course, beyond philosophical analysis — indescribable, non-conceptual — and hence Buddhist philosophy is paralleled by other practices which take the conceptual apparatus of Buddhist philosophy and turn it into the raw material for direct experience. It is meditation which does this, turning philosophy into praxis. Buddhists are simply not interested in only knowing something: the whole point of pushing philosophical positions into meditative practices is to turn knowledge into wisdom via experience. One cannot simply know Buddhism or even simply believe in it; one has to be it.

Meditation manuals are in the end manuals of praxis: it is here, if anywhere, that the performative aspects of Buddhism must — and will — be found.

Before, however, investigating meditation as a performative praxis, it is well to do what Buddhists do before they meditate: review the basic philosophical premises, the epistemological map.[13]

Beginning, as with performance epistemology, where one must always begin: with Time. . . .

1. Temporality

At all seasons Time constrains the world; Time does not exist in the highest good which leads to salvation.[14]

---

13. Most Buddhist meditation teachers require that students learn Buddhist philosophy first or at least simultaneously; otherwise, they argue, the meditational insights will not be distinctively Buddhist: cf. Kornfield, Jack, *Living Buddhist Masters,* Unity Press, Santa Cruz, 1977; Wayman, Alex, *Calming the Mind and Discerning the Real. Buddhist Meditation and the Middle Way,* New York, 1978, pp. 89-92, 174. Evans-Wentz, W.Y., *Tibetan Yoga and Secret Doctrines,* Oxford University Press, 1958, pp. 79-82.

14. Aśvaghoṣa, *The Buddhacarita or Acts of the Buddha,* Oriental Books Reprint, 1972, p. 131.

1.1. *Anicca* — impermanence — is one of the four basic truths of Buddhist experience: the fundamental temporality of existence. It was this fact of permanent change which already preoccupied the Buddha himself and set him out on his journey. It extends beyond epistemology to be a cognitive stand: all truths too are temporary; indeed truth is itself a dynamic process, never a stable or static position.

1.2. Philosophical inquiry into Temporality, however, then yielded a theory of moments as the early Buddhists joined in the Hindu philosophical debate about the size of an instant, the length of now. Examining time, they decided that it must be almost infinitely divisible — into moments which are almost infinitely and discretely small. This early theory of momentarism was the one espoused by the *Abhidharma*: in the *Abhidharma-mahāvibhāṣa-śāstra* it is calculated that a day of 24 hours must have 6,400,990,908 *kṣaṇa*s or moments (others calculated 66,499,099,980). . . . It is not so much the numbers that matter as the fact that what the Abhidharmists had done was convert the Buddha's notion of impermanence into a new doctrine of moments. And the danger of momentarism is clear: if something exists — albeit only for a minute fraction of a second — without changing, then what has been generated is another form of substantialism: once you establish a moment, you postulate stasis and in the process create substance.

An alternative was, however, soon found: namely to define moments not in terms of what lasts through them but as units of change. All theories of time have to confront a basic philosophical problem, one as much logical as empirical: the problem of continuity and change. They form a classic binary: everything changes, but to be recognized as the thing which changed, something — in everything — must continue. You can only have change if there is continuity, and vice versa. But, as Nāgārjuna would therefore point out gleefully: that means that 'things' are philosophically self-contradictory — both the same as they once were and different — unless you posit that they are made up of two component parts: a core — a soul or self, an *ātman* (which continues) — and a surface form, an appearance (which changes). That is the classic Western philosophical solution and the Hindu view — and for a while the early Buddhists succumbed to it too. The Sautrāntika argument that everything exists, in a discrete and unique form, for one brief moment raises the logical problem of how anything can therefore have any relationship with the next stage of its own life, or any other thing? Such a theory of moments questions the very possibility of any causal relationship between things, to which the Sautrāntika replied that a thing lasts only as long as it needs to in order to exert its effect. Since there is, however, still a gap between the life-stages of all things, the question remains how 'it' crosses that gap? Meanwhile, the other major Abhidharma school — the Sarvāstivādins — also had a problem: arguing that a moment has four phases and that one of them — the crucial one — is subsistence or stability, they were faced with the question, **what** subsides, what remains stable? Faced by such a question, they could not resist postulating some 'special dharma' — something which, unlike all the others, endures. They were back with *ātman*, with substantialist theories; they had done what the Buddha warned them not to do, forsake the Middle Way. . . .[15]

Now, the only solutions for this are:

(i)   to continue to insist on gaps between moments but therefore accept that the world must collapse and be recreated every instant (because the gaps cannot be crossed);

(ii) to deny that there are any gaps, to deny the divisibility of time completely and argue a case for flux time;

(iii) to argue that time is relational or a property of phenomena;

(iv) to argue that time, like all so-called phenomena themselves, is not something objective but something cognitive; that what we in fact analyze is never and can never be any thing as such but only ever our perceptions and then our thoughts about things — by which time the 'thing itself' has passed, changed.

---

15.   On this issue cf. Kalupahana, David J., *Causality: The Central Philosophy of Buddhism*, University Press of Hawaii, Honolulu, 1975.

As Geshe Lhundup Sopa writes:

> Yesterday's pot exists as a past pot. The past of a thing
> occurs after its present existence, that is, after its present
> existence has passed. Tomorrow's pot exists today as a
> future pot. The future of a thing occurs before its present
> existence, that is, when its present existence is yet to be.[16]

Sangharaksita writes:

> Seeing conditioned things as impermanent does not mean
> seeing them first as actually existing and afterwards as no
> longer existing but rather in reducing them to an absolutely
> continuous flow, or pure becoming.[17]

1.3. It is this solution which became the basis of both Nāgārjuna's
critical metaphysics and of Yogācārya idealism: momentarism
gave way to a theory of eternal flux, within which Time is simply
adjectival, a property of living matter, the basis of the Buddhist
perception that there are — really — no things, only events.

It was Nāgārjuna who provided the philosophical formulation:
time is, in the end, always associated with some substantialist
notion of 'Self' — some thing which exists in and through time. If
you remove that, you have no problem: if there is no 'Self' (substance)
in subject or object, then time is no longer a problem because no
thing has now to continue or change through time. Nothing is born,
nothing exists, nothing dies because there is *no thing:*

> Without an existent, occurrence as well as dissolution are
> not evident. Without occurrence as well as dissolution, an
> existent is not evident.

> If it is assumed that time exists depending upon an existent,
> how can there be time without an existent? No existent

---

16.   Sopa, Geshe Lhundrup and Hopkins, Jeffrey, *Practice and Theory of
       Tibetan Buddhism,* Grove Press, New York, 1976, p. 75.

17.   Sangharaksita, *op. cit.,* pp. 131f.

whatsoever is found to exist. Where can time be?[18]

To Nāgārjuna the whole question of time — and, therefore, the key to any philosophy of process or performance — is bound up with the problem of *anatta* (insubstantiality), which is the more fundamental of the issues. . . .

2. Insubstantiality

The elements of existence are momentary appearances, momentary flashings. . . . They disappear as soon as they appear, in order to be followed in the next moment by another momentary existence. . . . Disappearance is the very essence of existence; what does not disappear does not exist.[19]

2.1. If Time starts to make sense only when moments are redefined not as instants of stasis but as measures of change, then Things too make sense only when also radically redefined — as cognitive events: "experiential moments . . . each one unique but . . . infinitesimally small".[20]

To a Buddhist, all things are changing, and therefore any thing *can* only be discrete, unique, singular, particular. Mental habits will relate each thing as it occurs to other, similar things and in the process obscure this essential, discrete distinction of particulars. All experiences, all perceptions are marked by the impermanence both of the perception itself and of the thing perceived, an impermanence which can be so disturbing, so disorienting that, as Buddha went on to argue, our realization that things are empty and impermanent is usually, habitually, obscured by the four *ghanas*

---

18. *The Mulamadhyamakakarika of Nagarjuna,* Introduction and Text and Translation by Kalupahana, David J., Motilal Banarsidass, New Delhi, 1991, pp. 278, 295.

19. Stcherbatsky, T.I., *The Central Conception of Buddhism,* London, Royal Asiatic Society, 1928, pp. 37-38.

20. Inada, K.K. "Time and Temporality — A Buddhist Approach", *Essays on Time in Buddhism,* ed. by Prasad, H.S., Delhi, 1991, p. 469.

(or densities), namely our habit of perceiving things as having continuity, wholeness or closure, function or flow, and objectivity.

The result is that the three 'marks' of existence (*anatta, anicca, duḥkha*) are converted by the four *ghana*s into the false notions of permanence, wholeness, purposefulness, and substance.

This is the fundamental self-deception, one whose 'cure' lies in constantly rethinking the nature of things and their mode of being, learning to see that a thing *is* what it does.

2.2. The second of the Buddha's truths is that all things are empty — *anatta*. This has led to charges of nihilism but really it was only ever a matter of deconstructive redefinition. When the Abhidharmists came to make their lists of things — *dharma*s — they began by breaking them down into their properties, with the result that what we get is not so much a list of nouns describing substances but one of adjectives describing qualities.[21]

To illustrate: the early Buddhist philosophers began where all early philosophies, East and West, began — with the four so-called elements, earth, water, fire and air — but already began to reinterpret these four substances in terms of their qualities or functions. Earth, water, fire and air are redefined as attributes, and in the process converted into adjectives: rough, hard, viscous, hot, moveable.... Earth becomes the quality or attribute of solidity whose function is to hold things together; water becomes the quality or attribute of moisture whose function is to provide cohesion; fire is heat providing ripening; air is motion providing change and growth, etc., so that the resistance of things to each other is their earth-quality; the mutual attraction of things is their water quality and so on....

Apart from a couple of 'unconditioned *dharma*s' which became subjects for meditation, everything in the world was divided by the early Abhidharmists into conditioned *dharma*s. In some systems

21.   There are useful studies in Jayasuriya, W.J., *The Psychology and Philosophy of Buddhism,* Colombo, 1963; Sogen, Yamakami, *Systems of Buddhistic Thought,* Chinese Materials Center, San Francisco, 1976 and McGovern, W.M., *A Manual of Buddhist Philosophy,* Chinese Materials Center, San Francisco, 1977.

there are 172 of these; in others 75, 84, 100 but — one must emphasize — as adjectives, qualities or functions.

Things, in other words, do exist but only as aggregates; aggregates in turn exist only in and through things; nothing exists *per se*: the referent is always a reification. This is already a good example of The Middle Way: it does not deny that things exist but suggests that they exist only as attributes which in turn exist only as combinations which produce things but, in the end, all such things are, therefore, neither denied nor affirmed: nothing exists but nothing does not exist.

2.3. This early Buddhist philosophy is sometimes called 'atomism' in that it attempted to reduce the world to a set and series of fundamental entities. The term 'atomism' must, however, be used cautiously because what the Buddhists found was these atoms are ultimately 'empty': they have no core or substance, they are only compounds of qualities, attributes. This discovery is critical but is often obscured by the way that a number of Western Buddhologists have been misled and have in turn misled their readers by adopting —- from their Western tradition — the assumption that *dharmas*, the basic atoms of the universe, are things and cannot even see that they may be just properties. Thus Stcherbatsky, for example, probably because he was a Russian and heavily influenced by Russian Materialism, calls *dharma* 'elements'. Rhys Davids, who did so much to bring Buddhism to the attention of the West, in the process misrepresented it by her assumption that the Buddhists could not be serious in denying a soul to humans or fundamental substantiality to matter: she calls *dharmas* phenomena; Geiger translates *dharmas* as 'empirical things'. Collins writes:

> Behind all these mistaken views and 'unfit questions' lies the assumption that there is an entity which is denoted by the grammatical subject of verbs, while the Buddha's reply asserts the existence of an event described by the verbal notion, but denies that it is legitimate to infer the existence of a real subject from the verbal form.[22]

---

22. Steven Collins, *Selfless Persons*, Cambridge U.P., 1982, p. 105.

It took people such as Conze and Guenther to realize the mistake, to realize that *dharma* in Buddhism (though not in Hinduism) refers by and large to the properties or attributes of events, not things. Conze writes: "the own-being of the thing is dissolved into the conditions of its happening"[23] or as Guenther puts it: "Things ... are hypotheses symbolizing possible ways in which events may be connected."[24]

In other words, and summarizing the above: the world of things is examined, deconstructed and becomes a world of properties which is then further re-cognized as a world of events, happenings. The result is that the criterion of a thing's existence in Buddhism is not some moment of pure being but the performance of generative actions.

Stcherbatsky writes:

at the time when an element does not yet actually perform its function, it is future; when performing it, it becomes present; when, after having performed it, it stops, it becomes past.[25]

Vyas writes:

The criterion of existence is the performance of certain specific actions.[26]

Johansson writes:

There are no 'things' in Buddhism, only processes.[27]

"Things," Chang summarizes, "do not exist; only events exist."[28]

23.   Conze, *op. cit.* (1973), p. 240.
24.   Guenther, *op. cit.*, p. 141.
25.   *The Central Concept of Buddhism,* Calcutta, 1956, pp. 66f.
26.   Vyas, C.S., *Buddhist Theory of Perception,* Navrang, New Delhi, 1991, p. 12.
27.   Johansson, Rune E.A., *The Dynamic Psychology of Early Buddhism,* Curzon Press, Oxford, 1979, p. 217.
28.   Garma, C. C. Chang, *The Buddhist Teaching of Totality. The Philosophy of Hwa Yen Buddhism,* Penn State U.P., 1971, p. 81.

Temporality, particularity, singularity, process, event: Buddhism provides a rich philosophical speculation on the fundamental properties of a world in performance. It also provides a theory of doubles.

3. Other Universes

The sense organs are to be known as Maya, the sense-fields resemble a dream: actor, act, and setting —they do not at all in reality exist. . . .[29]

3.1. This quotation from the *Laṅkāvatāra Sūtra* may seem at first sight to resemble Western thinking about theatre and suggest some similar fundamental commitment to the notion of one 'really real' — material — universe of which all others are necessarily representations, illusions, deceptions.

But Buddhism has never had problems with other, parallel realities: Buddhist cosmologies, indeed, posit a virtually infinite number of parallel universe—necessary if every possible expression and manifestation of the basic forces in the universe is to be realized. None of these universes has any priority over the others: all of them are fictions, *māyā*-like. Indeed what Buddhism came to see is that every 'reality' is a creation, a construct of the mind: they are all 'theatres'. This is inherent already in an early basic text — the *Paticcasamuppāda* — where the combination of the first six steps in cognition[30] describes how we create a sense of a real world somehow 'out there' which we seek then to know, not recognizing, in our ignorance, that that world *is* something which we are creating. That does not mean that it does not exist; it does exist but not, as we in our ignorance, see it: we see 'things' when there are really only combinations of *dharmas* in flux; we see causality when there is really only a dance of interconnected *dharmas*. In this sense, the *Paticcasamuppāda* is no less than a blueprint for the

---

29. *Lankavatara Sutra*, tr. by Suzuki, D.T., Routledge, London, 1952, pp. 235 and cf. pp. 190, 193.

30. Ignorance; the 'dispositions' ['*sankharas*']:consciousness ['*vijñāna*']; the psychophysical complex ['*nāma-rūpa*']:the six senses; contact.

ongoing creation of the world of *saṁsāra*, the world in which we live, the theatre in which we believe.

To this extent it might appear as if Buddhism merely anticipated the Western Theatrum Mundi metaphor or borrowed the Hindu notion that reality is like a theatre in its *māyā*-quality. This is to some extent true but masks the real difference, namely that Buddhism — uniquely — resolves the whole problem of appearance and reality, illusion and truth by dissolving the distinction: form and emptiness are complements; things are their appearances.[31]

This applies not only to things; it applies also to "us". . . .

4. No Self

What are called 'individuals' are streams of momentary physiological-psychological events.[32]

4.1. Probably the most immediately attractive aspect of Buddhism to contemporary Deconstructionists and Cognitive Scientists is *anatta* — the decentred, dispersed, discontinuous self of Buddhism. It is also the topic which provides the most obvious of the analogies with Performance theory: the quotation above from Stephan Anacher's description of Buddhist *anatta* could be said about any performer.

Buddhism even arrived at this insight by the same route as Performance theory — first by identifying the 'Self' as a binary, and then by dispersing that binary through deconstructive reasoning.

4.2. Early Buddhism recognized a primary distinction between the I-as-Subject and the I-as-Self. The former is the spectator of the latter, which is, however, itself deconstructed into a series of evolving and transient me's. None of these is the 'real me': all are merely actors of parts.

'Parts' is taken literally: the ego is deconstructed into five

---

31.   Cf. Vyas, *op.cit.,* p. 140.
32.   Anacher, Stefan, "The Meditational Therapy of the Madhyanta-vibhagabhasya", in *Mahayana Buddhist Meditation. Theory and Practice,* ed. by Kiyota, Minoru, University of Hawaii Press, 1978, p. 86.

operations — the five *Skandhas* — with the result that a 'person' is never anything but a particular and temporary combination of functions producing and explaining experiences.

Skandhas are, then, also not things but activities; the 'Self' which they construct is a temporary product of activities. Identity — as some contemporary feminists are arguing in the West — is a practice.[33]

Malalasekera writes:

An individual is a being, i.e., something that is, but, in the Buddha's teaching, the individual's being is, in fact a *becoming,* a coming-to-be, something that happens, i.e., an event, a process.[34]

Ueda Yoshifumi summarizes:

The world exists, not only as an object seen by the individual, but, at the same time, as something being created by each individual it is in the process of becoming. The individual is not simply a seer, but also an actor.[35]

That was already the Buddha's insight and teaching:

Train yourself in such a way that there is only seeing in what is seen, there is only hearing in what is heard, there is only sensing in what is sensed, there is only cognising in what is cognised. Then you will not be recognised in terms of what is seen, heard, etc. (i.e., as the seer of something, as the hearer of something, etc.). . . . That will be the end of suffering.[36]

33. Cf. Klein, Anne Carolyn, *Meeting the Great Bliss Queen,* Beacon Press, Boston, 1995, p. 7.

34. Malalasekera, G.P., "The status of the individual in Theravada Buddhist philosophy", *The Status of the Individual in East and West,* ed. by Moore, C.A., University of Hawaii Press, Honolulu, 1968, p. 66.

35. Yoshifumi, Ueda, "The status of the individual in Mahayana Buddhist philosophy", *ibid.,* p. 83.

36. Translation by Lily de Silva of the passage in the *Bodhi-vagga* of the Udana, from "Sense Experience of the Liberated Being as reflected in early Buddhism", *Buddhist Philosophy and Culture,* ed. by Kalupahana, D.J., and Weeraratne, W.G., Colombo, 1987, p 17.

Mookerjee comments:

> How completely the Buddha had rid himself of the notion
> of a fixed being is well-established by all the passages
> where he replaces the actor by the act itself.[37]

Buddhist psychology is very close to performance psychology here,
recognizing the Self as only a mix of transient actor of roles (written
by *karma*), confronted by a spectator who is him/herself only a
transient point since the whole is in flux.

Truth, experience are to be found, in consequence, only ever in
the threshold.

5. In-between

> *When the notion of objectivity becomes problematic . . . , so*
> *too does the notion of subjectivity. If everything is ultimately*
> *specified through its appearance to us, then so is the knowing*
> *subject. Since the subject can represent itself to itself, it*
> *becomes an object for representation but is different from all*
> *other objects. Thus in the end the self becomes both an*
> *objectified subject and a subjectified object. This predicament*
> *discloses the shiftiness, the instability of the entire subjective /*
> *objective polarity.*[38]

5.1. Buddhism often draws no distinction between mental and
physical phenomena: *dharma* means natural phenomena [and
hence, by extension, nature or the world] but it also means mental
phenomena, mental states, ideas [and beyond that, by a similar
extension, doctrines or principles and even truth].

Buddhism did not make any distinction between these, partly
because, as Johansson argues, Buddhism does not divide the world
into concrete realities on the one hand and mental realities on the
other but rather sees these as only the two poles of a continuum,

---

37. Mookerjee, *op.cit.,* p. 168.
38. Varela, Francisco J., Thompson, Evan, and Rosch, Eleanor, *The*
     Embodied Mind, M.I.T. Press, Cambridge, Mass., 1991, p. 242.

seeing reality — as he terms it — as "psychophysical".[39] But it also uses the one word *dharma* for both objects and ideas, both things and concepts because, to a Buddhist, everything — concrete reality, mental reality, the world and even truth itself — are the same: all are fictions.

5.2. The word fiction is interesting: it meant originally 'to fashion, form, shape; to construct'. Buddhism argues that all epistemologies (all attempts to know what can be known) and their equivalent ontologies (their statements about what is) are and can be only constructs, hypotheses, fictions.

This has a number of implications:

(i) that Buddhists have less of a problem than those brought up in a Western philosophical tradition in seeing all 'realities' as somehow partly imaginative;

(ii) that they typically practise philosophy by recourse to continuum models, namely models defined by two extreme and opposite poles (Subject-Object; Phenomena-Noumena ...). These two poles appear always to offer a stark choice, but what Buddhists seek to do is not opt for one or the other, not try to prove that one is true and the other false but somehow find a position which does not occupy one end to the exclusion of the other, nor denies that they are opposites, but tries somehow to transcend or suspend their contradiction. For example and notably: Buddha identified the two extreme possible philosophical positions current at his time in Hindu philosophy as nihilism or annihilationism on the one hand and eternalism or substantialism on the other. Both, Buddha found to be false in themselves but instead of negating or affirming either, he sought to occupy some position in between them.

Buddhists are taught always to try to occupy positions — the Middle Way — in between a non-existent Self and an equally non-

39. Johansson, Rune E.A., *The Dynamic Psychology of Early Buddhism*, Curzon Press, Oxford, 1979, p. 49.

existent objective world, to inhabit, in other words, liminal spaces. That is the function of its meditative practices. . . .

It is to those that we may now turn because, although the above is, hopefully, sufficient to prove the point that Buddhism can provide Performance Theory with the kind of rich tradition of philosophizing which it needs at this point in its evolution as a new paradigm, if this is to be more than a philosophical analogy, if it is to be a meeting of praxes [which, I have been arguing, both Buddhism and Performance ultimately are] then all of this philosophy must be pursued now into the arena of meditation, for it is here that Buddhism is performed.[40]

6. Meditation as Performance

Contemplation is the stage of fruition of the theater of mind. When the practitioner has reached this stage, the multiple realities coded in cosmology and enacted in mythopoeic drama may 'come alive' in direct experience. . . .[41]

6.1. Detailed comparisons between specific meditation techniques and cultural performances will be attempted in the three chapters of Part Two; what needs noting here — in introduction — is the more general point, namely how every one of the philosophical insights of Buddhist epistemology outlined above becomes a topos for meditation, which, therefore, is a translation of the topic into a praxis, a performance. Whenever Buddhism reached historically — and whenever individual Buddhists still reach — a point in their empirical and sceptical philosophical inquiries when they decide that, beyond this point, we can only speculate, Buddhists then assign the inquiry to their meditational practices, which they have also investigated with another form of rigorous scientific method.

---

40.   On Meditation as Performance, cf. notably unpublished Honours thesis, *Meditation as Performance*, by Kok Cheng TSUNG, Murdoch University, Western Australia, 1995.

41.   Laughlin, Jr., Charies D. McManus, John and d'Aquili, Eugene G., "Mature Contemplation", *Zygon. Journal of Religion and Science*, Vol. 28., no. 2, p. 163.

This is because meditational practices are processes devised by people who, having decided, like Kant, that in the end, metaphysics is a science of cognition, that the 'Ding an sich' is, in the end, a 'Verstandeswesen' (a being of thought), that noumena are what Kant called 'pure beings of thought',[42] turned away from the objective world to the processes of consciousness and investigated them with a quite remarkable analytical rigour too.

Buddhists meditate because they have found that we can use consciousness in more ways than rationally, and that those other ways can be systematized too. Having reasoned something out, they decided, we can then subject that knowledge to other methods of consciousness, methods which will test that knowledge. . . .

Buddhists seek always to turn knowledge into experience; to know it not just intellectually but privately, deeply, personally, usefully, actively. Meditation turns ideas into truths, knowledge into experience and experiences into forms of action.

6.2. There are, of course, many and diverse systems and forms of meditational practice. Some — such as Chöd — are very theatrical; others — such as Zen — as obviously practices in improvisation and ambiguity, but even the most austere and classical — Vipassana — merits analysis in terms of performance.

Every meditation sets up a basic binary, splinters the 'Self' into 'I-spectator' of 'me-parts'. Yoshifumi writes:

'I' is divided into two parts, the really existing I, or the center of the knowing act, and the conceptual I, or the known I. . . . It is only the latter that is known."[43]

Or, as K.K. Inada writes in "Problematics of the Buddhist Nature of Self," Buddha asks one to be "both spectator and participant of the activities".[44]

---

42. Kant, Immanuel, *Prolegomena to Any Future Metaphysics,* Indianapolis, 1950, pp. 62, 109.

43. Yoshifumi, *op. cit.,* p. 87.

44. In *Buddhist and Western Philosophy,* ed. by Katz, Nathan, New Delhi, 1981, p. 275.

It might appear that there is, nevertheless, a real difference here: in performance it might appear that we become spectators of others rather than of our selves — except by empathetic identification. The whole point of a meditation, however, is to transform one's 'me's' into others — non-selves. It is basic to any meditation to objectify the me, to re-cognize it as non-self, to see that there is no self, for these me's are in constant flux. As for the 'I-spectator', it too becomes a 'me' as soon as it is cognized—by a new Subject-I which must, therefore, remain empty if it not to cross the threshold and become another bit-player. . . .

Inhibition of the creation of any reified or hypostatised 'Self' is the essence of Buddhist meditation; as Shwe Zan Aung comments: "In Buddhism there is no actor apart from action,"[45] or as Buddhadasa Bhikku puts it:

The doing is done but no doer is there
The path has been walked but no walker is there.[46]

6.3. This progressive emptying of all 'Selves' establishes only the event as 'real', and only the Threshold as a position of experiential truth, for it is paralleled by a progressive emptying of the other pole — the 'objective' world — too. All meditational systems have as basic topoi the deconstruction of things into their qualities, their attributes, thus reversing the linguistic fabrication of absolutes and substituting for them unique and transient events. 'Objects' are re-cognized as insubstantial, lasting only as long as their momentary, instantaneous apprehension by a sense-organ; by the time that sense-organ has registered an impression of the 'object', both 'it' and its channel have changed, gone. The Vipassana technique of 'noting' identifies the sensual medium and then deconstructs its contents, redefining them not as channels effecting communication but as 'factories' — fabricators of fictions masquerading as facts.

---

45.   Aung, Shwe Zan, "An Introductory Essay to the Compendium of Buddhist Philosophy", *Compendium of Philosophy*, Pali Text Society, O.U.P., London, 1929, p. 7.

46.   Translation from *Heart-Wood from the Bo Tree* by Bhikku Buddhadasa, Suan Mok, 1935, p. 23.

6.4. This experience of *anatta* is simultaneously experience of the truth of *anicca̅*, too, for every meditation re-establishes the primary fact of temporality, of ephemerality. This is indeed, in all systems, another of the basic meditational topoi: time becomes ever more segmented, ever more fractured into smaller and smaller units. This is an always disorientating and even terrifying experience of the rapid speed of change, a fundamental practice in de-mystification — cleansing the mind of its accumulated baggage of objects, absolutes, *a prioris*, and returning it to the contemplation of 'aesthetic' moments. . . .

6.5. There is much to be gained by drawing comparisons between performance and the Buddhist experience of truth; one can even speculate on a real similarity in goals, for every meditation offers a fundamental choice: either to return to the ka̅rmic scripts, write and enact new possiblities of being for other lives, or opt out, be the Empty Spectator of the dance — the ceaseless play of forms, arising interdependently, dissolving, re-assembling. Here one cannot only see the world as it is — *tathata* — but feel emotions without desire, occupy a seat of unattached equanimity. . . .

Conclusion

Analysis of meditation as a form of performance requires detailed case studies. A first attempt at this follows, because what has been claimed above about the analogies between meditation and performance needs paralleling with the reversed equation: performance as a form of meditation. To investigate this, we must now revisit Buddhist theatre which, in spite of injunctions banning it, can be found in Sri Lanka, Thailand, Burma, China, Japan, Nepal, Tibet. . . . Within this panorama, three main *kinds* of theatrical practice can be identified, each corresponding to one of the three *paths* open to a Buddhist — the *karma* path, the *bodhisattva* option, and Enlightenment — and each representative of one of the three main *cultures* of Buddhism — the Hi̅naya̅na, Maha̅ya̅na, and Vajraya̅na.

The former may be found best exemplified in Sri Lanka;

'*bodhisattva* theatre' is how I would want to redefine the Tibetan Theatre of the Vajrayāna while the final option — performance itself as a means of satori — can be best exemplified in Japan.

Part II

The Case Studies
Buddhism in Performance

3

Karma Drama
The Hīnayāna; Sri Lanka

Introduction

EVERY religion has its austere, 'puritanical' wing and it is invariably this wing which lays claim to being the most 'pure' expression of the original doctrine, constantly returning the religion to its most reductive, fundamentalist reading and practice.

Within Buddhism, the Hīnayāna ('Lesser Vehicle' or Path) — or, as they prefer, Theravāda ('Teaching of the Elders')—represents this wing. Of the countries practising this form of Buddhism, it is perhaps Sri Lanka which has the best credentials for representative status: it is in Sri Lanka that the Pāli scriptures are preserved and from Sri Lanka that both Burma (Myānmār) and Thailand switched from Mahāyāna to Theravāda in the eleventh and twelfth centuries.

The actual history of Buddhism in Sri Lanka is, nevertheless, a history of decay and reform, of sectarian conflict, recurrent disputes about orthodoxy, periodic revitalization campaigns, the purging of Mahāyānist and other revisionist influences.[1] The very fact that the order had to be reformed twelve times up to the fifteenth century illustrates the point but also the claim that it is Sri

---

1. Cf. Adikaram, E.W., *Early History of Buddhism in Ceylon,* Colombo, 1953; Rahula, Walpola, *History of Buddhism in Ceylon,* Colombo, 1966, pp. 87ff, 93ff; Paranavitana, S., "Mahayanism in Ceylon", *Ceylon Journal of Science,* Vol. 2, Pt. 1, 1928, pp. 35-71.

Lanka which has most rigorously and regularly, throughout its history, purged itself of both syncretic and Mahāyānist tendencies, sometimes with the return assistance of the Thai or Burmese Saṁgha.[2]

It is also in Sri Lanka that the more austere forms of meditation are practised.

As a praxis, Theravāda meditation can be summarized as emphasizing:

- solitude, isolation;

- desensualisation and consequent de-aestheticisation;

- the conversion of sensory filters into barriers, leading to the progressive emptying of the 'Self';

- the identification of all 'media' — all the *skandhas* — as supplying deceptive information, and their progressive clearing of any substantial content;

- a practice in 'emptiness'.

There is no formula here for the development of a theatre but there are many analogies to performance, because meditation in Pāli and Sinhalese — *bhāvanā* — describes not only the actual practice of seated contemplation but cultivation of a general attitude towards every action performed in life. Theravāda meditation falls into two stages: *samatha* (tranquillity) which is virtually identical with classical Indian techniques, and *vipassanā*, the unique Buddhist method designed to facilitate insight into the true nature of the psychophysical constitution. Already in *samatha*, the class of practices called 'Kasina' cultivates a technique of 'one-pointedness' designed to generate awareness of the unique particularity of all phenomena and the temporality of all being. *Vipassanā* takes the practitioner beyond these preparatory stages to regular and arduous concentration on the arising and passing of all phenomena —

---

2.   Cf. Gombrich, Richard F., *Theravada Buddhism*, Routledge, London, 1988; Carrithers Michael, *The Forest Monks of Sri Lanka*, Oxford University Press, Delhi, 1983.

including the 'self'. Here performance metaphors become compulsive: a leading contemporary Theravāda meditation teacher such as Achaan Naeb, for example, writes:

> The Vipassana meditator must be like a spectator at a play. Don't try to direct the activity. Simply watch mindfully the constant flow of matter and mental states as they come into consciousness. This balanced stance will lead to wisdom.[3]

To become such a 'spectator' necessitates first splitting oneself from one's role as actor, or rather deconstructing the actor in oneself into a series of actions. Another influential contemporary Theravāda teacher, Mahasi Sayadaw, describes this technique as re-cognition of the self as a series of present tense activities:

> When you stop walking, stopping.
> When you stretch the hand, stretching.
> When the hand touches the cup, touching.
> When the hand takes the cup, taking. . . [4]

Emphasis on splintering the actor-in-oneself into a series of actions, realization of the permanence only of change, the deconstruction of all things, including the self, into events: these reveal Theravāda meditation as a practice as much in the basic epistemologies of Performance as of Buddhist philosophy. Above all, Theravāda meditation separates the self into spectator and actor and frees consciousness from entrapment in illusion.

To this extent we may well conclude that the Theravāda is simultaneously positive towards Performance while remaining negative towards Theatre, thus rigorously adhering to the Buddha's own doubts about theatre and dance as promoting illusion and sensuality.

There is, nevertheless, theatre and dance in Sri Lanka; the dominant forms — Sanni exorcism, Kolam and Kandy dance — will be examined in detail below but the phenomenon itself is ancient:

---

3. Kornfield, *op. cit.,* p. 158.
4. *Ibid.,* p. 61.

there are terracotta images of dancing girls dating back to the fifth/ sixth centuries and they are prominent in wooden carvings at Embekke. The *Mahāvaṁsa* records that King Pandukabhaya (377-307 BC) had "gods and men dance before him on festival days" and there is ample evidence that the courts since Dutthagamini's times (101-77 BC) sponsored dancing girls.[5] 'Sinhala Natum' is mentioned as a discrete dance form in the Tamil epic, *Cilappadikaram* of the second century, and the evidence can be followed, with little discontinuity, through to the graphic descriptions of the *Saṁdeśa Kāvyas* of the fourteenth and fifteenth centuries, and the evidence of stone, wood and metal carvings, ivory combs. . . Some dances, it appears, were performed in front of gods, in the nude.[6] Nor was this all and only dance: Senarat Paranavitana in *The Story of Sigiri* (Colombo, 1972) recounts how King Kaśyapa (477-95) built a 'theatre' in the North-West part of Simhagiri Hill where he had plays performed. He did more than that: needing to establish himself as a 'god-king' both for his personal pride and so that his new gold coins would be accepted as trading currency, he staged a remarkable piece of political-religious theatre: "he got up early and, having dressed up and adorned himself in the manner of Kuvera and accompanied by his queen dressed and adorned in the manner of Sri Devi, took their stand in the theatre established in the north-western slope of the rock and presented themselves to the assembly of over a thousand notables who had gathered there. The assembled multitude shouted at the top of their voices: 'Hail! The Great king Kasyapa, the Lord of Alaka. Hail! Kuvera, the consort of the goddess Sri.' " This piece of political-religious theatre evidently worked and even established a precedent: when Kaśyapa's younger brother, Moggallan, seized the throne after 18 years in exile, he dressed himself up as Yama, the God of Death, complete with a contraption which fitted inside his mouth enabling him to project four long canine teeth. The impersonation worked: his soldiers

---

5. Cf. Raghavan, M.D., *Sinhala Natum. Dances of the Sinhalese,* Colombo, 1967, p. 21.

6. *Ibid.,* pp. 27ff.

seized his dazed enemies and hurled them into the inferno he had prepared for them.[7]

Now it would be simple to conclude that these 'ritual performances' involved the impersonation of Hindu gods and to extend that argument to all the evidence: this is not Buddhist but Hindu — the argument put by Nandadeva Wijesekera is one of the more comprehensive studies of Sri Lankan dance: *Deities and Demons, Magic and Masks* (Colombo, 1987). Such a conclusion is not hard to validate: Sri Lanka remained under Indian cultural influence and even domination for long periods after its conversion to Buddhism; even Buddhist kings took Hindu wives.[8] Field research in Sri Lanka reveals that the friezes depicting dancing girls on the Hatadage (the second — main — Temple of the Tooth) in Polonnaruwa are remarkably similar to those of the Chidambaram Śiva Temple in Southern India. There are even two actual Śiva Temples at Polonnaruwa, built evidently for the Queen: all this suggests that the whole phenomenon is Hindu.[9]

It is, however, not as straightforward as that: King Parakramabahu and his wife Rupavati (1153-86) were both skilled dancers themselves and used hundreds of dancing girls at the worship of that most holy of all Buddhist relics: the Sacred Tooth.[10] This practice continued into the reign of his son and then the reigns

---

7. Paranavitana, S., *The Story of Sigiri*, Colombo, 1972, pp. 69-70. Moggallan was under the influence at the time of a Christian (Manichean) general who convinced him that his impersonation of Yama would blend in well with what should be his real role: that of Christ at the Second Coming! (cf. Paranavitana, *op. cit.* (1972), p. 93).

8. Cf. Iyer, P. Sarvesvara, "Puranic Saivism in Ceylon during the Polunnaruva Period", *Proccedings of the First Conference — Seminar of Tamil Studies,* K.L., 1968, Vol. 1, pp. 462-74.

9. Makulloluwa, W.B., writes in *Dances of Sri Lanka,* (Colombo, N.D.) that "The testimony borne by Sinhalese literature establishes beyond doubt that the form and content of the dance patronised by the Court and the Devalas were those of Bharata Natyam." (p. 2 and cf. p. 7).

10. Cf. Raghavan, *op. cit.*, p. 22; Geiger, Wilhelm, *Culture of Ceylon in Medieval Times,* Wiesbaden, 1960, p. 64.

of Vijayabahu IV (1270-72) and Parakramabahu IV (1303-33).[11] This is not Hindu and so a new explanation is found: it is Mahāyānist — not only the dance but the whole ritual and cult of the Sacred Tooth itself.[12] It is certainly true that worship of the Sacred Tooth bears distinct resemblances to Mahāyānist and Hindu practices, for it is treated to all intents and purposes as a living being: everyday it is washed, dressed, offered betel, lunch, sweets and, on Wednesdays, symbolically bathed.

But, in that case, given that the cult of the Sacred Tooth is the single most important Buddhist ritual in Sri Lanka, conferring not only religious authority but political legitimacy too,[13] then one might question whether any culture can possibly be Theravāda as a whole, or whether it is reserved only ever for a few.

These — classical, syncretic — explanations may be tested and first examined by reference to one of the most famous expressions of dance in Sri Lanka: Kandy dancing.

Kandy Dance; the Classical Case

The dancers who participate in the annual parade of the Sacred

---

11.   Cf. Seneviratna, A., *Traditional Dances of Sri Lanka,* Colombo, 1984; Ilangasinha, H.B.M., *Buddhism in Medieval Sri Lanka,* Delhi, 1972, pp. 179, 205, 210, 217.

12.   Cf. Rahula, Walpola, *op. cit.,* pp. 97, 128; Smith, Bardwell, "Varieties of Religious Assimilation in Early Medieval Sri Lanka", *Buddhist Philosophy and Culture, op. cit.,* pp. 266f; Mudiyanse, Nandasena, *Mahayana Monuments in Ceylon,* Gunasena and Co., Colombo, 1967 (notably pp. 49f. for evidence of dancing, Tāntric forms of *bodhisattvas* in Ceylon).

13.   It is not accidental that the establishment of Buddhism and of a monarchical system occurred simultaneously, Tissa (250-210 BC) being the first to assume the title of "Beloved of the Gods". The arrival in Ceylon of first the Bodhi tree and then the Sacred Tooth relic were as much acts and symbols of political unity and authority as religious legitimacy and it is a connection which remains in force today: the Sri Lankan President openly and regularly participates in religious ceremonies — including the Kandy Perahera, when it is noticeable that the best dancers perform for the Rajah, dancing with their backs to the Sacred Tooth; it is the Rajah who will award the gold medal and cash prize for the best dancer.

Tooth — the so-called Kandy dancers —, though assigned to a caste below that of scavengers and even executioners, have no doubts about their Buddhist credentials: they are attached to the temples and supply drumming and dancing in exchange for grants of cultivable land. Their origins are, however, animistic: Kandy dancing grew out of the Kohomba Kankariya which can be dated back to the fourth century BC.[14]A healing ritual lasting seven days and nights, originally danced to ensure fertility and specifically to bring rain, later to protect kings from demons, its myth of origin tells how Śakra, King of the gods and supreme Protector of Buddhism in Lanka, had King Mala (or Malaya) come down from the Himalayas to dance for the king and thus exorcise an evil spell put on him by a leopard: a ritual of propitiation which, significantly, records the divine origin of dance and thus validates it.[15] Kandy dance evolved by the simple expedient of taking passages from the elaborate episodic ritual of the Kohomba and performing them in their own right — but now as Buddhist dances: the Dance in Imitation of the Horse, for example (Turanga Vannama), describes how Prince Siddhārtha went into retirement riding on the horse Kaṇṭhaka, while praise of the Sacred Tooth itself is sung to the tune of the Dance in Imitation of the Elephant (Gajaga Vannama).[16] Today the Kohomba Kankariya is performed after the first reaping of the harvest in February/March and can be commissioned on other occasions by individuals to discharge vows made during an illness, but it is used also for the investiture of a Kandy Dancer into a Buddhist temple when, after ten years of apprenticeship, he is granted the right to wear the 'Jatava'. This is the centrepiece of the

---

14. Cf. Molamure, Arthur H.E., "Aspects of the Kohomba Kankariya", *Ceylon Journal of Historical and Social Studies,* Peradeniya, January 1958, pp. 63-72; Seneviratna, A., "Kohomba Kankariya", in *Senarat Paranavitana Commemoration Volume,* Leiden, 1978, pp. 204-14; Makulloluwa, W.B., *op. cit.*; Godakumbura, C.E., *The Cult of the Kohomba,* R.A.S., 1946., pp. 185-91.

15. Cf. Seneviratna, *op. cit.* (1978), p. 210.

16. There is speculation on Kathakali influence here: cf. Raghavan, *op. cit.*, pp. 61-69; Seneviratna, A., "Kandyan Dance", in *Sangeet Natak,* 32, 1974, pp. 5-25.

'Ves-Tattuva' (the headpiece) and represents no less than a miniature, Buddhist *stūpa*. Molamure has described this initiation ceremony in detail: the *bhikkhus* chant *sūtras* and administer the Five Precepts to the neophyte, the drummers play, and then the *Jatava* — which has been purified by coconut milk mixed with sandalwood paste — is placed in front of the neophyte on a green banana leaf surrounded by areca, betel, a mirror, a comb, a wisp of hair, silver coins and a lighted lamp. All except the *guru* and pupil leave. The *guru* places the *Jatava* on the pupil's head at precisely the auspicious moment previously identified by an astrologer. After worship of the Buddha, both leave, the pupil veiled in a white cloth; he then dances a homage to the four Guardian deities.[17]

The secret of the *Jatava* is, then, that it is the flame of the sun and a Buddhist *stūpa* at the same time; before performing, the Kandy dancer venerates the *Jatava* and then ritualistically ties it on the top of his head before attaching the silver flame in front of it and then the silver coronet — of bo-leaves.

As such Kandy dance might appear to support the thesis that dance and theatre in Sri Lanka represent a fusion of older — animistic — rites with later Buddhism on the pattern of Mahāyānist syncretism. This Mahāyānist argument needs, however, modifying by the historical facts: worship of the Sacred Tooth during the Kandy Perahera was an innovation of Siamese — Theravada — monks who had come to Sri Lanka to purify the *saṁgha*! Because the order had become once again corrupt, dominated by 'ganinnanses' — improperly ordained priests who were little better than shamans. Thai monks were brought over (in 1753 and again in 1756) to re-establish orthodox ordination and cleanse the *saṁgha*. They saw the Perahera, then a ceremony honouring the Guardian Deities only. Malalgoda writes:

> This festival, as celebrated during the early Kandyan period, was purely an occasion for the ceremonial worship of gods and had no connection with the Temple of the Tooth

---

17.   Cf. Molamure, *op. cit.* for a full description of this ceremony.

or with any other Buddhist temple. During the festival, the divinites themselves or their insignia were carried in procession through the streets of the capital — a sight, it is said, which shocked the Siamese monks, as no similar ceremony was performed in honour of the Buddha. They pressed the king to reorganise the perahera and as a result, a new dalada (tooth relic) perahera was introduced into the general ritual complex and was given primacy over all the other peraheras.[18]

Clearly these orthodox — Theravāda — monks had no problem permitting dancing in Buddhist rituals, though it is important to note that, though dance is thus approved for worship by the ordinary people, it remained banned for monks: a ninth-century Sinhalese text, the *Sikhavalanda Vinisa* forbids monks to perform or watch dances, and Parākramabāhu II (1236-70), even while putting on a huge dance festival in honour of the Sacred Tooth, forbade monks to practise it, reaffirming that it is a "despicable art".[19]

And so we have the equation: whatever the origin and continuing sponsorship of dance and theatre in Sri Lanka — animist, Hindu, Mahāyānist or simply proselytizing expediency — for the purist, it cannot be legitimized, and hence must be explained away.

This is essentially the task taken on by the doyen of Sri Lankan theatre scholars, E.R. Sarathchandra (*The Folk Drama of Ceylon,* Colombo, 2nd edn., 1966) who may be taken as representative of the classical — Theravāda — case.

Sarathchandra is nothing if not fundamentalist: the Teravāda, he writes, is "a highly philosophical creed, inculcating individual salvation by contemplation on the vanity of life".[20] However, "though Buddhism is the predominant faith of the people, a great part of their lives happens to be ordered by beliefs and practices which are

---

18.   Malalgoda, Kitsiri, *Buddhism in Sinhalese Society 1750-1900,* University of California Press, 1976, p. 64.

19.   Cf. De Silva, K.M., *A History of Sri Lanka,* O.U.P., 1981, p. 202.

20.   Sarathchandra, *op. cit.*, p. x.

really not of Buddhist origin."[21] A typical Sri Lankan, according to Sarathchandra, practises, in other words, two religious systems in parallel: Buddhism for their ultimate salvation and, meanwhile, a complex of folk practices which help resolve the everyday problems of material existence. The two systems are, he insists, parallel and unrelated: being a purist Theravāda culture, Sri Lanka did not absorb such folk practices into its Buddhism "thereby tainting the original creed, as it did in most other countries".[22]

Sarathchandra's is, in the end, a dogmatic argument: drama, he argues, always derives from ritual; Buddhism eschews ritual and all ceremonialism; therefore 'Buddhist theatre' is impossible by definition.[23] Any theatre in any Buddhist country can arise only as the result of some compromise — with animistic exorcistic rites. Since Theravāda Buddhism — "puritanical and strict"[24] — does not permit this, it could not happen. This dogmatic argument is indeed a source of national and religious pride: Theravāda Buddhism is a better — purer — Buddhism for not having made the compromises found in other — Mahāyānist — cultures. The nationalist and sectarian biases are quite explicit, and the historical evidence that such compromises, albeit prohibited on doctrinal grounds, did nevertheless occur, does not ruffle the general thesis: phenomena such as the proto-dramatic elements in Pirit chanting are ascribed to "Mahāyānist" contamination[25] whilst the development of "Buddhist hymns" is ascribed to "Tamil influence" as is Kandy dancing.[26] That Kandy dancing later received explicit Buddhist patronage is a problem which Sarathchandra resolves by arguing that, though there is indeed historical evidence of repeated slippages from the Theravāda ideal, these "in no wise affected, substantially, the character of early Buddhism, as it did in countries like Tibet and China."[27]

21.   Sarathchandra, *op.cit.*, p. 1.

22.   *Ibid.*, p. 2.

23.   Cf. *ibid.*, pp. viii, 1-2.

24.   *Ibid.*, p. 8.

25.   *Ibid.*, p. 5.

26.   *Ibid.*, pp. 12-13.

27.   *Ibid.*, p. 6.

All Sarathchandra will admit is that this pure Buddhism does become inevitably compromised: when it turns from the solitary path of contemplation to cater for those who have no such option, then it "becomes reconciled with a system of cults connected with the propitiation of gods and demons, in order to suit the exigencies of day-to-day living."[28] Such cults include magical rites to ward off disease and ensure good crops: these are the 'ritual origins' of Sri Lankan dance-drama but, the argument concludes, for a Sri Lankan Buddhist such cults are not really religious at all; they are a form of "positive science," a system of psychosomatic therapy within which gods and demons are evoked not to be worshipped but simply to be used.[29]

Now there is no doubt that the Sanni Yakuma and other, similar exorcist rituals are the most theatrical phenomena in Sri Lanka and Sarathchandra's thesis that they are not Buddhist [and, indeed, not really religious at all] has been taken up by other scholars — such as Michael Ames who argues similarly that Sinhalese exorcistic plays are "practical sciences akin to Western or indigenous or Ayurvedic medical system;" all they do is "turn sick Buddhists into healthy Buddhists."[30]

Other scholars, such as Obeyesekere, have proposed a different solution — both to the question of the purported parallelism of the rites and of their theatrical expression. Recognising that it is not a simple question of Buddhist religion on the one hand and animistic magic on the other, he argued in "The Buddhist Pantheon in Ceylon and its Extensions"[31] that the actual relation between Buddhism, Brāhmaṇism and animism in Sri Lanka are neither a parallel dualism nor a syncretic mix but rather a systemic fusion in which the whole is "held together by the morality of *karma*."[32]

---

28. Sarathchandra, *op. cit.*, p. x.
29. *Ibid.*
30. Ames, Michael, "Buddha and the Dancing Goblins: A Theory of Magic and Religion", *American Anthropologist,* Vol. 66(1), Feb. 1964, pp. 77, 79.
31. *Anthropological Studies in Theravada Buddhism*, ed. by M. Nash, Cultural Report Series, no. 13, Yale U.P., 1966.
32. *Anthropological Studies in Theravada Buddhism*, ed. by M. Nash, Cultural Report Series, no. 13, Yale U.P., 1966.

Karma Drama

Karma is the cornerstone of Buddhist ethics; it is also the way that Buddhism influences the lives of the vast majority of its followers: a moral code for those effectively denied access to the path of ultimate salvation. One of the best known terms, *karma* is, however, also one of the most misunderstood concepts in Buddhism, not least because though the Buddhists took *karma* straight from Hinduism, they were forced by their radical rejection of *ātman* and redefinition of Self to revise the whole system.

Buddhist ethics contain all the obvious injunctions one finds in most religions: anti-sex, anti-sensuality, anti-hate, anti-murder, anti-anger, anti-selfishness, promoting the usual social virtues, necessary in any social order. But, in Buddhism, virtue by itself cannot lead, as in other religions, to ultimate salvation. As the major text of Buddhist ethics, the *Dhammapada*, makes clear:

> Some people are born on this earth; those who do evil are reborn in hell; the righteous go to heaven; but those who are pure reach Nirvana. (9/126)

This distinction between purity and virtue — and therefore between *nirvāṇa* and heaven — is crucial: Buddhism offers not one but two goals in life — ultimate salvation or better rebirth, and the path of *karma*, the path of virtue and its rewards cannot, by itself, lead the Buddhist to *nirvāṇa*, only to heaven. In heaven, he or she may, if they have been very good, be reborn as a god, gods being simply reincarnated mortals who have earned sufficient merit to enjoy a period of sheer bliss in heaven. But it will not last for ever: the actions gods perform in heaven will now dictate their next rebirth. Already in Hinduism, *karma* had raised profound questions about the status of gods: if their futures too are dependent on the results of their actions, they could in theory fall out of heaven. The Hindu solution was to elevate to supreme status the relatively impersonal and inactive *Brahman* — as a god beyond *karma*. The Buddhist solution was more radical: it was to deny the immutable position and hence the supreme status of gods as such.

Buddhism, however, had other problems with *karma*: as a theory of reincarnation, it implies some 'self' which migrates from existence to existence, thus threatening the *anatta* doctrine. Various solutions were proposed, of which the most consistent was — and is — to separate the notion of action from that of an *actor*, thus turning it all into a *performative morality*. *Karma* means 'action' and, in Buddhism, is a theory of rebirth, not reincarnation; of the moral causality of actions, not of actors; of performances, not of performers.[33]

This distinction is, it must be admitted, often blurred in folk beliefs and practices; not, however, the causal logic which is worth reviewing: in Buddhist *karma* theory, once an action is performed, the effects become a force of which the *performer* is the victim. . . .

In other words, whatever the effect on someone else of whatever good or evil actions one may perform, what one can be sure of is that the action will affect one's own future.

Given the contemporary trivialisation of *karma* in the West, it is important to understand this: if *X* hurts *Y* and *Y* suffers, then *X* will be made to suffer but, strictly speaking, *Y*'s suffering, though occasioned by *X*, was actually *caused* by *Y* him/herself — in their previous existence!

In other words, *Y* suffers *directly* because *X* hurts her but *causally* the suffering is self-induced — the result of some previous action which they once performed.

Karma is, then, a theory that all actions have consequences *for the actors themselves*. Indeed, radically, one could argue that no-one ever really hurts anyone else, only themselves: when *X* hurts *Y*, *Y* actually had it coming in any case. . . .

This is where Obeyesekere steps in with a new perspective on the Sri Lankan Pantheon and on the Sanni rituals and their Buddhism. Obeyesekere establishes Sri Lankan religion as a pyramid, at the top of which is Buddha who, however, "is not viewed

---

33. Cf. O'Flaherty, W.D., *Karma and Rebirth in Classical Indian Tradition,* University of California Press, 1980, pp. 166 f.

as a deity in the conventional sense of a being who intercedes on behalf of humans and brings fertility, prosperity, weal, or woe to humans who propitiate him."[34] For this purpose, there are the 'Guardian Deities' of the second stratum: Saman, Viṣṇu, Kataragama (Skandha), Pattini, Nātha, Śakra. . . .[35] These are gods; they grant favours in the here-and-now — but only because they themselves have converted to Buddhism.[36]

On the third level are humans at various stages of perfection and, below them, the demons. They are the devils of the exorcist plays and they are now in the most unfortunate position of all: born as demons because of bad *karma*, they are now doomed to go on performing further evil acts, their only chance of escaping the vicious cycle and hoping for a better rebirth being to leave the bodies of those they are afflicting. And it is precisely this that they are requested, bullied, invited, coaxed and threatened into doing in the exorcistic rites. From this perspective, 'devil-dancing' is not just a form of therapy for a superstitious patient but also *a Buddhist ritual for the demons* through which they are helped to desist from further evil-doing — for the sake of their own kārmic destiny.[37]

Buddhism stresses 'mutual causality', the reciprocal interaction of all events: in the exorcistic rites, the patient's cure is simultaneous with the demon's improved *karma*. For the patient the performance may be medicine; for the demon it is a Buddhist ritual of release. It may be asked how actors can influence demons — when they are possessed by them? The answer lies in the notion of 'transfer of merit' — a popular development of Buddhist *karma* theory which helps to remove selfishness from otherwise 'self-serving' acts of virtue.[38]

Building on this, R.F. Gombrich, in *Precept and Practice:*

---

34.   Obeyesekere, *op. cit.,* p. 5.
35.   In other lists and other regions: Upulvan, Vibhisana. . . .
36.   Cf. Geiger, *op. cit.,* p.177.
37.   Dala Kumara, for example, became a demon because of committing incest with his sister. . . .
38.   Cf. O'Flaherty, *op. cit.,* pp. 190f.

Traditional Buddhism in the Rural Highlands of Ceylon (Oxford, 1971), most effectively [and at times even playfully] set about demolishing most of the remaining myths and confusions regarding Buddhism in Sri Lanka — and its theatre.

Gombrich does not deny Sri Lanka's Theravāda credentials; he insists on them, arguing that much of the confusion disappears when the 'gods' who are held to be Mahāyānist or Hindu contaminations of a — therefore — syncretic Buddhism, are recognized as really, actually, irrelevant as religious entities. These gods have power but they have very little to do with religion as Buddhism has redefined it: a path of release from endless rebirth and the attainment of *nibbāna*.[39] The invocation of gods such as Saman, Kataragama, Nātha and so forth does not contaminate or diminish Sri Lanka's Buddhist credentials nor make it a syncretic religion: these gods, he argues (following Obeyesekere), are themselves subject to and manifestations of *karma*. They have achieved their present status and power by merit earned in earlier lives but they live not on the Buddha's lonely peak but are, rather, simply advanced human beings—which is why they so conspicuously share the appetites and needs of humans. The power which they have accumulated by merit in previous lives is to be respected and can be used to relieve suffering in this life but [reinserting the classic 'scientific' argument here] Gombrich agrees that this has no more to do with religion than a visit to a doctor compromises a Christian's belief in Divine Grace.

The religious status of such gods is that they are *bodhisattvas* — in the Theravāda sense of that term: converts to Buddhism who have determined to become Buddhas themselves [Nātha is indeed Maitreya, the Buddha-to-come]. Having accumulated merit, they are in the position of any other advanced candidate for *nibbāna*: they can help. Indeed, just as demons can be helped on their kārmic journey by being persuaded to stop afflicting humans, so too these gods, by helping humans, will themselves accumulate still further merit. For a god to help a human is actually to help himself too.

---

39.   Gombrich, *op. cit.*, pp. 46f.

This is also where the monks come in. The *vanavāsi* [or *vidassanādhura*: forest-dwellers] — namely monks who dedicate their lives to solitary meditation in tiny huts or cells on the way to *nibbāna* — are highly respected but very few in number. Michael Carrithers, in *The Forest Monks of Sri Lanka* (O.U.P., Delhi, 1983), calculated that there are some 600 of them gathered in 150 hermitages compared to 20,000 village monks. Most monks, though not priests, are *ganthadhura*: they spend most of their time teaching and otherwise helping their fellow human beings, united with them in the same slow accumulation of merit. Indeed, Gombrich argues that, for the average monk, *nibbāna* is considered difficult to attain, postponed, and "we are not sure that we want it anyway;"[40] far better to accumulate merit and work toward a better rebirth — on earth or with the gods in heaven. Such monks — the majority — mix periods of meditation with periods of serving the people, largely through preaching.

This is where performance — again — comes in.

Gombrich cites the example of *suvisi pinkama* which sings and dances the 24 previous Buddhas and was, Gombrich claims, inspired by certain rituals in the Temple of the Sacred Tooth in Kandy,[41] and the *Alavaka-yaksa-Damane*. This latter is a dramatic interlude incorporated into preaching and relates how the Buddha subdued and converted a fierce demon called Alavaka. The story is narrated up to the point where the King of Alav, who had been captured by a demon and freed only after promising to sacrifice a child to him every day, found, after twelve years, that he now had to sacrifice his own son. Buddha, seeing this and knowing that both King and son had the potentiality for spiritual insight, went to the demon's abode. It is at this point that narrative is replaced with drama: the demon Gadrabha, who guards Alavaka's abode, now enters the preaching hall, costumed, with matted hair and face blackened by soot and carrying a sword. He and the chief monk now engage in dialogue, the monk narrating what the Buddha said. Gadrabha

---

40.   Gombrich, *op.cit.*, p. 322.

41.   *Ibid.*, p.130.

leaves and, after a sermon, Alavaka himself enters the preaching hall, costumed in the same style as demons in exorcistic rituals. He runs wildly up and down in front of the congregation, miming his fury at the Buddha, creating a hurricane, then a rainstorm, a rain of coals, a shower of stones and finally thick black darkness. All in vain: Buddha's power is such that the demon is converted; a child (a doll) is brought in and handed over to him but he is now ashamed, offers it to the Buddha and thus becomes himself a *sotapanna* (stream-enterer).[42] Costumes, dialogue, props: Gombrich argues that these are not transgressions of the Buddha's ban on theatricality; they are *bana* — preaching — and therefore not covered by the injunction which was, in any case, only of enjoyment and indulgence in music, dance and drama. In *suvisi pinkama*, the dancers face a screen displaying images of the Buddha and have their backs to the audience; it is performed not for entertainment but to raise money for the temple and hence as an act of merit. Were such performances to be put on for pleasure, they would be 'despicable'; as media to teach and preach Buddhism and/or as *pinkama* — acts of merit — they are exempt from censure: positive steps on the kārmic path.

Such an explanation would cover the proto-dramatic elements of 'Pirit' too, which is also used to cure illness: Wijesekera writes that,

> The Sinhala Buddhists repose greater faith in the effectiveness of pirit chanting than in any other extra medical means of curing illness.[43]

Probably of ancient origin,[44] Pirit is also used "for protection from robbers, sickness, and evil spirits . . . and is also chanted to induce rain, to ease labour pains in women, to bring down a high fever and to guard a house from evil spirits."[45] The most dramatic are those sequences connected to the chanting of the *Ratana Sūtra* which are

---

42. Cf. Sarathchandra, *op. cit.*, pp. 20-22.
43. Wijesekera, Nandadeva, *Deities and Demons Magic and Masks,* Part I, Colombo, 1987, p. 203.
44. Sarathchandra, *op. cit.*, p. 4.
45. Wijesekera, *op. cit.*, p. 203.

performed by a young boy who has spent a week in the temple eating only vegetarian foods, and who now enters dressed up as a messenger of the gods, accompanied by guards also in costume and sometimes even riding on an elephant. His role is to summon the gods to listen to the reading of the *Ratana Sūtra*: he delivers passports to them to enable them to attend. Significantly, this *sūtra* tells of one of the very few occasions when the Buddha actually intervened in human affairs, visiting Visala when it was struck with disease and famine, and chanting away the demons. This practice connects Pirit with the exorcist rituals, for a version of the same events and the same *sūtra* is held to be the origin of the Sanni Yakuma.[46]

In other words, and summarising for now: it is not so much that there are two (or three or four) religions in Sri Lanka, either co-existing in parallel or blended into some syncretic mix: rather it is the case that *within* (even Theravāda) Buddhism itself there are always *two* options, *two* paths: the arduous, solitary practice of meditative withdrawal, necessarily reserved for the few, and the longer, slower path of *karma* and the accumulation of merit. Sri Lanka has clearly decided to adopt the theatre·to serve *these* Buddhists — in all their manifestations: humans, demons and gods. For those travelling the long *karma* path either as monks or as laymen, for those resigned to the slow pace of multiple rebirths and, therefore, the accumulation of merit [a perfectly legitimate and orthodox Buddhist ambition and aspiration]: for them there can be dance and even theatre, after all.

Buddhist Performance Epistemology in Practice

Sri Lankan theatre — both in its various 'preaching' forms and in the exorcistic plays — offers case studies in, and contributions to, kārmic dynamics: that is the most obvious way in which it could be argued to serve Buddhist paedagogy and ethics. In the context of this present study what, however, needs to be noted is that the

---

46.   Goonatilleka, M.H., "Sanni Yakuma: its mythical dimensions and religious interaction", *Ananda. Papers on Buddhism and Indology*, ed. by Y. Karunadasa, Colombo, 1990, pp. 131f.

actual medium of both exorcistic cure and kārmic change are not plot or character but performance: it is the shifting relationships between actor and role, between spectators and actors, and between theatrical illusion and 'normal' epistemology which are the key. To this extent, the 'Buddhist connection' could be argued to extend further and deeper than the provision of illustrative theatrical case studies — into the dynamics and dialectics of altered cognition which only performance can supply.

For demons are, conspicuously and explicitly, masters of illusion, and the object of the exercise and the methodology of the cure is to break the hold that illusion has on a patient. This is the agrument put by Bruce Kapferer,[47] namely that the cure occurs through the creating and then dispelling of theatrical illusions:

> They enable a reality, constructed in the course of ritual performance, to be destroyed and re-assembled in accordance with a conception of reality consistent with that of those who must participate in the 'normal' everyday secular world.[48]

To this extent the significance of such performances extends beyond the cure of a particular patient; they re-affirm an epistemological system in which

Theatre = illusion + emotion = attachment = suffering (*duḥkha*).

Sri Lankan exorcists, it could be argued in other words, employ basic Buddhist epistemological paradigms to structure a cognitive approach to disease and to healing in which the methodology is that of performance dynamics, because what the exorcists do is, first, set up two worlds — one where demons are 'real', the world of illusion, of overt theatricality, separated from the healthy ordered world of normal social intercourse. The patient is — spatially and cognitively — entrapped in this malignant world. Sometimes the cure occurs

---

47. Kapferer, Bruce, "First Class to Maradana. Secular Drama in Sinhalese Healing Rites", *Secular Ritual*, ed. by Sally Falk Moore and Barbara Myerhoff, Assen, Netherlands, 1977, pp. 91-123.

48. *Op. cit.*, p. 92.

here — by the classical Shamanistic method: the chief exorcist
takes the malignant spirit into himself and thus frees the patient.
But this is not always the method and it is in any case itself preceded
and prepared by the exorcist using the demons' very own powers —
mastery of illusion — to f ool *them*, beat them at their own game!

> The exorcist stretches out on a mat in front of the patient.
> A number of further offerings are made. This episode itself
> takes the form of an elaborate subterfuge or trick whereby
> the exorcist presents himself as a corpse in an effort to lure
> the demon's attention away from the patient.[49]

The contest is clear: as performers, exorcists have the same powers
as demons: they can "step into the world of the patient and by dint
of magical art and clever subterfuge domesticate, control and tame
the afflicting devils."[50] This is, however, only a prelude to the 'real'
cure which is not magical but cognitive: as described in detail by
Kapferer and confirmed by field-research, the patient is then
persuaded to step out of belief in the illusory world of demons and
sickness in which (s)he is the victim, and become a spectator. All the
while that the construction of an illusory, demonic world has been
happening and the patient locked into it, the same actors have been
simultaneously conversing with the spectators, drawing here on
the secular world, exposing themselves and the demons they
represent as just actors. Through comic banter and satirical
reference, they affirm the greater reality of the normal world, one
in which they are not so much exorcists as comedians, rupturing
any identification of actor and role and replacing it with an 'alienation
effect' which Brecht would have admired. Brecht, argued that such
'alienation' disrupts emotional involvement and enables analytical
distance and it is this which then occurs, because it is into this world
that the patient is then transported, converted from the former
status as actor, trapped in *karma*, into a spectator:

> Once a patient expresses enjoyment in a publicly received

---

49.   Kapferer, *op. cit.*, p. 99.
50.   *Ibid.*, p. 100.

and understood manner then he is regarded as having crossed the threshold from a frightening malign world into a mundane reality as the more healthy and non-afflicted should perceive it. The patient is no more a patient but now one with the audience. Like the others gathered around, he is outside, apart from those elements of a malign, supernatural world performed before him ... psychologically separated from an involvement in a demonic world.[51]

Theatre is a highly suitable medium to demonstrate *karma*; a Buddhist seeing a Shakespeare play would have no problems recognizing the fate of characters trapped in a cycle of attachment, desire, craving, illusion and retribution. The secret is to enable people to step out: become spectators. Buddhism's basic approach to salvation is to change perception, alter the basic way we see reality, and the exorcist rituals offer exercises in such a basic step too. It is impossible not to observe Sri Lanka's relative poverty in theatre and speculate what connection this might have with the fundamental Buddhist belief that illusion and deception are the constant threats and sources of evil. Theatre is, of course, a deceptive illusion, though a peculiar one in that an audience knows it is being deceived. Enjoyment of such willing deceptions is not considered by all cultures to be a dangerous thing, though most cultures have had their moral critics of theatre. But Buddhism is a very special religion, one which seeks ultimately to change the way we see reality: part of every Buddhist's education is to learn to see through illusion. As practised — uniquely — in Sri Lanka, exorcicm confirms this paradigm and draws on it: as masters of illusion, demons control and dominate by manipulating forms, appearances:

> Demons in their illusions of form mask what in actuality they are.[52]

The conflict — both within the plays themselves and in the world

51   Kapferer, *op.cit.*, p. 114.
52.   Kapferer, Bruce, *A Celebration of Demons*, Indiana U.P., Bloomington, 1983, p. 125.

at large — is always one between deceitful, malignant illusion and Truth:

> Demons are tricksters. The falsity of the illusion they spin
> is implicit in popular understanding of the meaning of the
> name of Vesamuni, the demon lord, as 'false face'. . . To be
> tricked — whether this be in the events told in myth or in
> everyday life — to be fooled by the disguise or by the mask,
> to be trapped by appearances, is to be under the control of
> the trickster and the dissembler. But to see through illusion,
> to apperceive correctly what is directly hidden from
> perception, is to dispel the illusion and to assert mastery
> over the trickster. This is the power of the Buddha.[53]

There is no Sri Lankan theatre in which anyone ever impersonates the Buddha; in the 'preaching' forms, the monks — though they do sometimes use the first person — conspicuously make no attempt to create an illusion of the Buddha's presence. Buddha does not work through such means, indeed eschews them, but some of his power to assert mastery over demon-tricksters resides with the exorcists and is demonstrated by their control over performance dialectics. Ultimately this power has to be transferred into every individual's own cognitive patterning and this process too can be achieved as much by exploitation of performance dialectics as by Buddhist psychological paradigms. Victor Turner has noted Bruce Kapferer's debt to George Herbert Mead who

> discriminates between the Me, the object one forms of
> oneself . . . and the I, the response of the unique individual
> to his perception of the concrete historical situation in
> which he finds himself. The Me is multiple, consisting of
> the sum-total of the role-statuses. . . .[54]

Kapferer himself acknowledges his extended use of Meadian psychology[55] but — curiously — makes no effort to relate it to

---

53.   Kapferer, *op.cit.*, p. 127

54.   *Ibid.*, p. xi.

55.   *Ibid.*, pp. 198-202.

Buddhist psychology and thus investigate how the system might reflect not Western sociological truisms but the perspectives of the participants themselves. But it could be argued that, in a Buddhist culture, the 'Me' does not necessarily arise only out of the intersection between the self and social others. Buddhist meditation, drawing on basic Buddhist psychology, also stresses the need to distinguish the I from the Me's but recognizes the latter as not only social constructs but also cognitive operations. The Me does not have to arise only out of adopting the attitude of the social other; it can [and indeed always will] arise whenever there is a self-conscious I. This cognitive operation — practised both in meditation and performance — is actually quite different from the Meadian pattern in which a 'complete self' is constituted out of the multiple 'Me's'; in Buddhism there is no such complete self, and the object is not to fuse but to distingush sharply between I and Me's. But then the ultimate goal in Buddhism is not to become a well-integrated social being — which is Mead's and Kapferer's definition of 'health'; rather it is to hive off all such Me's and learn how to inhabit empty subject-I positions. How this operates in classic Theravāda meditation is by substituting cognitions such as 'I am thinking', 'I am feeling' by 'a thinking is going on, a feeling is occurring'. The meditator establishes the door through which such cognitions are entering — the specific *skandha* or sense/sense-consciousness medium — and, by 'noting' this door, effectively converts it into a 'fourth wall', splitting the meditator into a spectator of a now increasingly objectified performer. Such is *Buddhist* psychological health, and such — it could be argued — is achieved by and thus constitues the 'Buddhism' of the exorcist plays.

Conclusion: From Karma to Nirvāṇa

The more traditionally theatrical cousin of Sri Lankan exorcistic rites is called Kolam. At first sight, the evidence seems again to be negative towards theatre: the mythic origin of Kolam is retold at the opening of every performance — a Queen's pregnancy craving, taking the form of a passionate desire to see masked dances. Nothing, it seems, could express better the purely negative quality of theatre than to see it as a craving associated with (re)birth. The king, however — Maha Samatha — is a *bodhisattva* and grants her wish, thus demonstrating his compassion for those not yet able to break the chain of desire, craving and illusion. Every Kolam thus re-enacts the mythic origin of masked dance-drama in that Śakra is again asked to use his celestial artisan — Viśvakarmā — to provide not a dancer this time but the masks and the texts for plays. These texts — and the plays which therefore follow this prelude — are all taken from the *Jātakas* — moral tales which re-enact the Buddha's own earlier births and demonstrate his own steady kārmic progression. Every Kolam ends traditionally with the entry of Gara Yakka — a demon who, through accumulated merit, has now joined the gods. Kolam thus offers more lessons in kārmic dynamics but it does perhaps more than that: Buddha, at the end of his *Jātakas*, achieved *nirvāṇa* so that the implicit message now is: even for the *karma* traveller, *nibbāna* can be the ultimate hope.

It is clear from the analyses above that Sri Lankan Buddhism has concentrated most on exploiting the paedagogic function of theatre, employing it as a medium of instruction in Buddhist morality and legend. As such it is lodged — as theatre must be — firmly in the saṁsāric world of *karma*. But *karma* and *nirvāṇa*, though separate paths, are no more mutually exclusive than the actor-spectator dualism: the *karma*-path should ideally always culminate in the *nirvāṇa*-path, and one can be helped in this transition by performance epistemology which can convert actors into spectators. Such, it has been argued above, is the common and basic methodology of the Sanni rituals, the Kolam and *bhāvanā:* the conversion of actors trapped in *karma* into spectators.

Those who make such transitions are potentially on the way from *karma* to *nirvāṇa*. . . . This is because *karma* is, in the end, itself an illusion. Buddhist *karma* is a theory of the moral causality of *actions*; Buddhism, denying any substantial 'Self', deconstructs all 'actors' into the five *skandhas*. The *skandhas* are the functions of the mind-body system; the sum of all the functions which create subject-object relationships — the senses, perception, feeling, habits, memories, consciousness. . . . Together they construct a false sense of reality, a reality in which there appear to *be* things and to be a Self. This is the world of *saṁsāra*, the world of *karma*.

Reduced to its essence, what Buddhism proposes therefore is that it is the *skandha*s which create *karma*.

From this extended perspective, *karma* appears even more like a performance, for what it means is that, living in the world, performing intentional acts of sensory perception, feeling, cognition, the *skandha*s project a world of forms, a world in which a 'myself' appears to move and to live. That 'myself' performs acts — also through the *skandha*s, notably the fourth. Those acts are cognised by the *skandha*s as causal — notably through the fourth and fifth *skandha*s. Through the construction of a myself which performs causal acts, the *skandha*s construct *karma*.[56]

The conclusion is startling, but logical: *karma* has, therefore, no real ontological status; at best only a phenomenal status. It is a socially useful, rational explanation but it operates only in the world of *saṁsāra*, the world of delusion and illusion. *Karma* is a construct of the *skandha*s, intended, willed by them — for their own perpetuation. . .

Both *karma* and the false self through which it operates are constructed simultaneously by the *skandha*s and they disappear, melt away as soon as the *skandha*s are transcended.

The shift from theatre-as-metaphor to performance-as-paradigm now receives an additional dimension: in the old metaphor, the

---

56. More: they **perpetuate** it, for so attached does the false 'myself' become to living in such worlds that, at death, its *vijñāna skandha* seeks out a new womb and reincarnates in that womb, inhabiting a new life-form which will now act out the consequences of the deeds performed in its previous incarnation. Chandra explains the process: "Birth means only a fresh grouping of the *khandhas,* the basic elements constituting the personality, whose reality has never been doubted. The process begins with the actual descent of *vinnāna* in a new womb and ends with the breaking up of the factors of existence, leaving the *vinnāna* free to move on to create yet another personality in accordance with the deeds of the erstwhile combination." Chandra, Pratap, *Metaphysics of Perpetual Change*, Bombay, New Delhi, 1978.

world is like the theatre because it is the best model of a world of *māyā* — delusion. But for Buddhists there is no 'True Reality' behind the curtain of *māyā*: there is only *śūnyatā* — Emptiness. For them, performance becomes a much more useful paradigm, for in *śūnyatā* as in performance, appearances *are* reality: *rūpa* = *śūnya*.

Śūnyatā is the necessary gateway to *nirvāṇa*: only an emptied mind can be enlightened. The means of this emptying is, of course, meditation. This path necessitates a radical change in consciousness: through practice in meditation and mindfulness, the *skandhas* can be turned off, Subject-I positions separated from Object-Me's ('Myselves') and then themselves progressively emptied of all contents. Here performance provides an ideal metaphor and even praxis, for it is when one can sit back and begin to observe one's false Object-Me's operating in their foolish pursuit of desires and grasping in the world of *saṁsāra* that one can begin to see that there is no Self either doing or receiving the results of actions: it is then that one begins to get free from *karma*.

Karma goes on until one gives up a Self to be reborn, until one recognizes that the phenomenal self [along with *karma* as such] is not really real. Constructed by the *skandhas*, tying us to life through the *Paticcasamuppāda* series, causality along with its moral form — *karma* — and its medium — the self — are all exposed by Buddhism as constructs, inferences, deductions.

Again performance provides a superior model to theatre, for in all theatre, the parts have always implicitly been written by an author: all characters are predestined in their fates. But in *karma* as in performance, there is no divine author: you are the author of your parts: you write the scripts for all future rebirths and, whatever the consequences may be for others you encounter along the way, your actions will decide your fate.

Summarizing: Karma is something which Buddhists themselves don't really believe in any ultimate, ontological sense. It is a construct, a temporary teaching for those who either aren't ready to try getting to *nirvāna* or who don't even want *nirvāna* but want to remain attached to life after life and hence construct a theory which tells them that they will be reborn from saṃsāric life to saṃsāric life if that is what they want (and it is what most Buddhists do want).

Buddhists are like other people: they want to live; indeed they want to live so badly that they have created a theory that they will be reborn, will play another part. And, Buddhism argues, if that is what you want, that is what you will get; more: that is what you will deserve. Desire, *karma*, causality and the false self form a logically coherent system, one which creates and perpetuates a world in which to operate — the theatre of *saṃsāra*.

Kārmic travellers are saṃsāric performers, but for those seeking ultimate release, there is the other — complementary — model provided by performance: the spectator, still involved in the affairs of *saṃsāra* but detached. Such is the path towards which Sri Lankan theatre and Theravāda meditation point; such is the path trodden by the Mahāyāna *bodhisattva*; we may move from Sri Lanka up to the heady pastures of Tibet.

4

Theatre of Compassion
The Vajrayāna; Tibet

DANCING Buddhas, dancing oracles, dancing meditations: if the Hīnayāna permits some theatricalisation of its Buddhism only reluctantly, the Tibetans seem to have gone to the other extreme. As a major contemporary Tibetologist, Stephan Beyer, writes: "a scholar from our secular societies, I discovered, may all too easily ignore the fact that Buddhism is basically a performing art".[1]

There is a simple (superficial) explanation, based (again) on the assumption of syncretic contamination: the Vajrayāna represents the fusion of Buddhism with Tantra; all one has to do is equate Tantra with Śiva, and the 'answer' is clear: this is not Buddhism but some corrupt "charlatanism of a mean necromantic order".[2] The quotation is from Waddell, one of the earliest Western 'authorities' on Tibet, for whom Lamaism is "devil worship and sorcery",[3] their *mantras* "unmeaning gibberish",[4] and their meditation "contemptible mummery"[5] — the whole charade due to the influence of Tantra which is a "parasite" which "crushed and cankered most

1. Beyer, Stephan, *The Cult of Tara. Magic and Ritual in Tibet,* University of California Press, 1973, p. xii.
2. Waddell, L.A., *The Buddhism of Tibet or Lamaism,* 2nd edn, Heffer and Sons, Cambridge, 1971 (first published 1894), p. 129.
3. *Ibid.,* p. xl.
4. *Ibid.,* p. 143.
5. *Ibid.,* p. 145.

of the little life of purely Buddhist stock yet left in the Mahāyāna".[6]

Now this Tāntric connection will need to be examined; what this 'explanation' overlooks is that the Mahāyāna itself had already and in any case transformed early Buddhism in fundamental ways, some of the most significaint of which presaged and promoted a distinctively performance-orientated Buddhism. It is with that doctrinal evolution that we must begin.

The Mahāyāna

The Mahayana was a complex religious and social phenomenon. It was a religious revitalization movement and a reworking of metaphysics, a revival of archaic contemplative modes and a reordering of religious priorities. The very mood of meditation changed from peace and tranquillity to action and concern, from transcendence to immanence.[7]

Evolving between the second century BC and the first century AD, the changes brought into Buddhism by the Mahāyāna were largely those inevitable after the Buddha's own *nirvāṇa*. Every religion changes after its founder passes on, needing some new source of authority and of ongoing revelation. Buddha's own insistence on personal experience as the only reliable basis of true knowledge inhibited the usual development — the establishment of an authoritative, mediating church and clergy — and instead pointed the way to what did in fact evolve, namely, the multiplication and

---

6.   L.A. Waddell, *op. cit.*, p. 14. But then Waddell was intent on promoting the supremacy of the Aryan Race as "the originators and chief propagators of the world's civilisations, including the higher religions" (p. vii and cf. his *Makers of Civilisation and History,* London, 1929). Waddell dismisses the Tibetan lamas as 'naïve' (xii), Buddhism as "a doctrine of sheer negation and despair" (xiv), and a "morose nihilistic doctrine" (xv) in which the monks are mere "parasites" (xvii). He had time only for Aśoka's reforms which he interprets as adopting and bringing into Buddhism an Aryan Ethical code (xxiii), and its later transformation into a theistic creed under Christian influence (xxix).

7.   Beyer, Stephan in Prebish, *op. cit.*, p. 148.

transcendentalization of the founder, extending into the belief that everyone is a potential Buddha. Buddha is reinterpreted not as a person but as a state of mind attainable by all, Śākyamuni being only one — the most recent — of the manifestations of this primordial Buddhahood. In contrast to the early Pāli teachings in which the Buddha, once in *nirvāṇa*, was effectively dead and gone, the new *Mahāyāna Sūtras* reveal Buddha's immortality and ongoing presence, a kind of Buddha-consciousness present in all living things.[8] As Dayal summarizes:

> The Buddhas were subjected to a sixfold process of evolution: they were multiplied, immortalized, deified, spiritualised, universalised and unified.[9]

Such a Buddha cannot, of course, be identical with his physical body: "if a Buddha is immortal and superhuman, his physical body cannot represent his true nature".[10] This insight into a fundamental distinction between physical appearance and essential being — and the recognized need for some mediating link between them — gave rise in turn to the important new theory of the *trikāya* or Three Bodies which became so prominent in Mahāyānist epistemology and meditation practices. Every Buddha has a *dharmakāya* (Truth-body) namely the essence of Buddhahood, realized through the direct experience of Emptiness (*śūnyatā*) and hence the body of a being in *prajñā* (*prajñāpāramitā* — Perfect Wisdom). At the same time, so long as he lives in this material reality, he has also a mundane and particular body, the physical body we all have — the *nirmāṇakāya* (Actual Body). In between is the *sambhogakāya* (Enjoyment Body), attained when one reaches the stage of being able to enter *nirvāṇa* but decides to postpone it for the sake of others: the *sambhogakāya* is the body of a *bodhisattva*.

These bodies are, however, conceived not just as stages on some historical or biographical path from material incarnation to

---

8. Cf. Har Dayal, *The bodhisattva doctrine in Buddhist Sanskrit Literature,* Motilal Banarsidass, Delhi, 1970, pp. 25f.

9. *Ibid.*, p. 28.

10. *Ibid.*, p. 26.

transcendent emptiness: they are co-existent in any Buddha — and in any *potential* Buddha too who must cultivate these three bodies which are conceived as epistemological strata (and even, since the Mahāyāna is prone to ontological extensions, planes of Being), namely:

- the physical/material,

- the absolute/empty,

- and a third stratum, mediating between them, bringing the former to an imaginative intuition of the latter, and the latter to its ideal manifestation in the phenomenal.

We will return to this later in an analysis of Tibetan dance-drama; for now it is important to note that, of the three bodies, it is the second, the *sambhogakāya*, which is of most interest to this study, because by forming a link between the physical and the absolute, at once transcendent and phenomenal, the *sambhogakāya* is the realm of dreams, inner visions and the imagination, and as such a foundation for Buddhist aesthetics. As Guenther writes:

> Such imaginative and affective appreciation of the significance of Buddhahood is similar to the best aesthetic experience as a means of apprehending most vividly what is there for intrinsic, value-sustained perception.[11]

To this extent and by this doctrine, no aesthetic experiences or media are rejected *a priori*, not even the theatre which, as a physical but also ideal medium, one simultaneously material but also symbolic, can stake its claim to belong to the *sambhogakāya* — a "temporal and spatial presentation of the absolute dharma-nature".[12]

This multiplication of Buddhas and the doctrine of their three bodies were paralleled by and expounded in a multiplication of the

---

11.   Guenther, *op. cit.* (1971), p. 103 and cf. Odin, Steve, *Process Metaphysics and Hua-Yen Buddhism*, State University of New York Press, Albany, 1982, p. 6.

12.   Park Sung Bae, *Buddhist Faith and Sudden Enlightenment*, State University of New York Press, 1983, p. 32.

sūtras too, the acceptance of new works as authentic records of the Buddha — the *prajñāpāramitās* which probe the higher stages of enlightenment and the attainment of Buddhahood. Philosophically, the most important aspect of these new *sūtras* was their integration into the canon of later developments in Budddhist philosophy, above all the works of Nāgārjuna and the adoption of *śūnyatā* (Emptiness) as the central doctrinal concept. Nāgārjuna's dialectics do not need to preoccupy us too much here: the adoption of Emptiness as the key to the ultimate identity of all beings is no more or less than a philosophical complement to the Mahāyānist notion of a universal Buddhahood accessible to all, for it is in our universal and common emptiness that we are one. As the fourteenth Dalai Lama explains:

> The minds of beings are, in reality, always void, being really not-self-nature. This natural voidness of the mind is variously called 'the lineage of self-existent', 'the lineage of the Buddhas', 'the seed of the Buddhas'. . . This Buddha lineage exists in the minds of all beings and it is for this reason that all beings are able (given suitable conditions) to attain to Buddhahood.[13]

Important though many of these philosophical revisions were, what really distinguishes the Mahāyāna path was — and is — a new accent on practice, the active effort to attain Buddha-consciousness. This emphasis on achieving Buddhahood, combined with the notion that ultimate reality is a shared Voidness, are what led to the next major development, perhaps the one most distinctive of the Mahāyāna: the replacement of the old ideal of the *arhat* by a new saint, the Bodhisattva, with a new driving motive — compassion — and a new goal, the enlightenment of all. Because the Hīnayāna *arhat* seeks, in the end, a personal salvation in *nirvāṇa*, in the process of which he does become perfect [eradicating the four *āsavas* of sense-desire, love of existence, ignorance and speculative opinion; practising the seven factors of enlightenment (mindfulness,

---

13.   Dalai Lama, *The Opening of the Wisdom-Eye*, Theosophical Publishing House, Wheaton, Illinois, 1972, p. 121.

investigation, energy, joy, serenity, concentration and equanimity),
free of the five hindrances (sensuality, malice, sloth, worry and
doubt), freed of the three roots of evil (sense-desire, hatred and
delusion), abstaining from killing, theft, unchastity, falsehood,
slander, harsh speech, frivolous talk, covetousness, malice and
wrong views. . . .] Pure, free, concentrated, powerful, the *arhat*
enters *nirvāṇa* and will not be reborn:

> He had accomplished what was to be done. He had laid
> down his burden. He had lived the holy life. He attained
> undefiled and final emancipation of mind and heart. . . .
> Such was the ideal of the *arhat*, as it was understood during
> the three centuries after Gautama Buddha's death.[14]

But such an ideal was soon also open to criticism — for its
selfishness, its passivity, its indifference to others:

> They seem to have cared only for their own liberation from
> sin and sorrow.[15]

From this criticism sprang the *bodhisattva* doctrine, for the
bodhisattva is compassionate where the old *arhat* was merely wise:
as Beyer notes, in place of the earlier training in morality for the
individual aspirant:

> the Mahayana demands specific training in compassion; it
> is through constant meditation upon compassion that
> there spontaneously arises the intention to achieve nothing
> less than Buddhahood itself for the sake of these suffering
> creatures. The meditator begins to yearn for the omniscience
> of Buddhahood, to think of it constantly: he hopes for
> supreme and perfect enlightenment that he may save all
> beings from their sorrow.[16]

This doctrine of compassion is one preached especially today — and
notably by Tibetan Buddhists — as demonstrating their affiliation

---

14.   Dayal, *op. cit.*, p. 3.
15.   Eadem.
16.   Beyer, in Prebish, *op. cit.*, p.149.

to some kind of universal religion; one can understand the motive even as one must question the distortion, for Buddhist compassion — *karunā* — should not be confused with Divine Grace and certainly not with Christian charity. Buddhist *karunā* is a state of indifference in which selflessness is only one aspect of a general philosophy of soul-lessness. A *bodhisattva* is not compassionate because he feels sorry for people caught up in *samsāra*; he is compassionate because he can't see any difference between himself and others. Unlike the *karma*-traveller, there is no sense of merit in his compassion, indeed, he is not really **morally** compassionate at all since the aim of morality is happiness whereas a *bodhisattva* lives in a state of tranquillity and equanimity. The *prajñāpāramitā* makes this very clear:

> when the notion of suffering and beings leads him to think:
> 'Suffering I shall remove, the weal of the world I shall work !'
> Beings are then imagined, a self is imagined, —
> The practice of wisdom, the highest perfection, is lacking.[17]

Where the Hīnayāna had gone wrong (according to the new doctrine) was not only in the selfishness of the *arhat*'s ambition; it was also philosophically naïve, because if one essential aspect of the experience of Enlightenment is the realization of the identity of the One and the All, how can One achieve true Enlightenment unless and until the All can and have? As Govinda argues:

> With the extinction of the ego-illusion, nay, even with the mere recognition of the fact that there is no such thing as a separate 'I', how can there be anything like one's 'own salvation'? As long as we know about the suffering of our fellow beings and experience it as our own (or, more correctly, if we do not make any more a distinction between 'self' and 'others'), our liberation can only be equated with the liberation of all.[18]

---

17. *The Perfection of Wisdom in Eight Thousand Lines and its Verse Summary*, ed. by Edward Conze, Bolinas, California, 1973, p. 12.

18. Lama Anagarika Govinda, *Foundations of Tibetan Mysticism*, Bombay, 1977, p. 235.

In other words, the *'bodhisattva* option' is not really an option at all; compassion is part and parcel of true Enlightenment.

A *bodhisattva*'s compassion is, then, detached from virtue and merit: a product of many previous lives of slow maturation, he has gone beyond all sense of self, replacing that with an ever-present awareness of the equality-in-emptiness of all because this redefinition of the ideal human path and saint necessitated a parallel redefinition of the *summum bonum* too — not *nirvāṇa* but *śūnyatā*. A *bodhisattva* cultivates not *nirvāṇa* but *bodhi* ('*bodhi-sattva*' means 'essence of enlightenment', or 'one who has perfect wisdom as his essence'[19]). Bodhisattva meditations aim at the generation of *bodhicitta*, of which there are two — complementary — types: compassion on the one hand, but also the simultaneous realization of Voidness on the other.[20]

Buddhist compassion has been much misunderstood, as has the *bodhisattva* who does not so much voluntarily postpone *nirvāṇa* for himself so as to stay on or be reborn and help others; he *cannot* enter *nirvāṇa* until everyone does. It is not so much a question of saying 'I have found Enlightenment, now I will help others' — this is expressly ruled out in the *Perfection of Wisdom Sutra* [XXVI/6] because it implies an ongoing I-consciousness which a *bodhisattva* must already have transcended. Rather, a *bodhisattva* is compassionate because *śūnyatā* is Sameness, is Equality: ultimate personal enlightenment is simply not possible without universal Enlightenment. Dwelling himself in Emptiness, the *bodhisattva* must lead everyone else to it, otherwise Emptiness would not be empty.

While it is true then that the new compassion frees the search for Enlightenment from the charge of selfishness, *karuṇā* consists in realizing the equality of oneself and others, a habit of regarding others as oneself.[21] *Karuṇā* means the identity of Me and not-Me: it is not a sentimental goodness but a philosophical equanimity.

---

19.   Dayal, *op. cit.*, p. 4f.
20.   *The Preliminary Practices of Tibetan Buddhism,* ed. by Georges Driessens, Washington, 1974, p. 47.
21.   Dayal, *op. cit.*, p. 179.

Beyond that, this new saint is an eminently active being, one who not only does not shirk future rebirths, knowing them to be essential until everyone enters *nirvāṇa*, but one who does something even more significant for this study too: he complements his own wisdom — *prajñā* — with a new skill or set of skills — *upāya*. *Upāya* means strategy, device, expedient, means; it is a major Mahāyānist concept, according to which the Buddha himself at first declined to teach what he had learned, recognizing it to be incommunicable; the god Brahma Sahampati pleaded with him to teach it nevertheless and the Buddha decided that he would, after all, teach the *dharma,* recognizing that *any* truth is only as good as the ability of its receiver to respond to it.[22] Distinguishing between absolute truth and relative, provisional truths but promoting the latter as useful and even necessary steps towards the former, *upāya* becomes in the Mahāyāna a paedagogic duty, the necessary complement of *prajñā* and the means to realize *karuṇā*. To this end, almost any medium is legitimized if it brings the listener closer to truth — even the theatre: in a parable such as that of the burning house, even deception is welcomed as a means to bring people to enlightenment while in the parable of the son who did not recognize his father, disguise and even the assumption of a false identity are similarly acceptable *upāya*.[23] The criterion is not truth but the suitability of the means to the listener, their capacity to submit to the 'enticement'; as Pye writes: "without a certain amount of dissimulating packaging it would not be possible to convey the essence at all".[24] Indeed, the early Buddhas themselves concealed their own true nature,[25] while the supreme *bodhisattva* of the Mahāyāna — Avalokiteśvara — takes many different forms, depending on the readiness of the viewer/disciple to recognize him.

This strategic use of any expedient means expanded vastly the range of the permissible: "the bodhisattva is permitted much that

---

22. Cf. Pye, Michael, *Skilful Means: A Concept in Mahayana Buddhism*, London, 1978, p. 123.
23. *Ibid.*, p. 43.
24. Eadem.
25. *Ibid.*, pp. 69, 70.

is forbidden the monastic — anything, in fact, that has at heart the welfare of others".[26] It includes — explicitly — theatre: in his commentary on Candragomin's *Twenty Verses* — the foundational document setting out the *bodhisattva* path — Śāntarakṣita wrote:

> Accordingly, the bodhisattva, for sentient beings inclined to dance, song and instrumental music, and for those inclined to tales of kings and robbers, food and drink, prostitutes and street scenes, is learned in the varieties of dance, song, music and narrative. With a merciful intention he pleases them with varieties of narrative containing dance, song and music.[27]

Candragomin himself — the central theorist of the *bodhisattva* path — wrote works on drama (*Lokānandanāṭaka*) as well as on logic, medicine and philosophy.

In sum: the Mahāyāna gave Buddhism both a new emphasis on practice, on performance — the ambition to be a Buddha, to act like a Buddha — and a fundamental soteriological promotion of expedient means which predisposed it to look kindly on dance and drama. These were tendencies which it found it shared with what then attracted the Northern Mahāyānists: Tantra.

Tantra

It is a common mistake to assume that the Tantras were originally Hindu an only later became Buddhist;[28] an even worse mistake to assume that it was through the Tantras that Vajrayāna Buddhism was influenced by Śaivism. Pre-Buddhist in origin and "independent of any abstruse metaphysical speculation,"[29] the Tantras were

26. Tatz, Mark, *Difficult Beginnings, Three Works on the Bodhisattva Path*, Shambhala, Boston and London, 1983, p. 6.

27. *Ibid.*, p. 9.

28. Bhattacharya argues that it was the Buddhists who first incorporated the Tantras: cf. Matsunaga, Alicia, *The Buddhist Philosophy of Assimilation*, Tokyo, 1969, p. 91.

29. Dasgupta, Shashibhusun, *Obscure Religious Cults*, Calcutta, 1976, p. 26.

adopted as expedient means by Mahāyāna Buddhism and also — independently — by Śaivism but, as Govinda argues, Vajrayāna Buddhism does not represent a fusion with Śaivism through Tantra so much as an invigoration by Tantra — out of which later Śaivism also developed.[30] The fact that the Vajrayāna uses Tāntric symbols and even what appear to be Hindu icons to symbolize forces and facilitate meditative experiences does not signal adoption of a Hindu religious outlook. Though it is true that the *prajñā-upāya* and *śūnyatā-karuṇā* pairings became readily associated with Tāntric sex-yoga polarities and rites, within Buddhism the female figure represented in conjunction with the male is not, as in Hinduism, a symbol of Power or Energy (*śakti*) but a symbol of Wisdom: she is the *prajñā* to his *upāya*, *śūnyatā* to his *karuṇā*. What the male/female — Yab/yum — couples of Buddhist Tantra represent are not the invigoration of a meditating ascetic Śiva by a dynamic *śakti* to generate a world-creating eroticism but something quite different: the union of Wisdom with Compassion, of Enlightenment with Universal Love, *prajñā* with *upāya* — the Buddhist *bodhisattva* ideal for which there is no Śaivite equivalent until the much later *bhakti* cults.[31]

The 'message' of the Yab-yum figures is that Enlightenment is imperfect unless accompanied by action: it was this shared focus on action — on praxis — which brought the Mahāyāna and the Tantra together, and brought them to performance too, for the Tantras promote the idea of the body as a microcosmic epitome of the universe within which all truth is already innate, an attitude well in accord with the Mahāyānist idea that everyone is born with an innate Buddhahood. 'All' the Tantras ultimately do is mobilize the energy of human desires, believing that you can and should use everything on the path — anger, lust, passion — but purged of attachment and thus transformed into awareness.[32] Step one along the Tāntric path is always to realize that grasping at sensory

30. Govinda, *op. cit.*, p. 95.
31. *Ibid.*, pp. 96ff.
32. Chögyam Trungpa, *Journey Without Goal. The Tantric Wisdom of the Buddha*, Shambala, Boston and London, 1985, p. 68.

pleasures won't work, will lead to disillusionment, loss, dissatisfaction, suffering: the Tāntric *yogin* must first renounce hope or belief that essentially transient pleasures can lead to happiness.

The Tantras have had a bad press: even those who defend them as ways to enlightenment concede that a purely symbolic interpretation is not all there is: *yogins* would — and do — assemble on the eighth and fifteenth days of the dark fortnight and eat meat, drink wine, sing and dance and all the rest of it.[33] Adopted into Buddhist monasteries, such practices "no longer describe these orgiastic gatherings of *yogins* and *yoginis,* but the inner process of self-integration of a man in meditation."[34] But these practices too remain, to a large extent, shrouded in secrecy: the Dalai Lama in *The Opening of the Wisdom Eye,* after a lengthy exposition of classical *bodhisattva* meditation, concludes that one can practice Vajrayāna as an alternative and then attain Buddhahood in one lifetime but that this can only be imparted from a *guru* to a *yogin*; all he will say is that such a seeker "should first be endowed with detachment and renunciation," and then practice visualization and meditation on emptiness.[35] Enough is known about visualization meditation, however, to complete our trek to the borders of ritual theatre, for if it can be argued that the Mahāyāna revision of Buddhism already predicted a turn towards performance, then it can also be shown that its fusion with Tantra produced a form of meditation which is already effectively a full-scale solo theatre performance.

The Vajrayāna's special techniques of meditation consist in the use of *mantras, mudrās, maṇḍalas* and sex and elaborate methods of visualization. These must be practised for several years, passed in absolute solitude, until the yogin "has become so skilled in creating mental constructions that he clearly perceives the external world in its real character as a manifestation of mind."[36] As such,

33.   Eadem.
34.   *Ibid.*, p. 18.
35.   Dalai Lama, *op. cit.*, p. 119.
36.   Blofeld, John, *The Tantric Mysticism of Tibet,* Dutton, New York, 1970, p. 84.

Vajrayāna meditation leads first to a realization of the illusive 'theatricality' of the world — on the surface something apparently similar to the Medieval Western 'Theatrum Mundi' topos: hence, in addition to the metaphors of dream, mirage, reflection in a mirror, etc., the use of the simile of the world as a play.[37] But one soon realizes that the Vajrayāna goes much further, based as it is on a vastly different myth of creation; as Tucci writes in *The Religions of Tibet*:

> All this is directed to a single goal: to reproduce in oneself the process of emanation and reabsorption, and in this way to divest all appearances of their pretence of reality.[38]

What visualization meditation does is no less than repeat the process whereby the world itself was originally created — out of Light and Emptiness — leading to the realization that the world *is* our creation, its reality only our cognition of it.[39] To the Vajrayāna Buddhist, creating a visualized world through and in the contemplative imagination is not creating an ontologically different world but one the same as the 'real' world — except that this one is created under one's total control and is all semiotically meaningful. Beyer writes:

> The Buddhist philosophers in India had long made an axiom of the 'softness' of reality and given an ontological status to the omnipotence of the imagination. . . . Much of Buddhist 'ontological psychology' is an attempt to explain in historical terms why we make a systemic epistemological error in our apprehension of the world, why we attribute to it a solidity that in fact it does not possess. In answering these questions, the philosophers planted many of the seeds that would flower in the Tantric manipulations of reality; they asserted the possibility and provided a model, but the Tantrics built a contemplative technique upon the structures of earlier

---

37. Cf. e.g. Dasgupta, *op. cit.*, p. 37.
38. Tucci, Guiseppe, *The Religions of Tibet*, University of California Press, Berkeley and Los Angeles, 1980, p. 96f.
39. Cf. Beyer, *op. cit.*, 137.

meditation and gave it a new symbolic potency.[40]

Realization that reality is an illusion and that we co-create it ourselves could never, however, be enough for a potential *bodhisattva*; he must seek to use that insight: the ultimate purpose of visualization meditation is to give the lama power and control over the world of appearances. This he does by creating in his mind a world every bit as convincing as the one apprehended through the senses: "the meditator actually produces an alternative reality for himself, a reality as real (and as unreal) as the one we know".[41] Or, as Beyer writes in *The Cult of Tara:*

> The ability to control 'appearances' is the affirmation of the practitioner's control of reality itself. This point is worth repeating: in a universe where all events dissolve ontologically into Emptiness, the touching of Emptiness in the ritual is the re-creation of the world in actuality; where solid reality is but a fabric of constructions.[42]

The Tāntric Buddhist in meditation is, then, at first, a kind of psychic dramatist and director, fabricating an hallucinatorily real theatre-in-the-mind, but he then becomes also an actor in that world, one who exchanges his own personality for that of his favourite character — the deity he visualizes:

> Not only must the practitioner visualize the deity as vividly as possible, but he must also, in any ritual of evocation (that is, whenever he generates himself as the deity), exchange for his own ordinary ego the ego of the deity, which is the subjective correlative of the exchange of ordinary appearances for the special appearance of the deity and his retinue of the mandala.[43]

These visualizations are minutely detailed, involving rehearsals, costumes, props, sets. They begin with the visualization of a

40.   Beyer, *op.cit.*, p. 92.

41.   Beyer, in Prebish, *op. cit.*, p. 154.

42.   Beyer, *op. cit.*, p. 69.

43.   *Ibid.*, p. 76f.

maṇḍala — as a palace for the deity to reside in[44] — and then go
on to people this stage, visualizing

> posture, clothes, ornaments, hair, body-colour, eyes,
> expression, arms, hands, fingers, feet and sometimes
> environment. Beginners have to create the parts separately
> and, as more and more are envisioned, those created first
> vanish. . . . With practice, however, the adept learns to
> evoke instantaneously a figure complete in all its parts. . . .
> Mastering the art of visualizing a coloured figure that is
> perfect in every detail is only the first step, for the figure
> will be static — a mere picture. With further practice, it
> comes alive like a being seen in a dream.[45]

The performative function of these techniques is clear: it is to
activate the deity's power through the body and being of the lama;[46]
their theatricality is also transparent: as Blofeld writes

> The mind becomes a stage which can be lit up at will for
> enacting the brilliantly coloured, vivid transformation
> scenes which cut through the sense barriers and permit
> mystical union with the sacred Source.[47]

The connection with the *bodhisattva* ideal is also clear, for successful
visualization requires the adept to lose all sense of ego because
visualization is not merely conjuring up hallucinatory images in
the pursuit of wisdom; the visualized deity is reabsorbed by a sort
of Stanislavskian mystical empathy, the point of the whole technique
being to see oneself *as* a deity in order to *become* the qualities which
that deity represents, and then to act them out — for the benefit of
all. As Lama Yeshe Thubten writes in his *Introduction to Tantra*:
one must "act now as if he or she were already a fully enlightened
Buddha".[48] Beyer writes:

---

44. Beyer gives one detailed example (*op. cit.*, pp. 31-33 and 72-73) and
    there is another example of this in Blofeld (*op. cit.*, pp. 104-110).
45. Blofeld, *op. cit.*, p. 86f. and cf. Beyer in Prebish, *op. cit.*, pp. 155ff.
46. Beyer, *op. cit.*, p. 72.
47. *Ibid.*, p. 149; cf. Tucci, *op. cit.*, (1980), p. 88f.
48. *Introduction to Tantra*, Boston, 1987, p. 15f.

he vividly visualizes himself as the deity and grasps the divine pride or ego; he directs the power of the deity into himself and becomes, in effect, the transformer through which the divine power can pass out of the realm of knowledge and into the world of events.[49]

Visualization meditation is, in sum, the basic practice for a potential *bodhisattva,* whose aim is not merely to enable the meditator to achieve some kind of wisdom but to create a reality, adopt a persona and perform this wisdom for the benefit of others:

A practitioner who can thus form, at will, these special appearances and special ego is in conscious control of both his external and internal reality: the world he lives in is one of his own choosing, one that he owns; even more striking is the assertion that the yogin not only creates his own reality but also imposes it at will upon others, that his ability to control the universe extends also to the appearances perceived by other people.[50]

So it is not surprising that Tibetan monks learn not only the use of *mudrā*s and *mantra*s and how to make *maṇḍala*s, but also ritual dancing:[51] we are on the borders of full scale Tibetan dance-drama.

Tibet

Tibet was converted from Bon to Tāntric Mahāyāna Buddhism in the seventh century, traditionally by Padmasambhava.

Bon was and still is a form of Shamanism which believes in a world of spirits who roam the mountains and valleys and live in trees and rocks.[52] These spirits are friendly when propitiated, malignant when annoyed, and hence Bon typically employs exorcists to contact them, trance to communicate with them, and sacrifice

---

49.   Beyer, *op. cit.*, p.66.

50.   *Ibid.*, p. 81.

51.   *Ibid.*, p. 24.

52.   Cf. Kenneth Kuan-sheng Ch'en, *Buddhism, the Light of Asia,* Baron's educational series, 1968, p. 189.

(even of humans) to appease them.[53] To counteract their power, Padmasambhava had to perform miracles, demonstrate powers he had derived from Tāntric practices and already fused with Buddhist lore.

It is this fusion which is called the Vajrayāna — the Buddhism of Nepal, Bhutan, Sikkim, Ladakh and Mongolia as well as Tibet — considered by its adherents to be the highest form of Buddhism, because the most effective. Thus Ngawang Tenzin Zangbu, the Reincarnate Lama of Tengpoche Monastery where the Mani Rimdu is performed, says that his own sect — the 'Old' Nyingmapa sect:

> uses all three schools of Buddhism: Hinayana to improve one's character, Mahayana to think about others, and Vajrayana to follow a short-cut to spiritual liberation.[54]

Later he writes:

> The three schools of Buddhism are often explained as paths up a mountain. Hinayana leads to the base of the mountain. Mahayana is the long gentle road that winds around the mountain to its summit. Vajrayana takes the most direct, but risky, route straight up the cliffs to enlightenment and liberation at the mountain's summit,

and in what we could read as an indirect reference to their respective attitudes towards dance and drama too, he continues:

> Often a story about a poisonous plant in a beautiful garden is told. The student of Hinayana, upon seeing the plant, is most likely to leave the garden altogether. A Mahayana follower, realizing that small amounts of poison may also

---

53. On Bon: Cf. Tucci, *op.cit.* (1980), pp. 214-16, 221f., 228f. What we know about pre-Buddhist Bon is however very little, for Bon was early on influenced by Buddhism itself and before that by Śaivism and Zurvanism (*ibid.*, p. 214f.). Like Shinto in Japan, Bon was strengthened philosophically by contact with Buddhism just as it in turn influenced Buddhist mythology and ritual. . . .

54. Ngawang Tenzin Zangbu, *Stories and Customs of the Sherpas*, Khumbu Cultural Conservation Committee, Kathmandu, 1988, p. 3.

act as a medicine, will examine the plant. Afterwards, a practitioner of Vajrayana comes along. Believing that poisons often only appear to be dangerous, he eats the whole plant.[55]

The Vajrayāna is named after the Vajra — sometimes called a thunderbolt, properly called a Diamond. It is the Diamond Path, like a diamond changeless, pure, radiant; colourless, though latent with all colours, the Diamond represents the Void, the Emptiness — *śūnyatā* — at the core of Wisdom and of Being. Iconographically, this diamond contains a disc at its centre in the form of a spiral — the seed or germ of the Universe and of Consciousness, turned in on itself as pure but unlimited potential.... It may seem strange, given the visual extravagance of Tibetan Buddhism, to find Emptiness so prominent in its outlook but one key to the Vajrayāna is to realize that the more abstract it becomes, the more it courts complementary visualization. More aware of the dangers of empty intellectualism and abstraction than afraid of anthropomorphism, the Vajrayāna constantly translates abstract concepts into visual — and often humanoid — forms. This is most clear in its *maṇḍalas*, themselves maps of its meditative universe at the centre of which is the Ādi-Buddha, the primordial, universal and infinite Buddhahood latent in all beings. Though venerated as the founder and expositor of the *dharma*, Gautama is not considered to be the originator of Buddhism; this is the Ādi-Buddha, the "Self-Existent", emanating from the mystic syllable *oṁ* in the original Great Void (*mahāśūnyatā*) in the form of a blue flame issuing from the cosmic lotus. The Ādi-Buddha is pure, perfect and absolutely latent Buddha-consciousness, sometimes represented with a consort, called *ādi-dharma* or *prajñāpāramitā* — Perfect Wisdom — personified as a naked female.

In order to understand the nature of this primordial Buddha-consciousness, the Vajrayāna analyzed it into five basic aspects of meditative consciousness: the 'radiant/universal', 'immutable/noetic', 'luminous equality', 'discriminating' and 'all-accomplishing'.

---

55.   Ngawang Tenzin Zangbu, *op.cit.*, p. 5.

These five aspects are also visualized — as the five 'Dhyānī Buddhas' (meditating Buddhas) — surrounding and emanating from the core Ādi-Buddha. They are respectively Vairocana, Akṣobhaya, Ratnasambhava, Amitābha and Amoghasiddhi. Each of them governs one of the five *skandhas* and occupies one of the five directions; each has a colour, a vehicle, and a consort but while all these provide the basis for inconographic representation and meditative visualization, what each represents is a kind of wisdom, a form of meditative insight, the sum and combination of which make up perfect Enlightenment.

The interested reader is referred to Govinda for details;[56] the Dhyānī Buddha who most interests us is Amoghasiddhi: as the Buddha of All-Accomplishing Wisdom where *prajñā* is *upāya* he combines static meditation with dynamic dance, and is sometimes known as 'The Lotus Lord of Dance'.[57]

The five Dhyānī-Buddhas are major aids in meditation but, though they do help to make the Ādi-Buddha more explicit, they too are, in fact, engaged in perpetual deep meditation. They cannot and are not to be disturbed and hence the care of the world is left to the Dhyānī-Bodhisattvas. In some systems there are five of these, one for each Dhyānī-Buddha, in others there are eight but in all systems they are distinguished from the Buddhas by being immanent, active, and often incarnate in mortals. They are the *karuṇā* side of the Buddhas' *śūnyatā*-nature, the *upāya* aspect of their *prajñā*. Each presides over a material age or world, after which they are absorbed into *nirvāṇa*. Our present age is the fourth in the current cycle; it is presided over by Avalokiteśvara: he has already manifested himself as Gautama Buddha and continues to reincarnate in every Dalai Lama.

Avalokiteśvara is the Dhyānī-Bodhisattva of Infinite Compassion (known as Lokeśvara in Cambodia and Thailand, Kwannon in Japan, Kuan-Yin in China); his *mantra* is *oṁ maṇi padme huṁ* and he is the most popular deity in the Mahāyāna

---

56.   Govinda, *op.cit.*, pp. 120ff.

57   *Ibid.*, p. 263.

pantheon, iconographically close to Śiva (who is worshipped as a form of Avalokiteśvara) and sometimes represented as dancing. His consort is White Tārā, born, it is said, of a tear when Avalokiteśvara wept at the depth of human suffering. As Lord of the Dance, Avalokiteśvara becomes Padmanarteśvara, represented with eighteen hands, all of which hold double lotuses. Significantly, he is an emanation of the *sambhogakāya* and is the Tutelary Deity of the Nyingmapas.[58]

To complete the Vajrayāna pantheon, each *bodhisattva* can assume a fierce or terrible form, as can their consorts, and beyond them are the 'Eight Terrible Ones' (Dharmapāla) — Tāntric divinities with the rank of *bodhisattvas* who wage war against the enemies of Buddhism. They belong to the huge number of Tāntric and Bon deities whose worship was integrated into Buddhism by Padmasambhava in the eighth century along with other protective gods, calendrical gods, place deities, *ḍākinīs*, tutelary gods, reincarnate lamas and deified humans such as Nāgārjuna, Milarepa and Padmasambhava himself, known as Guru Rinpoche: the interested reader is referred to Alice Getty for further detail. . . .[59]

This whole wonderful pantheon is dominated by the need for visualization, and comes alive in the great mystery plays.

These are performed by all the major sects, the origins of which date back to the 'Great Debate' at Samye (792-94) — essentially a dispute between the sudden (Chinese, Ch'an) and the gradual (Indian, Mādhyamika) schools.[60] The substance of this debate (which was to define Tibetan Buddhism for the future) was Śāntarakṣita's insistence on the gradual path, whereby "the achievement of Buddhahood (is) the end-result of a long drawn-out process, which necessarily went through different stages before the

---

58.   Cf. Sangharakshita Bhikshu, *The Three Jewels: An Introduction to Buddhism,* London, 1967, p. 195 and Snellgrove, D.L., *Buddhist Himalaya,* Oxford, 1957, pp. 235, 236.

59.   Cf. Getty, Alice, *The Gods of Northern Buddhism,* Tokyo, 1962.

60.   Cf. on this debate: Ch'en, *op.cit.*(1968), p.193, and Tucci, *op.cit.* (1980), p. 13.

conclusion was reached,"[61] the basis of the whole Tibetan *bodhisattva* system. Though the Prāsaṅgika-Mādhyamika position was thus vindicated and the Chinese lost the debate and were expelled from Tibet, their doctrines lived on — not least in the *siddha* (Tantra) tradition which similarly believed in a rapid path, albeit by other means.

Buddhism continued to grow and develop in Tibet, especially after the Islamic conquest of India and the Hindu reform movements swept it from India in the eleventh and twelfth centuries. During this process many texts were destroyed which are preserved now only in Tibetan which can thus claim with some justice to be the legitimate heir to Indian Buddhism. It remains a syncretic Buddhism, within which there are four main schools: the Nyingma-pa, Kargyut-pa, Sakya-pa and Gelug-pa. The former is the one which interests us most: it traces its lineage back to Padmasambhava but was also clearly affected by Ch'an notions of an instant or sudden illumination, especially in the practices of the Dzokchen branch of the Nyingmapa.[62] In Dzokchen, the Pure Mind is conceived as perfect — empty — Light which is the original, innate and only true reality and which can be achieved through Atiyoga without extensive practice or effort, consisting essentially in rediscovering the original mind before its defilement by transitory impurities — something which occurs in an instantaneous flash of insight. The Nyingmapa is the major sponsor and practitioner of Chams performances and the theatre metaphor is already powerful in its metaphysics: Tucci paraphrases Dzokchen beliefs:

> Gnosis only can lead to realization and this gnosis is not to be acquired by the long practice of very complicated meditation, for the very reason that being ourselves co-essential with the Buddha, and all representations which constitute the world . . . . being illusory or a magic play of the Absolute, pure shining consciousness, what we need is

---

61. Tucci, *op.cit.* (1980), p. 13.
62. On the Nyingmapa cf. Tucci, *op.cit.* (1980), pp. 14, 76-82; G. Tucci, *Minor Buddhist Texts,* Rome, 1956, p. 64.

only to jump, as it were, from the plane of the representations
into that of Buddhahood, our true nature.[63]

Different though the four schools are, doctrinal divergences are
minor compared to practices: "all along the line intellectual
understanding remains subordinate to lived experience."[64] The
Vajrayāna is essentially a set of practices, an intensely ritual path,
a method or sets of methods — all of which are already theatrical.
Beyer writes: "A Tibetan ritual is built up on . . . a set dramatic
form;"[65] "in many ways it is only the language of dramatic criticism
which is finally applicable to the description of a Tibetan ritual."[66]

Chams

Nebesky-Wojkowitz lists over 60 examples of Chams — the masked
ritual dance-drama performed by lamas. There is some dispute as
to their origin: in pre-Buddhist Bon, there was already masked
dance, and it remains an important and regular aspect of Bon
rituals.[67] Waddell and Evans-Wentz were both convinced of the Bon
source — and that it originally included human sacrifice and
cannibalism — and Tucci had little doubt: the Chams evolved out
of Tantric initiation rites which had themselves evolved from pre-
Buddhist fertility rites to become "a real liturgical drama, studied
in all its details, requiring from its actors, in the complexity of its
moments, an accurate and attentive participation."[68] In these
initiation rites the neophyte becomes possessed by the deity who
"then acts, through his person, tossing him about in a frenzied
dance;" Tucci concludes:

The origin of the sacred dances so frequent in Tibetan

63.   Tucci, *op.cit.* (1956), p. 103; and cf. Tucci *op. cit.*, (1980), pp. 82-89;
      Tucci, *op. cit.* (1956), pp. 60-65.
64.   Tucci, *op. cit.* (1980), p. 93.
65.   Beyer, *op. cit.*, p. 170.
66.   *Ibid.*, p. 171.
67.   Tucci, *op. cit.* (1980), p. 233.
68.   Tucci, G., *Tibetan Painted Scrolls,* Rome, 1949, p. 248, and cf. *Oracles
      and Demons of Tibet,* R. de Nebesky-Wojkowitz, Kathmandu, 1993.

convents should be sought precisely in these ceremonies, connected with pre-Buddhist rites of a chtonic character or intended to help the mysterious forces from which the earth draws its periodical fruitfulness.[69]

The whole question of the historical origin and development of Tibetan dance-drama requires much more serious research: apart from Nebesky-Wojkowitz's invaluable records and the full-length studies of Mani Rimdu by Fantin, Jerstad and Richard Kohn, information on Chams is scattered and bitty.[70] Much remains hidden: training is in secret and the printing blocks describing performances are kept under seal and may be printed only with — rare — official permission.[71]

One can reconstruct what Chams may have been like to some extent from Waddell, though it is difficult to separate fact from

---

69.   Tucci, *op. cit.* (1949), p. 248f. Evans-Wentz believes Chams is of Bon origin: "originally little more than a ritual dance of sacrificial exorcism," and compares it to Ceylonese devil-dances (*op. cit.*, p. 284f.)

70.   Nebesky-Wojkowitz, Rene de, *Tibetan Religious Dances*, Paris, 1976; Fantin, Mario, *Mani rimdu Nepal*, New Delhi, 1976; Jerstad, Luther G., *Mani-rimdu*, University of Washington Press, 1976; Kohn, Richard J., *Mani Rimdu. Text and Tradition in a Tibetan Ritual*, Ph. D. dissertation, University of Wisconsin, Madison, 1988 with its valuable record of actual texts. Cf. also Schrempf, Mona, *Der sakrale Maskentanz der Tibeter am Beispiel des Yak Sang 'Cham im Kloster Dzongkar Choede*, M. A. Dissertation, Berlin, 1990, and the very useful booklet put out by the Tengpoche Trust: *Myths, Mountains and Mandalas*, compiled by Bill Kite and Geoff Childs (1988).

        There are also relevant works by Paul Robert A., (*The Sherpas of Nepal in the Tibetan Cultural Context*, Delhi, 1989) and Fürer-Haimendorf, Christoph von, (*The Sherpas of Nepal*, New Delhi, 1964) but both these rely heavily on Jerstad and the former is marred by some entertaining but ultimately rather silly Freudianism [Paul admits that he was unable to get "extensive exegesis from the performers themselves because of circumstances of my own travel" (p. 109) but the real reason may well lie in the lamas' reactions to being told that the Vajra is simply a phallus and the sacred pills on which they meditate and into which they transfer compassion nothing but testicles].

71.   Nebesky-Wojkowitz, *op. cit.* (1976), pp. 9ff. Kohn contains translations of the ritual texts preceding the actual performances.

opinion. Chams can be seen today in Tibet, in exile, in Bhutan and Ladakh but the most accessible and also best documented versions are the Mani Rimdu performed in Upper Nepal,[72] of which there is even a documentary, 'Destroyer of Illusion',[73] which goes behind the scenes to record the accompanying rituals centred on the *maṇḍala* and the Chief Lama's meditations and *mantras*. Because the actual dance-drama performance is only a public climax, preparations having begun in fact fifteen days earlier with the creation of a multi-coloured sand *maṇḍala* and a fortnight of intense, concentrated meditation and chanting. The function of this play is not just to entertain or even just to teach and preach the Vajrayāna Gospel to a largely illiterate flock; it is an act of compassion motivated by the *bodhisattva* ideal which will cleanse the whole area of evil for the next twelve months.

In general, it can be said that an account of Chams from a Buddhist perspective has yet to be undertaken. And yet it could be argued that it is really a culmination of the whole religion: as Govinda writes in *Foundations of Tibetan Mysticism*: "A thing exists only insofar as it acts."[74] Chams is arguably the climax of:

- the basic pattern of the Vajrayāna whereby all abstractions are progressively symbolized and systematically personified — as means to enlightenment, as *upāya*;

- the basic practices of Vajrayāna *yoga* — as a path of dramatic visualization and empathetic identification;

- the overall ethical requirement to enlighten, teach; and

---

72. That the Mani Rimdu is an authentic Chams does not really need defending: a first rudimentary version of it was performed at the inauguration of Tengpoche monastery (founded 1923) when Zatul Ngawang Tenzin Norbu came from Rongbuk monastery on the other side of Everest and performed some of the dances. These had themselves been copied and borrowed from other gompas in Tibet though Ngawang Tenzin Norbu created some himself: cf. Zangbu, *op. cit.*, p. 37 and Führer-Haimendorf, *op. cit.*, p. 211.

73. "Destroyer of Illusion" by Kohn, Richard produced by Franz-Christoph Giercke and distributed by Sky Walker Productions, 1989.

74. Govinda, *op. cit.*, p. 105.

the fundamental commitment of the Vajrayāna to a polarity of Philosophy and Performance, Precept and Practice, Wisdom and Action. . .

All this could be seen as generating a cumulative momentum which inevitably led the Vajrayāna to full scale theatre.

Such a theatre would be ritualistic, allegorical, and therefore operate on more than one level at the same time, but according to *trikāya* or Three Bodies Theory, everything does exist simultaneously on three planes — the sensual, the formal, and the formless, accessible respectively through sense perception, reason and imagination, and enlightened inner vision. What this means is that any phenomenon — from the Buddha on down — is embodied, exists and can be apprehended either as an individual, particular manifestation, an ideal representation, or in its universal form. Govidnda writes that, in the latter, the *dharmakāya*, "all Enlightened Ones are the same", while in the *sambhogakāya*, "things are cognized in their pure form as Ideas", and in the third body, the *nirmāṇakaya*, "inspiration is transformed into visible form and becomes action . . . the human embodiment or individuality."[75] None of these is actually higher or lower or even independent of the others, the ultimate goal being to apprehend all three simultaneously and interdependently — in the 'Fourth body', the *vajrakāya*.[76] Govinda summarises the doctrine and suggests a useful extension into the field of aesthetic creativity and appreciation when he writes:

In states of rapture, trance and highest intuition, as characterized by the stages of deep absorption in meditation (*dhyana*), we experience the *Dharmakaya* as the luminous forms of purely spiritual perception — as pure, eternal principles of form, freed from all accidentals — or as the exalted visions of a higher reality. In them the *Sambhogakaya*, 'the Body of Bliss' is realized. From it flow all immortal art, all deep wisdom, all profound truths (*dharma*, in the sense of formulated or proclaimed truth).

75. Govinda, *op. cit.*, p. 213.
76. *Ibid*, 222.

Its enjoyment is of two kinds, like that of every great work
of art: the rapture of the creative act and the enjoyment of
those who contemplate the completed work by retrospectively
experiencing and reliving the act of creation. . . .[77]

Such is the ideal experience of meditating on a *mandala* but it could
be argued that such is also the ideal experience of a play in
performance: we see a particular character performed by an
individual, physical actor but behind that we glimpse a vision of the
ideal character and of what she/he represents, this in turn being the
formal expression of only one potential of the total 'Human Spirit'.

Certainly such a 'triple apprehension' should work for any
allegorical theatre if it is to fulfil its religious purpose which — in
Buddhist terms — would be no less than to apprehend the same co-
existence of Form and Emptiness as in a successful meditation on
a *mandala*. Indeed, it is not too fanciful to argue that a *mandala* is
itself an allegorical 'playscript': it has characters, frozen in dynamic
poses and postures with symbolic gestures, masked; there is a 'set',
an inscribed 'plot' or at least journey, and the whole is enacted in the
mind of the meditator. Such a *mandala* — made of coloured sand —
is indeed constructred as the necessary prelude for a Chams
performance.

It is not possible to construct a typical or core or representative
Chams.[78] All usually contain scenes reenacting the victories and
triumphs of Padmasambhava, and a crucial 'Cemetery Dance' (or
Liberation Dance) and exorcism of the *linga*; Black Hat dancers are
found in virtually all and the Comic Old Man.

There are variations between the three versions of the Mani
Rimdu too, as performed in the monasteries of Thami, Chiwong and
Tengpoche, all in Sherpa territory;[79] the following is based on

---

77. Govinda, *op. cit.*, p. 214.
78. There is much competition between monasteries who borrow freely
    from each other: cf. Nebesky-Wojkowitz, *op. cit.* (1976), pp. 75-79.
79. Sherpas are Buddhists, migrants from Tibet who originally fled to the
    Khumbu region during the Tibetan 'Reformation' under the fifth Dalai
    Lama (1617-82) when the Nyingmapa (Red Hats) were persecuted in

                                                                    →

fieldwork done at Tengpoche in 1992, this monastery providing as it does the superb backdrop of the Himālayan peaks as their set: Ama Dablam to the east, Tamserku and Kantaga to the south, Tawache to the north, Kwongde to the west and behind and above them all Chomolungma, the Sherpa name for Everest, lit by the full moon in October. Tengpoche is a strict Nyingmapa monastery in which sect a lama is — like the founder Padmasambhava — both a magician (able to fly, turn the hairs of his head into trees, and dogs into tigers) and a mystic. In the Nyingmapa tradition every reincarnate lama (Rinpoche) is a *bodhisattva* in that, after his death, his 'sem' has been stopped on its way to *nirvāṇa* and told by the Urken Rinpoche that he must wait, go back and be reborn for the sake of humanity as a whole. Unlike other reincarnated 'souls' he is able to retain knowledge of his past lives.[80]

The whole ritual begins on the first day of the ninth month when the monks begin to make 'torma' (small cones of butter and barley flour) while others begin the arduous task of making a *maṇḍala* by grating coloured rock and sand. This will take four full days and it effectively creates a sacred space.[81]

For the next ten years, the monks assemble day and night, worshipping and invoking Pawa Cherenzig (Avalokiteśvara) in his action aspect, Mahā-Kāla, the chief protector of Buddhism, and other gods, three each day. Twice a day the *liṅga* — a paper effigy representing the forces of evil, one of which has been buried in the courtyard for the dance and the other under the sand *maṇḍala* where its limbs have already been broken — has new sets of enemies drawn into it and there ritually speared.

The fifteenth day is the Teri Whong or Life Consecration

→   favour of the Yellow Hats and Tibet effectively became a Theocracy under the military protection of the Mongols. Tengpoche itself was inspired by Rongphu, the headquarters of the Nyingmapa; it was there that the monks were sent to learn the Mani Rimdu which was first performed at Thami in 1942 and in its present more elaborate form only since 1950.

80.   Cf. Fürer-Haimendorf, *op. cit.*, p. 156.

81.   Cf . Kite/Childs, *op. cit.*, pp. 22-24.

ceremony when Sherpas from all surrounding villages assemble to receive the lamas' blessings and the gift of Torma and 'Rilpu' (sacred pills). This, not the dances which occur the next day, is actually the spiritual climax of the Mani Rimdu whose name is derived from 'Mani' (the *mantra* of Avalokiteśvara), 'Ril' (the little red pills) and 'Du' (meaning blessing): the Tengpoche Rinpoche says that the blessing of the Rilpu "can be traced back to when Guru Rinpoche (Padmasambhava) brought religion to Tibet".[82]

The dances take up the whole of the sixteenth day and there seems little doubt that what the spectators witness is a kind of dramatized sermon and potted history of their religion: "a dramatic enactment of the victory of the divine and human protagonists of Buddhist doctrine over the forces of evil".[83]

It is, however, just as likely that what the *lamas themselves* experience, especially the presiding Rinpoche, is something quite different: as Tucci notes, there remains, in practice "a deep division between monastic Lamaism and religion as it is lived by the people."[84] Thus, what may be for the simple spectator a slice of mythological history is probably very different for the lamas who dance the parts: they, as Govinda points out, have through intense meditation become the vessels of the deities they represent.[85] As for the Rinpoche, he does not dance at all but performs an elaborate parallel set of rituals, aimed at exorcising evil, trapped in the *liṅga*. The temptation to suggest an interpretation based on the *trikāya* is irresistible — and entirely Buddhist, for it is the essence of Tibetan Buddhism that everything exists on different planes and degrees of hermeneutic significance, so that there is no reason why the

82. Cf. Kite/Childs, *op. cit.*, p. 37. These pills possibly contain Lamas' excrement or urine: they along with semen, flesh and blood being the five Tāntric 'ambrosias'. Reputedly there used to be a brisk trade in the Dalai Lama's excrement at the foot of the Potala in Llasa (Kohn, *op. cit.*, p. 159).

83. Fürer-Haimendorf, *op. cit.*, p. 223. Kite/Childs call it a "performed analogy of the Khumbu religious culture" (*op. cit.*, p. 21).

84. Tucci, *op. cit.* (1980), p. vii.

85. Govinda, *The Way of the White Clouds*, Shambhala, Berkeley, California, 1970, p. 175.

performance of a play cannot be simultaneously a dramatized sermon and history lesson and, on another level, a meditation.[86]

The most obvious — *nirmāṇakāya* — plane on which the Chams operates is to tell the story of the founding of the Vajrayāna, demonstrate its power, and offer a theatrical demonstration of its main ethical teachings. Thus, after a ceremonial entrance in which *chang* is offered to the Dhyānī Buddhas (when it becomes *amṛta*, the Ambrosia of Life) and then shared between performers and spectators to establish a community of deities, monks and laity, the second scene brings on the four heralds of Padmasambhava who himself then enters in the third dance. He is, of course, the historical founder of the whole system and the object of special veneration for the Nyingmapa: he appears now in his wrathful form as Dorje Throlo. Having been announced, then having arrived 'in person', his victories can now be danced: his conversion of the (Bon) demons into defenders of the faith.

It is at this point in any Chams that a shift occurs from historical to topical exorcism — centred on the *liṅga*. Evans-Wentz describes how at this point the (Bon) demons are made to enter an effigy of a sacrificial victim where they are effectively imprisoned: "I pierce their hearts with this hook", chants the officiant,

> I bind their hands with this snare of rope; I bind their bodies with this powerful chain; I keep them down with the tinkling bell. . . . Then the chief of the Fierce Ones is requested to 'tear out the hearts of the injuring evil spirits and utterly exterminate them'. The sacrifical effigy, which is visualized as being in actuality a corpse, is symbolically dipped in the blood of the demons and offered up to the Fierce Ones to the accompaniment of the following chant: 'Hum! O! ye hosts of gods of the magic circle! Open your mouths as wide as the earth and sky, clench your fangs like rocky mountains, and prepare to devour in their entirety

---

86. Such, after all, was the Catholic Mass: cf. Hardison, O.B., *Christian Rite and Christian Drama in the Middle Ages,* John Hopkins Press, 1965.

the bones, the blood and the entrails of all the injuring evil spirits.[87]

Today this *liṅga* is usually a folded paper effigy, contained in a triangular wooden frame, often abstract, though sometimes representing a highly sexualized human form. It represents "all the setbacks and misfortunes experienced by each person in the society"[88] and contains "highly compressed and concentrated negative forces."[89] In the old days this *liṅga* was quite realistic: the 'dance-book' of the Fifth Dalai Lama translated by Nebesky-Wojkowitz states that the *liṅga* should be "just like a real corpse . . . complete, with brain, heart, bowels, etc.;" it should be made of black dough, prepared from roasted barley flour, or of dough which had been coloured dark blue or red; the organs are to be made of symbolic materials: pieces of conch-shell for bones, a strip of saffron-coloured silk for the tongue, a pearl for the brain, and sometimes a bladder filled with blood which is pierced by a dancer and sprinkled in the four directions as an offering.[90] Waddell describes it as follows:

> Some days previous to the commencement of the play, an image of a young lad is made out of dough, in most elaborate fashion, and as life-like as possible. Organs representing the heart, lungs, liver, brain, stomach, intestines, etc. are inserted into it, and the heart and large blood-vessels and limbs are filled with a red-coloured fluid to represent blood. And occasionally, I am informed on good authority, actual flesh from the corpses of criminals is inserted into the image used in this ceremony at the established church of Potala.[91]

The climax of exorcism occurs in the next, the 'Cemetery Dance'

87. Evans-Wentz, *op. cit.*, p. 290.
88. Marko, Ann, "Cham: Ritual as Myth in a Ladakhi Gompa", in *Tantra and Popular Religion in Tibet,* ed. by Samuel, G., Gregor, H., and Stutchbury, E., New Delhi, 1994, p. 145.
89. *Ibid.*, p. 148.
90. Nebesky-Wijkowitz, *op. cit.* (1976), p. 106.
91. Waddell, *op. cit.*, p. 529.

(Thur-Dag), the moral core of the play, illustrating the fate of those who resist conversion to Buddhism, the tortures perpetrated by two servants of Yama on corpses — represented now by a rag doll but in Waddell's day much more grisly, culminating in the stabbing of the effigy, its dismemberment and the extraction of the bleeding heart, lungs and intestines which were then collected in a silver bowl shaped like a skull and tossed to the lamas and spectators who ate them or treasured them as talismans. But, even then as now, it was a paper image of a *linga* which was finally placed inside the skull and burned, thus completing the exorcism of evil.[92]

In its contemporary form, this scene has already caused some merriment among the spectators and it is followed by a long comic skit — the Dance of the Old Man. Fantin claims that this is a satire on Chinese — Ch'an — Buddhism, and Waddell and Nebesky-Wojkowitz both identify the Old Man as the Chinese priest, Hwashang, the loser in the Great Debate at Samye.[93] To this extent this scene continues the historical thread of the narrative, and this comic debunking of the unorthodox is then — in the logic of moral propaganda — followed naturally by the Dance of the Eight Guardians — wrathful terror to bring about what comic humiliation can not.

In the Nepalese version, this is in turn followed by the climax for the Sherpa audience: the entrance and dance of their own special tutelary god — Zur-ra — bringing the reconstructed history of their religion up to their migration to Khumbu Valley, discovered for them by Zur-ra.

The last five dances allow the tale to run down, each a variation on the theme: trust the monks, they will protect you: the Ḍākinīs of the Khon-dro dance which follows are unmasked and very much monks, while the comic skit of 'The Yogi and his Novice' is a satire on the alernative — Hindu *sādhu*s, exposed here as ostentatious

---

92. Waddell, *op. cit.*, pp. 531 ff.

93. *Ibid.*, p. 534; Nebesky-Wojkowitz, *op. cit.* (1976), p. 82. Kohn, though he has reservations, agrees that it is probably Hwashang (*op. cit.*, p. 286).

fakes. The Sword Dance and the final 'Zor-cham' all emphasize the protection now offered by the monks and their rituals.

In other words and summarizing: what has been experienced on one level is a religious history, a moral sermon and the comforting message that the monks dancing for us are our present and rightful protectors. Like all ritual dance, the Chams makes the old new again:

> commemorating and bringing to life once again that moment of origin in which the ancestors descended to the earth, in order to call down their help and protection on the society tracing its descent from them, and thus to ensure its continuation.[94]

It is unlikely that the performance has any more significance than that for the average spectator: Fürer-Haimendorf writes that his informants were often "vague about the meanings" even of the masks and saw the play simply as the ritual destruction of the enemies of Buddhism by Raja Dorje Torlo (Guru Rinpoche).[95] Jerstad says much the same:[96] certainly the regular and continuous consumption of chang encourages a very discontinuous concentration on any deeper message, and the audience clearly relishes most the comic skits, content to 'gain merit' simply by attending what to most of them is as much a social occasion as anything else. Fürer-Haimendorf concludes:

> The performance of the dancers, all of whom are known to be lamas, is viewed as a spectacle rather than as a ritual act. . . The laymen take the view that the propitiation and worship of the deities are safe in the hands of the lamas. . . . Pilgrims and spectators have hence no other function than to attend.[97]

---

94. Tucci, *op. cit.* (1980), p. 233.
95. Fürer-Haimendorf, *op. cit.*, p. 224.
96. *Op. cit.*, p. 126.
97. Fürer-Haimendorf, *op. cit.*, p. 224.

The performers — the lamas — have, however, one can conjecture, been undergoing a quite different experience. Each of the dances they dance refers back to a special *pūjāh* they have performed during the previous fifteen days' meditations; originally, the dances themselves were also performed in secret, at night, and no uninitiated spectator was allowed to witness them.[98] And this is not the only special reference in the lamas' minds as they perform: the Tengpoche Rinpoche says:

> The dances come from when Guru Rinpoche blessed Samye monastery. He pretended to be his favourite god by imitating its body and danced the blessing. Since then, some lamas think they will see these dances in Dewa Chan.[99]

Tantalizingly enigmatic though such statements are, it does mean that the dances must have a far deeper significance and wider reference for the monks than for the lay audience: implicitly these are sacred dances, re-enactments of those performed by the deified founder of the whole religion and performed even now in 'Heaven'. The Rinpoche says:

> For the different gods, there are different ways of worship, chanting or dance movements that help make the gods closer to the dancer *and eventually a part of him,* helping everyone.[100]

Does this mean that the dancers enter some kind of trance? Guardian deities possess mediums who, in trance, become their oracles; oracles, in possession, also dance. . . .[101] Fürer-Haimendorf suspected this might be the case in the Chams and according to Nebesky-Wojkowitz, trance is known, the masks are consecrated and have such magical power that the performers must be purified before performing.[102]

---

98. Nebesky-Wojkowitz, *op. cit.* (1976), p. 43.
99. Zangbu, *op. cit.*, p. 39.
100. Zangbu, *op. cit.*, p. 40 (emphasis added).
101. Nebesky-Wojkowitz, *op. cit.* (1993), pp. 430f.
102. Nebesky-Wojkowitz, *op. cit.*, (1976), p. 75.

Govinda is quite explicit: the Chams, for the lamas, is no more or less than an enacted visualization mediation:

> in which beings from the spiritual world were propitiated and invited to manifest themselves in the bearers of their symbols, who for the time being divested themselves of their own personality, by going through a ritual of purification and making themselves instruments and vessels of the divine powers which their masks represented.[103]

There is some dispute here: Nebesky-Wojkowitz and others agree with Govinda that the lamas become the deities they meditate upon;[104] others like Kohn argue that they don't:[105] no-one denies that, as in all Tibetan rituals, beings are first created mentally, then physically, and that the whole system therefore draws on Vajrayāna meditation techniques and theories.

It is certainly clear that the whole performance has references, subtexts and implications which make it a quite different experience for the lamas than for the spectators: an attempt now to read the play on a deeper allegorical level, on the second — ideal, symbolic — *sambhogakāya* plane, illustrates what could be happening.

Thus, even the first dance may not be only a consecration of the communion of deities, lamas and laity; Ann Marko suggests that, for the lamas, the courtyard where they perform is a *maṇḍala* and the dancers the deities in it;[106] according to the Tengpoche Rinpoche:

> This dance is done for the purpose of invoking Tse Gyawa (improving one's life, longevity, health and intelligence), Whong (spiritual power) and Took (the ability to fight bad spirits). The black hats represent Nagger or Vajrayana priests.[107]

---

103.   Govinda, *op. cit.* (1970), p. 175.
104.   Nebesky-Wojkowitz, *op. cit.* (1976), pp. 113 and 240; Schrempf, *op. cit.*, p. 8.
105.   Kohn, *op. cit.*, pp. 85ff.
106.   Marko, *op. cit.*, p. 135.
107.   Zangbu, *op. cit.*, p. 39.

Kite-Childs explicate:

> Also known as Sha-nak (Black Hats), Ngak-pa are common to most *cham* performances regardless of sect, monastery or region. Representing tantric practitioners, they are adept at dispelling demons manifested as inherent human deficiencies (greed, ignorance). . . . The black hat, denoting an unchanging, unalterable condition, is crowned by a single skull which portrays the impermanence of human existence. Inside, the hat is colored red thereby signifying the compassionate goals of the bearer.[108]

The second dance has a similarly deeper layer of symbolic and allegorical significance for those who know how to read it. The four Heralds are two females and two males and within this basic — yab/yum — polarity there is a red/white and green/blue colour symbolism at work. Kite/Childs write:

> Having bodies of light, King-pa can only be seen by the enlightened who have cleared the deceptive influences of ignorance and false conceptions from their minds. . . .[109]

But the dance which perhaps best illustrates the possiblities of polyvalent meanings is the climactic Thur-dag or Cemetery Dance, where the rag doll may not represent just a tormented soul in the power of the servants of Yama; the Rinpoche says that it represents evil[110] and as for the two skeleton dancers: they have their own history, representing two ascetics who went into such a deep level of meditation that they failed to notice when thieves came and chopped off their heads. They then vowed to fight all the forces of evil, and it should be noted that, though overshadowed by the macabre dance itself, there are two other dancers in this scene: they wear the same costume as Padmasambhava in scene three and, like him, they carry the sacred Phurbu dagger for killing evil; such a Phurbu is at the same time being manipulated by the Rinpoche

---

108. Kite/Childs, *op. cit.*, p. 32.
109. Kite/Childs, *op. cit.*, p. 32.
110. Zangbu, *op. cit.*, p. 39.

himself up in the gallery so that there is, in fact, a rich layering of messages being enacted here:

- warning of the fate awaiting those who resist conversion to Buddhism;

- ritual exorcism of the forces of evil;

- and even the initiation of a *bodhisttava*, because after the two skeleton dancers have hurled the rag-doll 'corpse' to the ground, the two Tāntric priests in Padmasambhava's costume remove the evil form it and bury it, effectively thus purging the corpse of evil. In the version described by Waddell, there were dozens of ghoulish skeleton-dancers surrounding the *liṅga* and attempting to harm it but prevented — first by the magic triangle which the lamas had placed around it, then by a *bodhisattva* figure who appeared from his mask to be one of the incarnations of Buddha. He had more control over the evil spirits than any other who had yet contended with them. The skeletons . . . grovelled before him, and with inarticulate and beast-like cries implored mercy. He yielded to their supplications, gave each one a little of the flour he carried with him, which the fiends ate gratefully, kneeling before him.[111]

In the Tengpoche Mani Rimdu, the whole scene concludes — significantly — with the two skeleton-dancers learning a new dance from the two black-hat *bodhisattva*-dancers. . . .

Even the comic interlude has a deeper message[112] and as for the dance of the Eight Guardians, it would take a serious adept to decode the full symbolism of their masks and costumes (Naksum Ma's mask, for example, represents the highest female *bodhisattva*: it has one eye, one breast and one tooth, the single eye being representative of her

---

111.   Waddell, *op. cit.*, p. 529.

112.   He bungles the rituals, even the simplest — offering a *khata* to the head lama — but is helped to learn the correct way by a lama who enters from the audience: Kite/Childs, *op. cit.*, p. 28.

universally maternal nature to love and protect all beings as if they were one. The single eye is the wisdom eye with which she can view all three realms of existence simultaneously, while the single tooth denotes her power to destroy all spiritual enemies as if they were actually one.[113]

Even Zur-ra is not merely the local protective deity; he is also a manifestation of Dorje Chang (Vajradhara) and guardian of Khanbalung, a valley hidden by the Guru Rinpoche and not yet opened, while the Ḍākinīs are very complex figures — 'sky dancers' whom lamas invoke for their ability to grant supernatural powers. They have bodies of pure light;[114] Padmasambhava himself had been initiatied by a Ḍākinī the Ḍākinīs being the "genii of meditation. . . ."[115]

At the very least, one can and must recognize that there are symbolic and allegorical levels of meaning here which are readable only by a highly literate Buddhist and really only by one with many years of practice in visualization meditation. How the lamas and the Rinpoche himself actually cognise and use the Chams may probably never be divulged in full but that does not prevent the claim that the play does clearly operate on a deeper, allegorical level where the physical and material have been converted into the symbolic — as occurs on the *sambhogakāya* plane of being. That may even be the level at which they originated: dances are often derived from meditation experiences, visualizations of the Guru, of Ḍākinīs dancing. . . .[116] At least one — highly informed — Tibetan Buddhist authority supports such a reading: Jamyang Norbu in *Zlos-Gar Performing Traditions of Tibet* (Dharamasala 1986) writes:

> Cham could, with some licence, be described essentially as a kind of meditation in movement. The dancer is by his actions (aided by chants, music and costumes) supposed to

113. Kite/Childs, *op. cit.*, p. 36.
114. Govinda, *op. cit.* (1977), p. 190.
115. *Ibid.*, p. 192.
116. Cf. Cantwell, Cathy, "The Dance of the Guru's Eight Aspects", *The Tibet Journal*, vol. 20, no. 4, 1995, pp. 47-63.

conceive himself as the deity he is representing. Every gesture he makes is not only symbolic, but is supposed to have power in itself.[117]

As for a third level — a *dharmakāya* stratum: Nebesky-Wojkowitz noted as a general principle of Tibetan monastic dance-drama:

Besides the actors who actually dance on this stage, a number of other persons have to be enumerated who, too, fulfil important functions in the *'chams.* In the first place, we have to mention the so-called *rdo rje slob dpon,* the 'Thunderbolt Religious Master' who sits outside the dance circle, often on a balcony overlooking the courtyard, and who, by prayers and secret spells addressed to the deities appearing on the scene, directs the *'chams* on a mystic plane.[118]

His 'performance' has escaped deep investigation (and will continue to do so while this activity and its texts remain so secret) but throughout the performance, the Rinpoche himself — the *rdo rje slob dpon* — has been sitting up on the balcony meditating, sometimes praying, reciting *mantra*s, manipulating his magical phurbu, and chanting. In this he is accompanied by other senior monks, for the play does have a text, one chanted throughout — the *Thuje Chenpo Deshe Kundu.* By tradition this is one of the books which Padmasambhava hid, its teachings reserved for some time in the future when wars and other vicissitudes would make them necessary. 'Thuje Chenpo' is *mahā-karuṇā* in Sanskrit, namely 'The Great Compassion'; it is also the name for Jigten Wangchuk, the aspect of Pawa Cherenzig (Avalokiteśvara) worshipped during the Mani Rimdu rituals. The Tengpoche Rinpoche writes:

This book is mostly about Duph, a very powerful pujah that is an imitation of Guru Rinpoche's body in order to worship Pawa Cherenzig.[119]

---

117. Jamyang Norbu, *Zlos-Gar Performing Traditions of Tibet,* Dharamasala 1986, p. 4.

118. Nebesky-Wojkowitz, *op. cit.* (1976), p. 68.

119. Zangbu, *op. cit.,* p. 38.

During the preceding two weeks, the Rinpoche has supervised the creation of the 'set' — the *maṇḍala* (though for him the real *maṇḍala* is in his mind); he has completed the incarnation of the other deities in the other dancers in pre-performance rituals, and then visualized himself as and finally *become* Cherenzig, the Sherpa name for Avalokiteśvara, the 'Lord of the Dance' — of which he is, indeed, the contemporary reincarnation! At the climax of the Flask empowerment ritual preceding the Mani Rimdu he chants: "From now on, do everything I say, I am Avalokiteśvara" and then:

> this body of mine that has become that of the Lord of the Dance Great Compassion burns like a butter lamp. Its shining light stimulates the gods of the mandala to project countless forms from their minds — bodies and syllables, symbols which blaze in a mass of beams of light, which come helter skelter like rain and snow, like a blizzard. They enter through my pores and fill my body to the brim. Bliss blazes unbearably.[120]

This in turn is followed by the actual empowerment itself in which the Chief Lama receives all five forms of awareness — the five Dhyānī Buddhas — all *dharmakāya* forms.[121]

Simultaneously spectator, performer and director, the *rdo rje slob dpon* performs here as Avalokiteśvara himself, motivated by and performing a combination of wisdom and compassion. . . .

Though much research remains to be done, we know enough to stake the claim: the polyvalence of performance supplies Tibet with a vehicle whereby a play can operate on the three planes: a physical plane of paedagogy and re-affirmation for its primary audience but also, simultaneously, an allegorical plane for the dancing lamas, and even on a *bodhisattva* plane for the presiding Rinpoche. Practising forms of meditation which are already intensely theatrical, Tibet has found in the peculiar psychology both of the performer and of the spectator models of its highest ideals.

---

120.   Kohn, *op. cit.*, p. 443f.

121.   *Ibid.*, pp. 448ff.

There are other dance-dramas in Tibet and even more in Nepal: plays in honour of Tārā, for example, investigated by Stephan Beyer,[122] and Lhamo, classical Tibetan opera all of whose stories have Buddhist messages to deliver.[123] But to illustrate how Tibet accepts the medium of performance for attaining even the highest levels of meditating consciousness one can do no better than turn in conclusion to Chöd.

Chöd

If Tāntric meditation in general comes close to theatre in its imaginative and empathetic rigour, then, sometimes, it spills over. Chöd is an advanced meditation of the Nyingmapa sect, possibly derived from Bon but adapted to the Buddhist 'direct path': a rite to achieve Enlightenment in this lifetime by a risk-taking venture. "If he succeeds," writes Evans-Wentz, "he may go straight to Nirvana, having penetrated beyond Maya."[124] As such, Chöd is an extreme example of visualization meditation in which the *yogin* creates imaginary figures of such hallucinatory vividness that he cannot distinguish them from material, physical beings. This, in all visualization meditations, leads to the realization that the material, physical world too is no more than a mind-emanation, no more real than imaginative constructs, the difference being that in Chöd this is taken to an extreme in that the *yogin* "may even make them physically as 'real' as his own body",[125] and be so convinced of their

---

122. Tārā is the female form of Avalokiteśvara, the goddess of compassion, skilled in means, who is made approachable to her devotees by narratives, some of which are dramatized, for Tārā 'is the goddess who lets herself be seen' (Beyer, *op. cit.*, p. 57). Known as "ach'e lhamo" these Tārā plays are performed by wandering troupes of actors who enact tales of her patronage, in the open air, often over several days "before enthusiastic and often vocal audiences, sung in a strangely impressive warbling chant and enlivened by ad-lib buffoonery and dance." (Beyer, *op. cit.*, p. 56). Cf. Duncan, Marion H., *Harvest Festival Dramas of Tibet,* Hong Kong, 1955, pp. 175ff.

123. Cf. Ross, Joanna, *Lhamo. Opera from the Roof of the World,* Paljor Publications, New Delhi, 1995.

124. Evans-Wentz, *op. cit.*, p. 282.

125. *Ibid.,* p. 281.

reality that they can kill him. Practised in solitary and sacred places, "amidst the most psychically favourable environments,"[126] the site chosen is usually a Himālayan snowfield or "commonly by preference it is a place where corpses are chopped to bits and given to the wolves and vultures."[127] Blofeld writes:

> The more unsophisticated type of Tibetan adept has a lively faith in the existence of actual demons quite apart from the beings mentally created during a sadhana. He will firmly believe that, if he fails to impose the mantric safeguards properly, real demons will materialize and, taking him at his word, strip his flesh to stay their hunger.[128]

Call this is superstitious fear or as inability to distinguish between imaginary and material constructs: it does not matter: only people immersed in *māyā* believe in the real existence of demons: as *The Tibetan Book of the Dead* states: "apart from one's own hallucinations, in reality there are no such things existing outside oneself."[129]

Evans-Wentz—who has published the Chöd text in translation in his invaluable collection *Tibetan Yoga and Secret Doctrines* — has no hesitation in calling it a

> mystic drama, performed by a single human actor, assisted by numerous spiritual beings, visualized, or imagined, as being present in response to his magic invocation.[130]

For the great gift of theatre to this religion is that it facilitates the cognition of reality as an illusion, "an imaginative creation given illusive existence by its creator."[131] Chöd goes further by both creating a theatrical illusion and then seeking to penetrate beyond, to the Void, for 'chöd' means, literally, 'to cut off' — all egoism, all passion, all kārmic inheritance, all Self:

---

126. Evans-Wentz, *op. cit.*, p. 280.
127. *Ibid.,* p. 282.
128. Blofeld, *op. cit.*, p. 189.
129. Quoted in Evans-Wentz, *op. cit.*, p. 282.
130. *Ibid.,* p. 282.
131. *Ibid.,* p. 281.

as represented by the human fleshly form together with all its passions and kārmically-inherited predispositions constituting the personality.[132]

Simultaneously director, choreographer, performer and spectator, the Lama must have put in years of preparation and rehearsal before attempting this rite: he must memorize the whole ritual including the dance steps, the *mantras*, the rhythmic beating of the *damaru* drum and the sounding of the thigh-bone trumpet; the right way to pitch the symbolic tent, employ the dorje, the bell and various other ritual objects must also be mastered to perfection.

Alone in the wilderness with no other aid at hand than his own *yogic* power, he must face the strange elemental beings which the ritual evokes and dominate them; or, failing, risk an unbalancing of mind and psychic constitution, possibly leading to madness or even death.[133]

Installed in his snow-cave or cremation ground, the lama first visualises himself as the 'Goddess of All-Fulfilling (or All-Performing) Wisdom', then sounds a trumpet made of a human thigh-bone and begins to dance — to the five directions, at each of which he invokes one of the five Dhyānī-Buddhas and their Dākinīs in order to defeat, one after the other, each of the five inhibiting passions (hatred, pride, lust, jealousy and stupidity).

Identifying his passions and desires with his own body, he offers it as a feast to the Dakinis. Next he visualizes it as a 'fat, luscious-looking corpse' of vast extent and, mentally withdrawing from it, watches the Goddess Vajra-yogini sever its head and convert his skull into a gigantic cauldron, into which she tosses chunks of his bone and slices of his flesh. Then, by using words of power, he transmutes the whole offering into pure amrita (nectar) and calls upon the various orders of supernatural being to devour it. For fear they should be impatient, he begs them not to hesitate to

---

132.   Quoted in Evans-Wentz, *op. cit.*, p. 277.

133.   Evans-Wentz, *op. cit.*, p. 280.

eat the offering raw instead of wasting time on cooking it.[134]

Then comes the — dangerous — climax: the Spearing of the Self using the spears of the five orders of Ḍākinīs, for the key here is to realize that it is the desire for sensuous existence, for separate, individual existence which *creates* the physical body: stop desiring sāṁsāric existence and the body will simply 'drop away' and the adept will enter the Clear Light of Buddha-Consciousness. Bernbaum writes that he

> merges with the deity and becomes the play, but without self-consciousness, since he is no longer his ego but the deity. In this way the sadhana as play or drama helps him to transcend his ego. And having done so, he is free to discard the props and constraints of symbols and ritual in the experience of the undifferentiated void.[135]

A candidate for *nirvāṇa* in the Tibetan tradition may, however, return, become instead a *bodhisattva*; Evans-Wentz suggests this conclusion himself, ending his own introduction to Chöd with extracts from *Mahāyāna sūtras* in which Bodhisattvas vow to donate everything they possess to those who may need it — including hands, feet, eyes, flesh, blood, giving the whole sacrificial aspect of the Chöd rite a quite different slant and relating it to the central theme of Tibetan Buddhism: the cult of compassion.

---

134. Blofeld, *op. cit.*, p. 189.

135. Bernbaum, Edwin M., "The Way of Symbols: The Use of Symbols in Tibetan Mysticism", *The Journal of Transpersonal Psychology*, Vol.6, no.2, 1974, p. 107f.

5

Bodhi-drama
Zen; Japan

Introductory: The Terms

THAT drama can offer case-studies in *karma*, that the theatre can offer opportunities for compassionate intervention, and that both *karma* and *karuṇā* are performative concepts and practices leads, inevitably, to the final question: Buddhism is, ultimately, a way to Enlightenment; can that too be enabled by performance?

The Hīnayāna did not think so, and the Vajrayāna reserved the possibility at most for advanced lamas, both schools accepting that only those who dedicate their lives to meditation can hope to achieve enlightenment. That conventional division of the Buddhist path into two basic options has not, however, gone unquestioned; at various times in its history Buddhism has spawned movements which have sought to break that elitist division and offer even laypersons some hope of achieving at least mini-enlightenments. Foremost among such movements is Zen — the subject of this final chapter.

Zen recognizes that whenever a new saviour arises, he is not aware at the time of the religious system which will later grow up in his name. At the time of his life, his teaching is inseparable from his personality; both live and grow; it is only after he dies that either teaching or personality (or both) are elevated to a status where they effectively put an end to further development. Either he is proclaimed to be God and thus of a different order of being from mere mortals who can only obey and emulate him, not repeat him, or his teaching is proclaimed to be definitive: the word with which one may not tamper. Either way, the normal course of any religion is to freeze insight at either the person or the teaching of the founder.

Zen will have none of this: radically, it recognizes that the only way to keep a religion truly alive is to deny both the personality of the founder and the authority of his teaching. As the Ch'an master I-hsüan put it:

> Kill everything that stands in your way. If you should meet the Buddha, kill the Buddha. If you should meet the Patriarchs, kill the Patriarchs.[1]

Hsüan-chien was even more outspoken:

> There are neither Buddhas nor Patriarchs; Bodhidharma was only an old bearded barbarian. Sakyamuni and Kasyapa, Manjusri and Samantabhadra only dungheap coolies.... Nirvana and bodhi are dead stumps to tie to your donkeys. The twelve divisions of the sacred teachings are only lists of ghosts, sheets of paper fit only for wiping pus from your boils.[2]

Both personality and teaching, argues Zen, must be replaced by cultivation of the state of consciousness which the founder achieved and which, it says, we too can and must also achieve.

The four principles of Zen as laid down by Bodhidharma are:

A special transmission outside the scriptures;
No dependence upon words and letters;
Direct pointing to the soul of man;
Seeing into one's nature and the attainment of Buddhahood.[3]

---

1.   Kenneth K.S. Ch'en, *Buddhism in China. A Historical Survey*, Princeton U.P., 1964, p. 358.

2.   Eadem.

3.   Suzuki, D.T., *Essays in Zen Buddhism*, London, 1949-53, Vol. I, p. 20.

Zen pursues its ambitions through two fundamental techniques — zazen and the koan. While the koan may appear to have dramatic possibilities in its dialogic structure, zazen would appear to be the very antithesis of performance, for zazen is simply sitting — for six and more hours at a time, facing a blank wall. And yet there are those who have argued that Zen influenced the most classical of Japanese theatrical arts, the Noh, basing their evidence on the writings and career of the founder — Zeami — and on the performance structure of Noh.

It is the purpose of this chapter to re-examine that claim — one which has not gone undisputed. Some re-examination is necessary: analogies between Zen and Noh have tended to take the form of nebulous concepts such as 'serenity', 'calm', 'self-control', 'restraint', even 'mystical ecstasy', or 'Zen mass'.[4] The superficiality of the comparisons and the vagueness of the terms deserved and provoked a counter-attack, one itself based on the writings of Zeami.

Until his writings were 'discovered' for the general public, Noh texts had traditionally been ascribed to 'Zen monks'; publication of the authentic Zeami since 1909 supplied the alternative, for in spite of his employment of Zen terminology, Zeami appeared in these writings as a theatre professional *par excellence*, and his works as manuals of stage-business. René Sieffert — the first Western scholar to make these writings available to a non-Japanese public — lead the attack:

> sachant l'usage que certains "zennistes" occidentaux et même japonais (ceux-là toujours ignorants, sinon de mauvaise foi) preténdent faire du *nô*, je tiens à déclarer que je m'inscris d'avance en faux contre toute interprétation mystique ou ésotérique des *Traités* de Zeami.[5]

Sieffert refers such people to Book VII, paragraph 6 of the *Fushi-Kaden* where they will find that the 'secrets' of Noh are not mystical

---

4. Cf. Arnold, P., *Le Théâtre japonais*, Paris, 1957, p. 164; Hoover, Thomas, *Zen Culture*, London, 1988, p. 6.
5. Sieffert, R., *La tradition secrète du Nô*, Paris, 1960, p. 54.

or mysterious doctrines but "rien de plus que des trucs de métier".[6] According to Sieffert, Zeami's writings are not philosophical or mystical treatises but textbooks for a successful career, an interpretation which — as developed further by such scholars as Benito Ortolani[7] — has indeed highlighted both the technical sophistication of Noh and its pragmatic focus on the audience.

A similar scholarly reference to texts then provided the basis for a second attack on the Zen-connection, for the plays themselves refer far more often to other Buddhist doctrines and sects than to Zen, and a number are not Buddhist at all in the myths and legends they relate, but Shinto.[8] This gave birth to a second argument: Noh derives from Shinto and/or Shamanistic practices.

One can therefore now identify three camps:

- a Shinto-and-Shamanism school, which bases its arguments on Noh texts and a general theory of the 'universal' origin of the theatre in Shamanistic practices;

- a Zen school which bases its arguments on metaphors between Zen experiences and Noh performance conventions and on the historical origin of Noh in the Muromachi age of Zen predominance;

- a 'theatre business' school which bases its arguments on Zeami's pragmatic, audience-orientated aesthetics.

The argument of this chapter is not that one is right and the others wrong, but that there need really be no dispute between them. Shinto was, historically, fused with Zen (a marriage celebrated, as we shall see, in a number of Noh plays themselves) while the 'contradiction' between theatre-business and Zen is a problem only for those who do not know that the theatre can provide moments

---

6. *Ibid*, p. 54 and cf. the opinion of a modern Noh actor, Kanze Hideo, in "Noh Business", *Concerned Theatre Japan*, Vol. 1, no. 4, 1971, p. 9.

7. Cf. Ortolani, B., "Zeami's Aesthetics of the No and Audience Participation", *Educational Theatre Journal*, Vol. 24, no. 2, May, 1972.

8. Cf. Gundert, W., *Der Schintoismus im japanischen No-Drama*, Tokyo, 1925.

which are at least analogous to 'enlightenment'. These moments are known to theatre professionals, and not only in Japan; Peter Brook, for example, has referred to the theatre

> touching at certain short moments a quite genuine but fleeting experience of what could be a higher level of evolution . . . an authentic vision . . . the shadow on a wall through which a reality can be perceived.[9]

Zeami described such moments as 'hana', the flower, a term which had its origins in a famous story about the Buddha who, when preaching one day at Vulture Peak, was confronted by a man asking him to tell the secret of Buddhism. Buddha did not reply, simply held out a flower; the man hesitated, took the flower and, it is claimed, achieved enlightenment, "and the silent teaching of Zen was born".[10]

But if we are to penetrate beyond anecdote, metaphor and allusive language, we must first decide what precisely Buddhist enlightenment is.

That cannot be easy: Enlightenment is by definition beyond words to describe and the Buddha himself refused to answer many questions about it. But generations of subsequent Buddhist scholars, philosophers and teachers did agonize over the need to find methods to achieve it and terms to describe it. It is these terms which need to be re-examined first:

- *nirvāṇa* as the general state,

- *śūnyatā* as the more precise description of the state of an enlightened mind,

---

9. Smith, A.C.H., *Orghast at Persepolis*, New York, 1972, p, 251. Cf. Brook, Peter, *There are no Secrets*, (London, 1993) where he uses the Sanskrit word *sphoṭa* (form) which he describes as "the virtual becoming manifest, the spirit taking body, the first sound, the big bang" (p.88) and "a single unrepeatable instant when a door opens and our vision is transformed" (*ibid.*, p. 95).

10. Arnott, P.D., *The Theatres of Japan*, London, 1969, p. 102; cf. *Sources of Japanese Tradition*, ed. by Tsunoda, de Bary and Keene, Columbia U.P., 1958, p. 291.

- *tathatā* as describing the epistemological insight achieved by an enlightened, empty mind,

- and finally 'satori' as the term describing the moment of breakthrough.

Nirvāṇa

"Annihilation of existence, or that of passions and desires, or the dispelling of ignorance, or a state of egolessness": *nirvāṇa* has been variously interpreted in existential, soteriological and philosophical terms.[11] *Nirvāṇa* is, of course, the solution and alternative to the problem of indefinite sāṁsāric existence: the end of suffering, of craving, the cessation of rebirth and hence the attainment of freedom.[12] But the question remains: is it a psychological (mystical) state of consciousness or a dimension of existence, some ultimate reality, or all of those? The question has especially preoccupied Western interpreters — who insist on making such distinctions between ultimate realities and states of consciousness;[13] Buddha himself refused to answer questions about *nirvāṇa* except negatively, recognizing that to engage with the question meant embracing the assumptions on which it was based. Rune E.A. Johansson (*The Psychology of Nirvana*, London 1969) has combed all the Pāli texts for all references to *nirvāṇa* — first the verbal terms, whereby *nirvāṇa* can be 'seen', 'known', 'entered', 'acquired', 'enjoyed' (pp.18f), then its cognates: peace, insight, calm, detachment, freedom from desire, the destruction of craving (p. 20). From this he concludes that *nirvāṇa* is at least a state of consciousness, one arrived at by purifying the mind (pp. 30f).

To this extent *nirvāṇa* is less the attainment of some special ability than freedom from false, everyday consciousness — hence

---

11.   Suzuki, *op. cit.*, I, p. 56.
12.   Cf. Johansson, Rune E. A., *The Psychology of Nirvana*, London, 1969, pp. 31, 32.
13.   Cf. Welbon, Guy Richard, *The Buddhist Nirvana and Its Western Interpreters*,University of Chicago Press, 1968.

the term, which means literally 'extinction'. Only a mind free from false consciousness is a mind which will not be reborn.

One question, however, will not therefore go away: can one, after entering *nirvāṇa*, remain in *saṁsāra*? As a state which marks the end of all discrimination, even that between *nirvāṇa* and *saṁsāra* must theoretically be dissolved. The Buddha himself spent the last 45 years of his life in *nirvāṇa*-in-*saṁsāra*, and hence anyone who — like a Zen monk — seeks to be a Buddha himself, to enter *nirvāṇa* as a state of Buddhahood, theoretically has such an option. For Zen, *nirvāṇa* is

> nothing else in its essence than Enlightenment . . . Enlightenment in Nirvana reached while yet in the flesh and no Nirvana is ever possible without obtaining Enlightenment.[14]

In which case one must ask: what characterizes such an enlightenned mind?

One of the most dominant metaphors for *nirvāṇa* is the experience of Space — as empty:

> an unlimited, disinterested and problem-free inner space . . . often described in terms of emptiness . . . especially the type of emptiness produced by means of meditation.[15]

To quote but one significant example, *The Lankavatara Sutra,* the basis for so much later *Mahāyāna* and especially Zen thinking, is explicit: "Nirvana", says the Buddha,

> is attained when the self-nature of all things is seen as non-entity . . ., when varieties of individual marks characterising all things are seen as non-entities . . ., when there is recognition of the non-existence of a being endowed with its

---

14. Suzuki, *op. cit.*, I, p. 63.

15. Johansson, *op. cit.*, p.110; Jahansson also quotes examples of *nirvāṇa* described as a level of consciousness "experienced as empty, impersonal, undifferentiated, peaceful" (*ibid.*, p. 56).

own specific attributes. . . .[16]

In other words, *nirvāṇa* — as a cognitive state, as a state of Enlightenment — is the realization of emptiness: *śūnyatā.*[17]

Śūnyatā

Śūnyatā is as central to Mahāyāna philosophy as the *bodhisattva* is to its ethics, though the distinction is false: a *bodhisattva* must have realized *śūnyatā* — it is the precondition of his equanimity and compassion. The centrality of the concept was developed in and by the Mādhyamika whose general ambition was to deconstruct all metaphysical assumptions about the possibility of objective knowledge, extending *anatta* from a subjective to an objective condition: the objective world is as insubstantial — as empty — as the self. What Nāgārjuna and the Mādhyamika attempted was to radically deny any ontological content to *dharmas,* practically establishing methods to cleanse the mind of its innate tendency towards reification. This it does by processes of radical deconstruction, for it soon became clear that consciousness is always consciousness *of* some thing: deconstruct the thing, and one can inhibit the filling of consciousness.

As such *śūnyatā* ends any distinction between subject and object: both are empty, united in emptiness. All subject-object dualism is transcended as one enters a state of consciousness able now to be enlightened: as Tao-hsin, the fourth patriarch of Zen, wrote in his description of the meditation on *śūnyatā*:

The mind in its absolute purity is the Void itself.[18]

Accused of nihilism by a superficial equation of emptiness with nothingness, the accusation had already been pre-empted by the

---

16. *Lankavatara Sutra, op. cit.,* pp. 108f.
17. Cf. Th. Stcherbatsky, *The Conception of Buddhist Nirvana,* New York, 1973 where he stresses the equation of *nirvāṇa* with *śūnyatā* as both involving the loss of personal self-consciousness.
18. Suzuki, *op. cit.,* III, p. 31.

Buddha in the *Lankavatara Sutra:* though the Mādhyamika rejected the atomistic pluralism of the Hīnayāna, they did not therefore deny that *dharmas* exist; they do but only connected as things, just as things are merely the sum of their *dharmas*. Both are empty; both are and are not. Everything, according to the Mādhyamika, is the sum of its parts; the parts exist only in conjunction as things: things and their parts therefore do exist but 'are' not anything beyond that. Though some later Mahāyāna schools did fall into the trap of reifying and hypostatizing *śūnyatā* into some existential, even cosmic, Void (demonstrating once again that it is always safer in Buddhism to use the adjectival form — *śūnya* — than the nominal—*śūnyatā*), it is not the case that in a state of Enlightenment, forms somehow disappear into the Void nor that the Void remains after the forms have disappeared: emptiness and form are co-extensive. The Middle-Way between annihilationism and eternalism, and between substantialism and nihilism is the cognitive tightrope which must be walked here: forms are empty, but emptiness is form, for emptiness itself exists only in and through phenomena, just as phenomena exist only 'emptily'.[19] To say that things have no 'self-existence' does not mean that they do not exist; to say that they exist does not mean that they are self-existent. As Tao-hsin wrote:

> Out of the midst of Emptiness there rise the six senses, and the six senses too are of Emptiness, while the six sense-objects are perceived as like a dream or a vision. It is like the eye perceiving its objects; they are not located in it. Like the mirror on which your features are reflected, they are perfectly perceived there in all clearness; the reflections are all there in the emptiness.[20]

Or as the Hua-Yen — the major philosophical influence on Zen — will have it:

---

19. Cleary, Thomas, *Entry Into the Inconceivable. An Introduction to Hua-Yen Buddhism*, University of Hawaii Press, 1982, p. 69 and cf. pp. 18f., 26, 27.

20. Suzuki, *op. cit.*, III, p. 32.

when a Bodhisattva observes form, he sees Voidness, and
when he observes Voidness, he sees the form.[21]

The apparent ambiguity is resolved when one realizes that *śūnyatā*
is, strictly speaking, a position and a process more than a truth, one
which must itself be constantly vacated, voided: emptiness too
must be emptied if it is not to become a new Absolute, or as the Hua
Yen *Heart Sutra* puts it:

> Therefore in the Emptiness there are no forms, no feelings,
> conceptions, impulses, or consciousness; no eye, ear, nose
> ... no ignorance and also no ending of ignorance; no old age
> and death ... no Truth of Suffering, no Truth of the Causes
> of Suffering, of the Cessation of Suffering, or of the Path.
> There is no wisdom, and there is no attainment whatsoever.[22]

Practically, one must learn to see all things as empty, but a
consciousness filled with Emptiness would still be a filled
consciousness; as Murti writes:

> The Madhyamika method is to deconceptualise the mind
> and to disburden it of all notions, empirical as well as
> apriori ... primarily a path of purification of the intellect.[23]

Nāgārjuna himself clearly realized already the danger of
hypostatizing *śūnyatā* and hence used only the adjective not the
noun and then always with the deictic 'this': "all this is empty," not
"All is Emptiness;" as Kalupahana writes in his introduction to
Nāgārjuna: "His conception of 'the empty' (sunya) is a particular."[24]
Once again it is crucial to understand Buddhism as a process, a
practice, one whereby every position is vacated as soon as it is
occupied — only thus can *śūnyatā* be a way-station to *nirvāna* in
which self-consciousness too is transcended.

---

21.   Chang, Garma C.C., *The Buddhist Teaching of Totality. The Philosophy of Hwa Yen Buddhism*, Penn State University Press, 1971, p. 211.

22.   *Ibid.*, p. 97f.

23.   Murti, *op. cit.*, p. 212.

24.   Kalupahana, *op. cit.* (1991), p. 86; cf. Streng, *op. cit.*, p. 150.

It is also thus that the performative paradigm again reasserts itself, for this emptying of phenomena of all substantialism means that what is left are acts, events, not objects. As Buddha already advised Bahiya Daruciriya in the *Bodhi-vagga* of the Udana:

> Train yourself in such a way that there is only seeing in what is seen, there is only hearing in what is heard, there is only sensing in what is sensed, there is only cognising in what is cognised.[25]

An enlightened mind — one which, in the midst of *samsāra*, has at least glimpsed *nirvāna* — is, then, empty in the sense that it ascribes no substance to either the things of which it is aware nor its own state of being aware. This, however, was for many potential — and especially Chinese and Japanese — Buddhists too abstract on the one hand and implicitly negative on the other. It does not have to be so: to see things as empty need only mean ceasing to see them *as* something, and beginning to see them simply 'as they are'. Though an empty mind may well be on the way to *nirvāna*, an empty mind which — like the Zen monk — remains in *samsāra* will continue to cognise things — 'as such'. Just as *nirvāna* is co-extensive with *śūnyatā*, so *śūnyatā* leads to *tathatā*: Suzuki writes:

> Emptiness does not mean a state of mere nothingness. It has a positive meaning, or rather a positive term designating the suchness of things (tathata). In a sense Tathata and Sunyata are interchangeable notions.[26]

Kalupahana therefore offers the following translation of the Buddha's advice quoted above as:

> Then, Bahuja, thus must you train yourself: In the seen there will be just the seen; in the heard, just the heard.[27]

---

25. Translated by Lily de Silva, "Sense Experience of the Liberated Being as reflected in early Buddhism", *Buddhist Philosophy and Culture*, Colombo, 1987, pp. 14ff.
26. Suzuki, *op. cit.*, III, p. 313.
27. Kalupahana, *op. cit.* (1991), p. 28.

In other words, things can be experienced without any conceptualization at all, and therefore 'just so'. Such is *tathatā*, the term preferred by Zen, for, as Suzuki writes:

> Emptiness is, however, a word greatly abused, suffering all kinds of maltreatment. Mahayana Buddhism has another term with an affirmative connotation. I mean "Suchness" or "Thusness" (tathata).[28]

Tathatā

Though *śūnyatā* is the more central term within the Mahāyāna as such, *tathatā* is the more Zen concept, cleansing emptiness of any remaining negative connotations, affirming things as they are, and the ability of the enlightened mind to see them simply 'just so'. An empty mind will no longer impose its own conceptual operations on its experiences but the Zen mind, for whom *nirvāṇa* does not mean obliteration (except of wrong-seeing) remains in *saṁsāra* and must therefore continue to receive sense-impressions. The question is therefore how one is to cognise them. 'Just as they are,' answers Zen.

One of the great distinctions of Zen is the affirmative attitude it adopts not just towards life as such but towards the uniqueness of every single moment, the particularity of every event, the singularity of every experience. It is these unique, particular, singular experiences which are to be cultivated: Hui-neng, the second founder of Zen, emphasized experience, meaning by it "an intuitive, direct, personal apprehension".[29]

Such an apprehension of 'thusness' is, nevertheless, a conundrum, for according to fundamental Buddhist theories of cognition, all experiences are almost instantaneously contaminated

---

28. Suzuki, *op. cit.*, III, p. 330: this itself firmly based on the *mahāprajñāpāramitā* equation: "By enlightenment (bodhi) is meant emptiness (sunyata), suchness (tathata)" (*ibid.*, p. 243).

29. Saunders, E. Dale, *Buddhism in Japan*, University of Pennsylvania Press, 1964, p. 212.

by conceptualization. How *can* any thing or event be known as such, 'an sich'? The answer is technical, involving a re-evaluation of 'apprehension' (*pratyakṣa*), the primary sense-contact, for as C.S. Vyas writes: "It is pratyaksa which is the dominant one in respect of efficacy to lead to the real."[30]

Classically, *pratyakṣa* is divided into *indriya* (sense perception), *manasa* (mental) and *yogī* (Yogic perception); it is Yogic *pratyakṣa* which is the supreme,[31] because, normally, perception is rapidly transformed into conceptualization. The classical sequence is that apprehension leads to sensation which leads to perception which leads to understanding, which leads to conceptualisation.[32] But the very fact that this is a sequence (albeit very rapid) leaves the door open for some fleeting moment before this series of transformations occurs. In such a moment, *pratyakṣa* would confirm that external objects exist and can be contacted while at the same time telling one nothing about them except that they are thus: *tathatā*.

Such a re-evaluation of *pratyakṣa* did occur historically. The early Vaibhāsikas had already claimed the possibility, through a moment of immediate apprehension, of apprehending a 'Ding-an-sich' in all and only its 'here-and-now-ness'.[33] The Sautrāntikas then insisted, however, that all sense-data are only of the image or appearance of a physical object, essentially always already therefore a mental event which only resembles a physical object which as such is therefore only hypothetical.[34] But, following a lead given by Vasubandhu, Diññāga then reached a further stage where *pratyakṣa* could be redefined as "that cognition which is free from conceptual construction" — inexpressible but for all that true[35] — and Dharmakīrti returned to *indriya-pratyakṣa* as a stage of pure

30. Vyas, C.S., *Buddhist Theory of Perception*, Navrang, New Delhi, 1991, p. vi.
31. *Ibid.*, p. 9.
32. *Ibid.*, p. 10.
33. *Ibid*, p. 24.
34. *Ibid.*, p. 28f.
35. *Ibid.*, pp. 35, 39 and 47.

perception antecedent to imagination or conceptualization; Vyas summarizes:

> Perception is thus related to a certain unique-particular which is devoid of all the qualifications — spatial, temporal and conceptual which the intellect foists on it after it has been apprehended by the sense. It is ineffable because the moment our understanding begins to encompass it within the categories and tries to give it a definite name, it vanishes, momentary and extreme particular that it is.[36]

In other words, the whole problem of perception (do we/can we know a thing, or only ever its image, representation, appearance?) is resolved by denying the basic distinction between thing (in itself, as such, *an sich*) and its presentation: a thing is a compound of dharmas, and its apprehension in a particular and instant form is the only way it exists: "perception grasps the unique particular, a point-instant".[37]

Such is the key to those otherwise baffling Zen experiences of grasping things in their here-and-now-ness. The aim of the basic Zen practice of zazen and then of all everyday activity is simply to ensure that there are no ideas in consciousness, only direct realizations.

Such moments of insight in which things are apprehended by an empty, enlightened consciousness 'just as they are' are satori's — themselves as instant and as momentary as the object cognised in its thusness.

Satori

Historically, it was the Hua-Yen doctrine of mutal interdependence and simultaneous interpenetration which provided the immediate philosophical basis for Zen practice: as Odin writes:

---

36.   Vyas, C.S., *Buddhist Theory of Perception*, Navrang, p. 93f.
37.   *Ibid.*, p. 81f.

The Hua-yen theory of the unhindered interpenetration of past-present-future into a single thought-instant ... must be comprehended in its proper soteriological context wherein it functions as an *upaya* or expedient means for achieving sudden enlightenment.[38]

One can reverse the equation: emphasis on the sudden, instantaneous and immediate nature of satori requires that any experience contain implicitly all experiences, and that any experience can be of thusness.

'Sudden' has to be understood as . . . related . . . to a philosophy of the immediate, the instantaneous. . . . Things are perceived 'all at once', intuitively, unconditionally, in a revolutionary manner.[39]

This 'sudden' school of enlightenment is not unique to Zen, nor was it shared by all Zen sects: it is common to all those Chinese and Japanese sects which argue that in place of the formula 'I can become a Buddha' one should recognize that 'I am already a Buddha'.[40] The most common formula is to argue that a sudden moment of enlightenment — a satori — is the necessary prelude to the more gradual, subsequent cultivation of *prajñā*: insight must precede wisdom.

It is important to stress the momentary nature of a satori:

Satori comes upon one abruptly and is a momentary experience. In fact, if it is not abrupt and momentary, it is not satori.[41]

---

38. Odin, Steve, *Process Metaphysics and Hua-Yen Buddhism,* State University of New York Press, Albany, 1982, p. 53.

39. *Sudden and Gradual. Approaches to Enlightenment in Chinese Thought,* ed. by Gregory, Peter N., University of Hawaii Press, Honolulu, 1987, p. 15.

40. Sung Bae Park, *op. cit.,* pp. 4, 19ff.

41. Suzuki, *op. cit.,* I, p. 36.

Satori is always sudden, immediate and sometimes defined (since the thirteenth century) as a "bursting out of the mental flower".[42]

We are back to Zeami: "hana. . . ."

Summarizing: if the equations above are accepted (*nirvāna*, as a state of emptied consciousness which, in its total unself-consciousness, apprehends things simply 'as such' in moments of satori . . .) then the question which must — and now can — be asked is whether performance in general and Noh specifically can provide the means for such realizations? Zeami seems to have believed so: he referred to them as 'hana' moments.

Hana

There need be no dispute with Sieffert that 'Hana' was probably in origin an experience which Zeami knew as a performer and company leader and later sought to theorize as a professional. Zeami was simultaneously an actor, playwright and producer and as such his descriptions of Hana combine acting theory, composition theory, directing theory (or, in his tradition, teaching) and in addition, since he was preoccupied as few other performance theorists with audience response, spectator theory too.

The term appears in his earliest writings — the *Fushikaden* or *Kadensho* ("Teachings of Style and the Flower", written in 1402, when he was forty); here already Hana is established as the key factor and supreme objective of performance:

The Flower represents the principle that lies at the deepest recesses of our art. To know the meaning of the Flower is the most important element in understanding the *no,* and its greatest secret.[43]

At this stage, the term appears to describe a special quality of

---

42. Dutt, Sukumar, *Buddhism in East Asia*, New Delhi, 1966, p. 179.
43. *On The Art of the No Drama, The Major Treatises of Zeami*, tr. and ed. by J. Thomas Rimer and Yamazaki Masakazu, Princeton University Press, 1984, p. 29.

performing, a quality beyond (or before) technique, what for want of a better term we might call 'presence' or 'grace'.[44] It is a quality, Zeami notes, which characterizes very young performers — a spontaneous, temporary 'blossoming', the problem (their problem) being that such naive grace is 'only a temporary bloom':[45] the actor will grow, his voice will break, his body will change, he will become awkward: "he loses his first Flower".[46]

The actor falters, but he has twenty years training ahead of him to learn how to get the Flower back — but now on the foundation of technique: the 'true Flower' will return — if at all — at the age of thirty-four or thirty-five. Just as 'sudden' satori must be followed by gradual, concentrated, arduous practice, so too the true flower; otherwise the actor will simply decline, imitate himself, any success he enjoys being accidental: the term is critical and leads into the heart of Zeami's professional ambition which was no less than to learn and be able to teach the conditions by which the creation of 'Flowers' could become reliable, dependable:

> The real hana is the hana of the mind, and its blossoming and its fading depend upon the mind.[47]

What we have here are the writings of a theatre perfessional who has himself produced, known, seen and experienced those moments in performance when an actor goes beyond mere technical perfection and achieves a sudden moment of communion with an audience. It is a moment and a quality known to theatre professionals the world over: Peter Brook writes about Paul Scofield:

> It was as though the act of speaking a word sent through him vibrations that echoed back meanings far more complex than his rational thinking could find: he would pronounce

---

44. Cf. Friedrich Schiller's essay on grace: *Über Anmut and Würde* (1793) where he writes about the necessary loss of naïve grace and its re-achievement on a higher level. . . .

45. Rimer/ Masakazu, *op. cit.*, p. 5.

46. Eadem.

47. Seami, *Kadensho,* Tokyo, 1968, p. 52.

a world like 'night' and then he would be compelled to
pause: listening with all his being into amazing impulses
stirring in some mysterious inner chamber, he would
experience the wonder of discovery at the moment when it
happened. Those breaks, those sallies in depth, give his
acting its absolutely personal structure of rhythms, its own
distinctive meanings: to rehearse a part, he let his whole
nature — a milliard of supersensitive scanners — pass to
and fro across the words. In performance the same process
makes everything that he has apparently fixed come back
again each night the same and absolutely different.[48]

Or Stanislavski:

Actors achieve the pinnacle of their art when they have
that quality of the unexpected which startles, overwhelms,
stuns me. Something that lifts the spectator off the ground,
sets him in a land where he has never walked, but which he
recognises easily through a sense of foreboding or conjecture.
He does, however, see this unexpected thing face to face,
and for the first time. It shakes, enthrals, and engulfs
him.[49]

Other Western theatre professionals have had recourse to language
even closer to Zen — Toller, for example, writing of the 'timeless
moments' in which we hear the "Silence of the Universe", or
Cocteau:

The poet must bring objects and feelings from behind their
veils and their mists; he must show them suddenly, so
nakedly and so swiftly that it hurts man to recognise them
. . . this peculiar range of sensiblity can be expressed by
dramatic poetry at its moments of greatest intensity;

---

48.   *Actors on Acting*, ed. by Cole, T., and Chinoy, H.K., New York, 1949,
      p. 424.

49.   Stanislavski, K., *Building a Character*, Methuen, London, 1979, p.
      298.

Maeterlinck:

> I had gone there [to the theatre] hoping that the beauty, the grandeur, and the earnestness of my humble day-to-day existence would, for one instant, be revealed to me;

or Yeats, writing about the theatre as the home of "moments of intense life".[50]

To Zeami these moments represented the essence of the craft, and he spent the rest of his life trying to find out — and to teach others — how to achieve them — not by mere 'tricks of the trade' which is "like looking for fish in the trees"[51] but by carefully identifying and analyzing their preconditions.

Zeamils early descriptions of Hana as the actor's only authentic professional goal and its initial designation as a form of 'presence', 'aura', or 'intensity' then received more precise orientation when Zeami describes it not from the perspective of the performer alone but from that of the spectator too. For hana is not only something which an actor achieves at the height of his craft; it also describes the audience's peak experience: it is these moments which make performances both unique and valuable, namely the experience of "a level of skill which will simply make the audience gasp, without reflection, in surprise and pleasure".[52] This appeared in the *Kakyo* ("Mirror of the Flower") written in 1424 where Zeami has very precise instructions to his performers how to achieve this by 'reading' the audience — gathering their energies, "collecting the audience's eyes", using the "objective eye":

> an actor must look at himself using his internalized outer image, come to share the same view as the audience.[53]

This ability of the actor to lose all narcissistic self-absorption and

---

50. Cf. *Playwrights on Playwriting*, ed. by Cole, T., New York, pp. 30, 37, 218, 241, 259.

51. Rimer/Masakazu, *op. cit.*, p. 68.

52. *Ibid.*, pp. 90f.

53. *Ibid.*, p. 81.

be 'objective' towards his own 'self' is, of course, already based on Buddhist psychology — and it applies to the spectator too, for Zeami is reassuring: concentration of the audience's perceptions by the actor is facilitated by the fact that the spectator is also losing 'self-awareness' and concentrating on the performer.[54]

"Flowers" then bloom when actors and spectators are simultaneously transcending self-consciousness and concentrating on something being created between them: they bloom, we might say, in liminal spaces. . . .

Timing is of crucial significance here[55] as is the performer's sensitivity towards the unique conditions of each particular performance, for Zeami was acutely aware how each and every performance is unique: the class of spectators, the size of the audience, the site of the theatre, the time of day, year, the mood: all this is variable, singular.[56] This, far from daunting him, confirmed his basic theory: the flower is always unique and particular, always different:

> When speaking of flowers, in all their myriad varieties, it can be said that they will bloom at their appointed time during the four seasons; and because they always seem fresh and novel when they bloom at that appointed season, they are highly appreciated. In performing *sarugaku*[57] as well, when this art appears novel to the spectators, they will be moved to find it attractive. Flower, charm, and novelty: all three of these partake of the same essence. There is no flower that remains and whose petals do not scatter. And just because the petals scatter, then when the flower blooms again, it will seem fresh and novel.[58]

Flowers — hana moments — then do not last, cannot last the whole

54.   Rimer/Masakazu, *op. cit.*, p. 102.
55.   *Ibid.*, pp. 18, 82.
56.   *Ibid.*, p. 157.
57.   The original term for Noh.
58.   *Ibid.*, p. 52.

performance: the flower is an 'instant', a 'moment' but it is for this that the play was written, the actor has trained and the whole audience waits in anticipation. It arises suddenly: the term 'hana' needs complementing by the term 'mezurashiki' meaning 'rare' or 'fresh' or 'novel'[59] — the same quality as a satori. The analogy is not far-fetched: reading through Zeami's treatises, one finds an increasing use of Zen terminology to describe these flower moments: in the *Kadensho* (or *Fushikaden*) of 1402, we find him writing that "Hana is in the mind, technique is the seed", this in turn being a paraphrase of a Chinese Buddhist poem:

> If you understand the mind of a flower, you will understand Bodhi, Supreme enlightenment.

By the *Yugaka shudo fuken* ("Disciplines for the Joy of Art") written in 1424, he is discoursing on Form and Emptiness.[60]

By the time he came to write the *Kyui Shidai*, in which he set out the nine 'rungs' of Noh perfection, his recourse to Zen terms and to koan-like Zen descriptions had become compulsive: the top three rungs of Noh are described as:

> Stage 7: "In a silver bowl, snow is heaped" (or "The whiteness and purity of snow lying in a silver garden");

> Stage 8: "The snow covers one hundred hills, how is it that only one peak is not white?" (or "among snow-covered mountains one peak has ceased to be white" about which Zeami comments: "A man of old once said, 'Mount Fuji is so high that the snow never melts.' A Chinese disagreed, saying, 'Mount Fuji is so deep. . .'. What is extremely deep is high");

> And, finally, Stage 9, the supreme stage of Noh perfection: "At Shiragi at midnight the sun shines bright" (or "the light of the sun at midnight" about which Zeami comments: "The

---

59. Rimer/Masakazu, *op. cit.*, pp. 7, 53.

60. *Kadensho, op. cit.*, p. 52; Rimer/Masakazu, *op. cit.*, pp. 115f.

miraculous transcends the power of speech and is where
the workings of the mind are defeated.").[61]

These three stages are all obviously Zen in inspiration; both the top
two reveal clearly that the supreme Noh is that which transcends
dualism and even cognition as such, for Zeami describes such
experiences as

> one of pure Feeling that transcends Cognition; there is no
> occasion for reflection, no time for a spectator to realize how
> well the performance is contrived;

> when true feeling is involved, there is no room in the
> concept for reflection as a function of the mind; it is an
> intensity of pure feeling that goes beyond the working of
> the mind.[62]

Transcendence of the 'self', communion in liminal space,
particularity/singularity, temporality: these are all performance
techniques which any professional needs to study and learn; they
are all analogous to Zen satori in their suddenness, their
momentariness, their uniqueness and unexpectedness and, not
least, in the way they somehow drop the spectator like the meditator
into an 'empty space'. Zeami himself has described moments when
an actor appears to be 'doing nothing'; it is, he writes, "the actor's
greatest, most secret skill".[63]

As we shall see later in an analysis of Noh music and dance, one
of the great secrets of Noh is to stretch the interval between two
physical actions or between a sound and an action so far as to create
a moment of total, silent stillness: these are supreme 'flowers' and
Zeami gives at times very detailed technical instructions how to
achieve them.[64] These 'empty spaces' between movements, or
between sound and movement, fascinated him as they would

---

61.   cf. *Sources of Japanese Tradition, op. cit.*, p. 116.
62.   Rimer/Masakazu, *op. cit.*, p. 91.
63.   *Ibid.*, p. 97.
64.   E.g. *ibid.*, p. 76.

anyone interested and versed in Zen notions, for they are analogous to moments of deep Zen meditational concentration: Zeami writes:

> to speak of an actor 'doing nothing' actually signifies that interval which exists between two physical actions. When one examines why this interval 'when nothing happens' may seem so fascinating, it is surely because of the fact that, at the bottom, the artist never relaxes his inner tension. At the moment when the dance has stopped, or the chant has ceased, or indeed at any of those intervals that can occur during the performance of a role, or, indeed, during any pause or interval, the actor must never abandon his concentration but must keep his consciousness of that inner tension. It is this sense of inner concentration that manifests itself to the audience.[65]

These 'moments when the flower blooms' are, then, planned by the writer, seeded in the text,[66] worked on by the actor as he learns the secrets of his craft and sought by the spectator: they last for a brief moment, possibly one of total concentrated stillness, but they are, for all that, what performance is all about — the ultimate goal of every performer and the peak experience for every spectator. As essentially momentary instants, as unexpected and therefore novel, fresh, unique, as dislocations of perception, beyond cognition, they invite description largely by allusion and metaphor. It is evident from Zeami's writings that these allusions and metaphors became increasingly drawn from Zen and if his choice of successor is anything to go by (and Zeami himself already established the system whereby transmission of the secrets should be only ever from one to one), he became more and more committed to Zen, for when his last son, Motomasa, died in 1431, he nominated not the new Shogun's favourite actor — Onami — to be his successor but his son-in-law Zenchiku. Zenchiku had studied Zen with Priest Ikkyu,

---

65. Rimer/Masakazu, *op. cit.*, p. 97.
66. Though 'hana' is primarily a theory of performance, Zeami realized that writers must already seed such moments in their scripts: cf. *ibid.*, p. 158f.

and his major work, *Rikurin Ichiro* ("Six Circles, one Dewdrop") is philosophical Buddhism of the most abstruse kind.[67] Zenchiku's theories are not readily appreciable by anyone without a background in Hua-Yen paradigms and a specific understanding of the *tathatā-śūnyatā-nirvāṇa* complex. In his special study of Zenchiku, Thornhill notes how in general at this time

> artistic discipline became a vehicle for spiritual growth, and so the mastery of one's art was implicitly equated with the attainment of religious salvation or transcendental wisdom.[68]

And if it is true that performing artists were moving ever closer towards Zen, it is also true that Zen monks were themselves finding art: Dogen himself compared the 'thusness' of blossoms blooming to Buddha's raising the *udumbara* flower in his sermon, and went on to call them "flowers of emptiness:"

> they are beyond birth and death, beyond past, present, and future. . . . *Nirvāṇa* and birth-and-death are none other than the flowers of emptiness.[69]

An explanation for this growing convergence of Noh and Zen is actually not hard to find: the relationship between the two need not be based only on textual analysis and speculative theory; it can be pursued historically. Zeami's career and the origins of Noh coincided with the Muromachi, the age of Zen during which it became the most Japanese form of Buddhism and, beyond that, the basis of Japanese aesthetics as such.

---

67.   Cf. Thornhill III, Arthur H., *Six Circles, One Dewdrop. The Religio-Aesthetic World of Komparu Zenchiku,* Princeton University Press, 1993.

68.   *Ibid.*, p. 6.

69.   Kim Hee-Jin, *Dogen Kigen Mystical Realist,* University of Arizona Press, Tucson, 1987, p. 192f.

Japanese Buddhism

THE CHINESE BACKGROUND

Japan took Zen from China and, already in China, Ch'an Buddhism represented a radical move against the tendency of any religion to become fixated in dogma, text and ritual. 'Ch'an' is the Chinese phonetic form of the Sanskrit *dhyāna*, meaning meditation and, from the sixth century onwards, what Ch'an promoted was a return to the direct and personal experience of Buddhist truth derivable only through and from meditation. This claim to represent some 'pure', original Buddhism must, however, be tempered by the observation that Ch'an — like every other form of Buddhism — is as much a cultural phenomenon as anything else. Ostensibly a reaction against what it saw as the contamination of Buddhism by indigenous assimilation, Ch'an's own emphasis on the practice of meditation was itself due as much to osmosis with pre-existent Taoist practices as any fundamentalist ambition.[70]

Infiltrating along the Silk Route since the first century BC, Buddhism at first represented for the Chinese just another form of supernatural magic, and adopted at first the policy of competing with indigenous belief systems in these terms.[71] This willingness of the Buddhist missionaries to affect compromises with local belief systems — what is called its Philosophy of Assimilation — may seem, on the surface, to be merely a political strategy. It is clear from the historical evidence that Buddhism first sought conversion through the ruling classes and hence accommodation with Taoism and Confucianism — to the extent that both Confucius and Lao-tzu came to be seen either as manifestation of Buddha or themselves the original of the reincarnated Śākyamuni.[72] As Buddhism

---

70.   Ch'en, *op. cit.* (1964), p. 49.

71.   Cf. Zürcher, E., *The Buddhist Conquest of China*, Leiden (E.J. Brill), 1972, pp. 33, 52.

72.   Matsunaga, Alicia, *The Buddhist Philosophy of Assimilation*, Tokyo, 1969, pp. 99-101; Zürcher, *op. cit.*, pp. 290f; Ch'en, *op. cit.* (1964), p. 50.

infiltrated China, it found that the Chinese already had a sophisticated ethical code (derived from Confucianism) and an equally spohisticated mysticism (drived from Taoism), including advanced practices of breathing and meditation, and that it could and needed to use them for its own proselytizing purposes. But this tactic has — as we have already seen in the previous chapter — philosophical and doctrinal as much as strategic sanction: a *bodhisattva* does not so much postpone enlightenment for the sake of others; he cannot enter *nirvāṇa* until everyone does so. He must therefore set about converting everyone — to do which he adopts the concept of *upāya* or means. But it must be admitted that the general political, strategic and philosophical policy of translating Buddhism into terms which the Chinese could understand resulted as much in the grafting of Chinese indigenous religious and philosophical concepts onto Buddhism as *vice versa*. There is no doubt that language played an important part in this: Chinese often does not distinguish nouns from verbs: things can be seen as events, objects as processes, a factor which this present study finds especially significant, of course. The necessary adoption of Taoist terminology to translate Buddhist concepts into Chinese led to many and profound changes in original meanings.[73]

This 'Sinicization of Buddhism' is a point made forcefully by K.S. Ch'en[74] and in it he includes Ch'an itself.[75] The same point is made by the foremost interpreter of Zen to the West — Daisetz Suzuki, who even provides the detail: Ch'an and Zen are 'Chinese' in their affirmative attitude towards the world, one which conceives of Buddha himself as a latent power present in everything. This

---

73. Cf. Ch'en, *op. cit.* (1964), p. 50; Matsunaga, *op. cit.*, p. Zürcher, *op. cit.*, p. 73.

74. Including the conversion of Avalokiteśvara into the female Kuan-yin, the transformation of Maitreya into the laughing Buddha, accommodation with Confucian notions of family ethics as opposed to traditional Buddhist emphasis on personal salvation; the submission of the *saṁgha* to political and secular authority; the economic power of Buddhism in China. . . .

75. Kenneth K.S. Ch'en, *The Chinese Transformation of Buddhism*, Princeton, 1973, p. 4.

'affirmative Buddhism' is indeed what distinguishes all four of the specifically Chinese forms of Buddhism: Pure Land, Tien Tai, Hua-yen and Ch'an. For Pure Land transformed the empty *nirvāṇa* into a beautiful paradise, one which with its immaculately beautiful inhabitants can only be visualized, creating a sort of 'theatre in the mind'. Tien-tai, based on veneration of the *Lotus Sutra* and its doctrine of the accessibility of salvation to all, preached both the notion that Śākyamuni is but the earthly manifestation (*nirmāṇakāya*) of the eternal Buddha (*dharmakāya*) and drew up a sophisticated classification of the *sūtra*s into a heirarchy of *upāya*,[76] the whole encapsulated in its theory that "in every particle of dust, in every moment of thought, the whole universe is contained".[77] An even more positive re-affirmation of the phenomenal as the necessary complement of the noumenal is found in Hua-yen, philosophically the most influential for Ch'an with its stress on sudden awakening — a theory derived in turn from the principle that every single 'thought-instant' contains infinity, every *dharma* all *dharmas*.[78] Hua-yen dialectics stress the notion that, though substantially empty, concrete reality has a positive value, as necessary for emptiness as *vice versa*.[79] As Steve Odin writes about Hua-Yen:

In its Madhyamika context then, emptiness designates the ontological vacuity and unsubstantiality of dharmas,

A negative position which Hua-Yen then transformed into a positive statement through its theory that the interdependent and interpenetrative character of events "emphasizes the ontological fullness and cosmic togetherness of dharmas as opposed to their utter vacuity";[80]

---

76. Ch'en, *op. cit.* (1964), pp. 305-10.

77. Ch'en, *op. cit.*, p. 310.

78. Odin, *op. cit.*, p. xix.

79. *Mahayana Buddhist Meditation, op. cit.*, p. 168f; Prebish, *op. cit.*, p. 206.

80. Odin, *op. cit.*, p. 20.

> Hua-yen has come to bestow an absolute value not only on
> the concrete world in its totality, but on each individual
> which participates in this whole.... What can be despicable
> if everything is the body of the Buddha?[81]

This is not the place to enter into detail about Chinese Buddhism,
except as the necessary background to Japanese Zen: Chinese
Buddhism never fully recovered from regular persecution since the
fifth century and later under the T'ang. Though not extirpated, the
attacks of both Confucians and Taoists relegated Buddhism to the
status of a tolerated and influential religion, one which doubtless
provided Taoism with considerable philosophical sophistication
·but which never escaped the charge of being somethow anti-
Chinese.[82]

It is, therefore, not surprising to find that Buddhism in China,
though it was transformed into a religion and a philosophy with a
much more positive attitude towards the concrete world and a
marked aestheticization, had little effect on its theatre compared to
Confucianism. The Buddhists did expolit the popularity of the
theatre for their own purposes — as an *upāya*: as Ch'en writes:

> During such festival days, when throngs of spectators
> gathered at the monastery grounds, there would often be
> dramatic performances by the monks to entertain the
> people. The themes of such performances were undoubtedly
> based on episodes in the Buddhist scriptures, especially
> those connected with the life of the Buddha during his
> previous rebirths or during his last rebirth just prior to
> attainment of nirvana. There were very likely also puppet
> shows just for pure entertainment. Then there were those
> performances of magic feats by Buddhist monks who were
> proficient in such arts. Buddhist philosophy considers all
> the dharmas as illusory and devoid of reality. The world is

---

81.   Odin, *op. cit.*, p.175.
82.   Ch'en, *op. cit.* (1964), p. 204; Zürcher, *op. cit.* p. 255; Ch'en, *op. cit.*,
      (1973), p. 4.

maya, an illusion. From such a philosophy, the idea of illusion was popularized, and this fostered and abetted the development of the magic art. . . . In this connection one recalls the words ascribed to the Buddha in the *Divyavadana*, 'A magical feat quickly wins over the minds of worldlings'.[83]

More detailed research still needs to be undertaken but it would appear for now that Buddhism did little for Chinese theatre beyond supplying a number of plots (notably from *The Journey to the West* and the story of Mu-lien) and a number of topoi, such as the world-weary government bureaucrat, tired of court intrigue, who takes up the idyllic life of a recluse.[84] This, though Buddhist, is, however, more often and just as much Taoist, while the Buddhist injunction against indulgence in music and drama, though re-inforced in the T'ang[85] was relatively insignificant compared to the much more frequent and severe Confucian attacks on the theatre. As Dolby has shown, it was Confucianism much more than Buddhism which provided both the ideological structure of Chinese drama on the one hand and its profound fears on the other.[86]

SHINTO

Chinese Ch'an became Japanese Zen from the sixth century on — after Japan had already imported mainstream Mahāyāna Buddhism from China, partly via Korea. But whereas in China, Buddhism had to compete with Confucianism and Taoism, in Japan the only pre-existing religious system which it found was the relatively unphilosophical Shinto.

Shinto is — and remains — the native religion of Japan: it received its name only in the eighth century — to distinguish it from imported Buddhism but it has "no founder, no sacred scriptures, no

83. Ch'en, *op. cit.* (1973), p. 272; cf. Victor H. Mair, *T'ang Transformation Texts*, Harvard U. P., 1989.

84. Cf Ch'en, *op. cit.*, (1973), pp. 179ff; Zürcher, *op. cit.*, p. 74.

85. Cf. Ch'en, *op. cit.*, (1973), p. 103.

86. Cf. Dolby, William, *A History of Chinese Drama*, London, 1976.

established dogma, no authentic interpreters".[87] Less a theology than a practice, Shinto rites are essentially pragmatic, utilitarian, a dealing in good luck.[88] Shinto festivals are opportunities to lodge requests or give thanks for protection and good fortune — for oneself, one's family, one's land. Originally, a "form of animism and clan-worship of a type common to other primitive agrarian communities. Things were believed to have souls or spirits, called kami."[89] Kami are "natural energies, animated matter and ubiquitous, invisible agents influencing man's behaviour and destiny".[90] Some are deities, others are human beings — national heroes or other ancestors; some are birds, animals, trees, plants, rocks, seas, mountains, wind, thunder; also occupations and skill: anything with power. They are virtually innumerable: 2,500 shrines are officially venerated but there are 80,000 altogether in Japan and perhaps a further 10,000 locations, for most kami are localized and operate only within their area of influence.

Priests, priestesses and Shamans were early on attached to such shrines where they functioned as mediators, though their basic role was and is to serve as caretakers and administrators, for Shinto practices do not really require any intermediary.[91] For a fee a priest will perform certain special rites[92] including on occasion ceremonial dances, performed by 'miko' — usually the daughters of priests.[93] These dances are called 'kagura' and have been held to be the predecessor and even the origin of Noh. As such there need be no dispute: Zeami himself authorized such an argument of origin, referring to the famous 'tub-dance' of Uzume to lure the sun-goddess Amaterasu from the cave where she had hidden.[94] Zeami

---

87.   Spae, J.J., *Shinto Man,* Tokyo, 1972, p. 17.

88.   Ono, S., *Shinto.The Kami Way,*Tokyo, 1962, p. 84.

89.   Spae, *op. cit.,* p. 20.

90.   *Ibid.,* p. 41.

91.   Ono, *op. cit,* p. 62.

92.   *Ibid.,* p. 62.

93.   *Ibid.,* p. 43.

94.   *Kadensho, op. cit.,* p. 54.

was clearly proud to ascribe his own profession to a divine ancestor (although his argument is based on a very fanciful etymology of the word 'Sarugaku' which means 'monkey-dance' and not, as he would have it, 'god-dance': Japanese scholars do not hesitate to designate this as a forgery designed to give a vulgar-art form legitimacy).[95] The dispute — as usual — is about putative origins and — more significantly — the unquestioned assumption that origin dictates ongoing function: the 'fallacy of emergence'. Those who promote the Shinto-origin case themselves delve even further back, arguing that kagura were originally Shamanistic dances of divine possession, and supporting that claim by reference to certain Noh plays, such as *Maki-Ginu* in which a priestess is possessed by the god Otonashi no Tenjin and dances the kagura.

Now there are records of a Shamaness-ruler (Pimiko) in the third century AD, and some 'Kaniwa' (clay figurines found in burial mounds) are held to represent Shamans and dancers.[96] But it takes an exegetical legerdemain to describe Uzume's dance as a "vivid shamanistic performance"[97] and, in any case: "all performing artists in Japan claim descent from the heavenly dancer Uzume".[98] Much the same caveat applies to the other 'evidence': the tree which figures on the rear wall of every Noh stage (and which is held by the Shamanists to be the 'lightning rod' for the descent of the spirit) represents the Yoro pine in the Kasuga shrine in Nara in front of

---

95. Peter Arnott among others has argued that this original kagura could be the origin of the characteristic stomping of Noh dance which is performed on a stage under which tubs are still strategically placed (*op. cit.*, p. 63f.) though O'Neill has shown that Noh owed its 'rock beat' to a much later dance form called Kusemai, popularized by prostitutes (O'Neill, P.G., *Early No Drama*, Westport, Conn, 1958).

96. Yoshinobu Inoura, *A History of Japnaese Theater*, Japan Cultural Society, 1971, Vol. 1, p. 3f.

97. Kirby, E.T., *Ur-Drama*, N.Y.U. Press, 1975, p. 77. Amaterasu was coaxed out of the cave in which she had hidden not by Shamanic magic but by the simpler psychology of curiosity: the gods had laughed at Uzume's dance, especially when she performed the original strip-tease exposing her genitals. . . .

98. Kirby, *op. cit.*, p. 77.

which Kagura is still danced annually; Uzume's branch is, however, a Sasaki or Camellia Japonica, not a pine, and one cannot simply graft branches onto alien trucks so casually. Tub-dances and trees do not exhaust the argument of Shinto and Shamanistic origin: Kirby proposed this as the explanation for the typical plot-sequence of Noh, drawing analogies betwen the *waki / shite* relationship and that between medium and exorcist in a Shamanistic rite — an argument supported by Honda Yasuji and most forcefully by Carmen Blacker.[99] In itself, this is no more objectionable than any other structural parallelism; the trick as always is the casual conversion of structural parallels into an evolutionary argument whereby the one 'directly derives from', 'can be traced to', or is the 'origin of' the other.[100] The whole Shinto-and-Shamanism argument is based on such a scissors-and-paste methodology, a confusion of origin with function, and a dogmatic theory of the 'universal' origin of all drama in Shamanism.[101] One might just as well argue that

---

99.   Cf. Hoff, R., and Flindt, W., "The Life Structure of Noh", *Concerned Theatre Japan*, Vol. II, nos 3 and 4, p. 256; Blacker, Carmen, *The Catalpa Bow, A Study of Shamanistic Practices in Japan*, London, 1975; cf. Ruch B., in Hall, J.W. and Takeshi, T., *Japan in the Muromachi Age*, University of California Press 1977. Blacker cites 16 plays as exemplifications of her thesis that Noh plays are disguised Shamanic rites in which the Shaman exorcises a ghost, but when one reexamines them one finds that in *Akogi*, the priest only comforts but does not exorcise the tormented ghost; in *Funabashi*, the two shite relate how they have already been redeemed — and not by the waki; in *Genji Kuyo*, the priest re-interprets the story in Buddhist terms rather than exorcising the ghost; there is no redemption through the waki in *Higaki* or in *Hotoke-No-Hara* where the shite is already redeemed — she is a nun; *Izutsu* has no redemption through the waki; in *Ebira*, the Part 2 shite relates the torments to which he remains subject, as in *Uto, Tsunemasa* and *Tomonaga;* in *Eguchi*, the shite is already converted to Buddhism; Yorimasa and Yashima are not redeemed, and only in *Yugao* does the shite thank the waki for his prayers; in *Tomoe*, he asks for prayers but is not exorcised.

100. Cf. Kirby, *op. cit.*, p. 79: Blacker, *op. cit.*, p. 31 *et al.*

101. The general theory is that the Shamans were driven underground or into the theatre (Kirby, *op. cit.*, p. 87; Blacker, *op. cit.*, p. 140; Ruch, *op. cit.*, p. 304).

Japanese Buddhism as a whole is 'Shamanistic', since, when first imported, it attempted to establish itself as another — and more powerful — form of exorcistic magic.[102] This invasion, in fact, provoked opposition from Shinto which in the process responded by freeing itself from any Shamanistic origins it may have had, as did Buddhism too.[103] The most interesting Noh play in this connection is perhaps *Aoi No Ue* — a play always quoted by the Shamanists and which does indeed show a Shaman being summoned to cure a sick woman: she conjures up the spirit, but she cannot exorcise it; for that a Buddhist hermit is needed and he not only succeeds, he converts the spirit to Buddhahood:

> When she heard the sound of the Scripture
> The demon's raging heart was stilled;
> Shapes of Pity and Sufferance
> The Bodhisats descend.
> Her soul casts off its bonds,
> She walks in Buddha's Way.[104]

One cannot find a clearer statement of the attitude of Noh towards Shamanism — a negative attitude in which Shamans are exposed, not confirmed and in which, under Buddhist influence, spirit-possession is redefined as enslavement to passion or attachment to the sensual world.[105]

As for the ongoing relationship of Shinto to Buddhism, that problem was resolved by making the kami *bodhisattvas* — the so-

---

102. Dutt, *op. cit.*, p. 160; Kidder, J. Edward, *Early Buddhist Japan*, London, 1972, p. 18; Saunders, *op. cit.*, p. 101; Matsunaga, *op. cit.*, pp. 168ff; Matsunaga, Daigan and Alicia, *Foundations of Japanese Buddhism*, Los Angeles and Tokyo, 1974-76, Vol. 1, pp. 10f., 17 and Vol. 2, p. 1; Hoover, *op. cit.*, p. 34.

103. The Taiho code of 701 and the Yoro of 718 banned divination and exorcism.

104. Waley, Arthur, *The No Plays of Japan*, New York, 1957, p. 189.

105. Cf *Yo-kihi* where possession is defined as attachment to the sensual world. *Kanawa* does dramatize Shamanism but again the play itself offers a Buddhist message; in *Dojoji*, the snake-witch is herself exorcised by a Buddhist priest.

called 'honji-suijaku' theory whereby all kami are partial manifestations of Buddha, able to save people and bring them to Enlightenment.[106] The solution was expedient: the immanence of the kami was retained intact while Buddha was established as the superior power, his omnipresence contrasted to the particularization of the Shinto shrine kami who become tokens through which He partially reveals Himself. Shinto shrines came to contain Buddhist temples but Shinto undoubtedly lost most in this marriage: the kami became mere bridges, visual testaments of Buddha's grace, the 'dust' which reveals his light: Gundert has examples of just this terminology.[107] More seriously, mainstream Buddhism threatened the very basis of Shinto by introducing into Japanese religiosity radically new elements, notably a focus on the after-life and a moralization of religion[108] so it comes as no surprise to find a revolt of Shinto against its forced marriage with Buddhism in the thirteenth and fourteenth centuries. It was a dispute which Zen, however, was uniquely placed to resolve, unlike other Buddhist sects able to absorb the Shinto base without debasing it. For Zen shared with Shinto a common respect for natural beauty and for intuition, a common disregard for mediators, a relative indifference to morality, and a common a- or non-theism.[109] The very lack of scriptural authority in Shinto, its lack of authentic interpreters and established dogma — which other Buddhist sects sought to make good — could be embraced by Zen with its similar and fundamental contempt for transmission through scripture and authority:

> To ears,
> defiled by sermons:
> a cuckoo.[110]

---

106.   Cf. Matsunaga, *op. cit.* (1969).

107.   Gundert, *op. cit.*, p. 187.

108.   Because kami are amoral: "neither good nor bad, but can manifest itself as benign or destructive to human interests according to the treatment it receives". (Blacker, *op. cit.*, p. 41).

109.   Cf. Spae, *op. cit.*, p. 54.

110.   A haiku by Shiki.

In sum: it was not so much a metaphysics or a morality which Zen was able to share with Shinto — both were fundamentally disinclined towards both; it was a common aesthetic. Storry writes:

> There was much in Zen that was congruous with the standards established and implied by the world of Shinto. The appeal here, we can say, was aesthetic rather than moral; although in Japan these terms are often interchangeable.[111]

There was — and is — no difficulty for a Shinto worshipper contemplating a Zen landscape garden or a flower arrangement in which Zen has embodied its practice of spiritual training through aesthetic refinement; the immanence of the kami in nature was not hard to blend with the Zen doctrine of intuitive access to the numinous through aesthetic contemplation. Indeed, it can be argued that the tea ceremony is as much Shinto as Zen, as is landscape gardening, blossom viewing, the contemplation of mountains, and Noh too, because though there are copious references to Shinto in Noh, that does not make the plays Shinto in spirit. Always the Shinto images are reinterpreted in the new Buddhist terms;[112] a typical example is *Yoro:*

Shite: I am the God of this mountain shrine,
Chorus: Who is one with Yoriu Kannon Bosatsu.
Shite: A deity called God.
Chorus: And that called Buddha.
Shite: Differ but as water from wave,
Chorus: Voices instrumental for the delivery of mankind.[113]

Kamo is another example. Ostensibly a celebration of the Shinto kami of rain and thus a fertility-rite, the Noh play converts the water symbolism into a state of consciousness:

---

111. Storry, R., *The Way of the Samurai*, London, 1978, p. 46; cf. Spae, *op. cit.*, p. 20.
112. Cf. Gundert, *op. cit.*, pp. 198-200.
113. Quoted from Shimazaki, Chifumi, *The Noh, Vol. 1. God Noh*, Tokyo, 1972, p. 198.

The sacred stream
Flows, its water clear as the divine mind;
Clear our minds as the water in the pails.[114]

It should be noted here that Japanese rhetoric and poetics make much use of a technique called the *kake-kotoba* ('hanging word') whereby an adjective can qualify not just the word preceding it but simultaneously also the word following it: in the example above, 'clear' modifies both 'mind' and 'water', thus beautifully merging the old Shinto with the new Buddhist theme.[115] As a result, the opening lines of the *Kamo* quotation above ('In quest of the source crystal clear') are turned from describing a shrine-pilgrimage into a psychic, mystical journey.

Ema is a third example: another play with obvious fertility symbolism, in its second part it re-enacts Uzume's famous dance, but this fertility theme again receives psychic re-orientation in a line such as "Spring, the mind as young grass" in which the word 'young' modifies both 'grass' and 'mind'. . . . These plays are all Shinto in their evocation of natural beauty, all Buddhist in exploiting sensuous imagery for new mystical purposes. The *Hoka Priests* has a section chanted by the chorus in which the natural beauty of a spring morning is expressly celebrated as the voice of the Buddha:

On mornings of green spring
When at the valley's shining gate
First melt the hawthorn-warbler's frozen tears
Or when by singing foam
Of snow-fed waters echoes the discourse
Of neighbourly frogs: — then speaks
The voice of Buddha's heart.[116]

---

114.   Quoted from Shimazaki, Chifumi, *The Noh, Vol. 1. God Noh*, p. 210.

115.   Cf. Shimazaki, *op. cit.*, pp. xi-xii. There are about a dozen plays in the Noh repertoire in which plants attain enlightenment, and eighteen more which refer to this doctrine (Cf. Shively, D.H., "Buddhahood for the Nonsentient: a theme in No plays", *Harvard Journal of Asiatic Studies*, Vol. 20, June, 1957, pp. 135-61).

116.   Waley, *op. cit.*, p. 209.

In sum: one must have serious reservations about any direct Shinto or Shamanistic influence on Noh and recognize rather a religious syncretism at work under the umbrella of Zen. It is true that Shinto bequeathed to Noh and to Japanese Buddhism in general an affirmative attitude towards nature, but this was a tendency it inherited in any case from China, because by the eighth century all the major Chinese forms of Buddhism had been introduced into Japan; by the Heian, Buddhism began to receive a distinctively Japanese flavour.

ZEN AESTHETICS

Japanese Buddhism retained the primarily affirmative aspect of Chinese Buddhism; where it differed was in its distinctively aesthetic bent:

> Japanese Buddhism is perhaps unique in the extent to which it is expressed in artistic or esthetic modes. Buddhism may be the actual source of the art, as in the tea ceremony, it may supply the ideological foundation for the art, or it may be practised using an art form or esthetic expression as a vehicle.[117]

To quote but one Zen master, Kukai wrote:

> The secret of the *sutras* and commentaries can be depicted in art, and the essential truths of the esoteric teachings set forth therein. Neither teachers nor students can dispense with it. Art is what reveals to us the state of perfection.[118]

Among these art forms was dance: when Prince Shotuku, the first regal convert, had a Buddhist Temple built at Osaka in the early fifth century, he already included an academy for the cultivation of

---

117. Cook, Francis H., "Japanese innovations in Buddhism", Prebish, *op. cit.*, p. 230 and cf. Suzuki, *op. cit.*, III, p. 340: Dutt, *op. cit.*, pp. 168, 175, 189 ("it is scarcely possible to imagine Japanese civilisation without the influence of Buddhism, for its aesthetic quality is one of its essential characteristics").

118. Quoted in Dutt, *op. cit.*, p. 168.

dance; Zeami himself ascribes the origin of Noh to Prince Shotuku.[119]

Some sects such as the Kuya (or Koya) spread the message of Nembutsu through dance (Yuyaku) as well as the more usual method of chanting, and this practice of dancing the Nembutsu was taken up again later by Ippen's Jishu sect and three Jodo Shinshu sects (Joshoji, Yamamoto and Sanmonto-ha of Fukui and Echizen). ... All this already emphasizes performance — probably inevitably so given the general preoccupation with temporality in Japanese Buddhist culture[120] — so it is not surprising to find that the precursors of Noh had already been adopted by pre-Zen Buddhist sects. This is because, whatever speculation there may be about Shamanistic or Shinto origins, Noh arose historically out of Sarugaku, Dengaku, Kusemai and Ennen, all of which had Buddhist affiliations as did even earlier forms such as Gigaku and Bugaku. Only Dengaku and Kagura could be argued to be strictly indigenous and to have any kind of Shinto or Shamanistic connection. Literally meaning 'field music', Dengaku evolved out of fertility rites:

> Dengaku had been performed for centuries in the farming society of Japan. When performed at the time of rice planting, it was in the form of prayers for a rich harvest which were often officiated over by a priest and involved ceremonial embracing between men and women, or dances symbolizing the chasing off of deer and boars to prevent harm to the crops, plus various other dances to appease the gods and bring rain and sunshine.[121]

---

119. Rimer/Masakazu, *op. cit.*, pp. 33 and cf. Dutt, *op. cit.*, p. 162.
120. Matsunaga (*op. cit.*, p. 1976) writes of the "bittersweet flavour of impermanence and the transitory nature of life" as the distinction of Japanese Buddhism and its aesthetics (p.1). Cf. Kim Hee-Jin, *op. cit.*, p. 102f. Dale Saunders, writing about why the Kamakura should cultivate both Zen and the theatre when there were already a dozen other Buddhist sects in Japan, describes Kamakura Samurai culture as follows: "Emphasis was placed on the evanescence, the impermanence of things, on the gradual disintegration of the world" (*op. cit.*, p. 185).
121. Y. Nakamura, *Noh. The Classical Theatre*, N.Y, Tokyo, 1971, p. 60.

It, however, fell under Buddhist influence as did Kagura, which had its origin in Shinto rites and was ostensibly a copy of Uzume's famous dance (traditionally performed by the family of Sarume-no-Kimi who claimed to be descendants of Ame-no-Uzume and were by profession Shamans).[122]

Everything else came in from China, beginning with Gigaku, brought to Japan by Mimashi — a Korean dancer trained at the Chinese court and taken in by Prince Shotoku 'with a view to disseminating Buddhism'.[123] Gigaku took the form of a masked procession with dance and comic pantomime and was used to teach Buddhist doctrine; Ortolani gives an example: four girls appear; two men dance; a mythological figure — Konron — appears and makes obscene overtures to the girls with his phallus; they protect themselves with their fans until a Buddhist protector — Kongo Rikishi — comes to their aid and, in a grotesque dance, tears off the demon's phallus.[124] Gigaku decayed since the tenth century "because it did not match the Buddhism and the aesthetic attitudes of the new age".[125]

Bugaku came next — also a masked dance from China, taken up by the court and performed there by professional dancers, it was also performed at some Shinto and Buddhist shrines during prayers for rain and in worship of Buddha and Shinto kami.[126]

The direct ancestors of Noh were, however, Ennen and Sarugaku, the former a mix of song, dance and dialogue performed by priests and altar boys after Buddhist services at larger temples; by the early part of the twelfth century it had become so luxurious and popular that it was suppressed by the government.[127] Sarugaku was also attached to Buddhist temples and itself derived from Sangaku: miscellaneous entertainment combining acrobatics,

122. Inoura, *op. cit.*, p. 8.
123. *Ibid.*, p. 23.
124. Kindermann, H. (ed.), *Fernöstliches,* Stuttgart, 1966, p. 404.
125. Inoura, *op. cit.*, p. 7.
126. *Ibid.*, p. 34.
127. Inoura, *op. cit.*, p. 52.

clowning, dance, conjuring tricks, juggling and simple comic plays. Zeami's father, Kannami, blended in Kusemai — a dance which related the history of a temple or the life of a noted priest. Sarugaku too was attached to temples, though this does not in itself necessarily indicate any religious function: as the ranks of performers shifted from lower-class priests to full professionals, temple affiliation was sought as an exemption from taxes and forced labour, while the temples sought to attract crowds to their festivals which were important commercial undertakings.[128]

What one observes, then, is a very clear pattern of Buddhism adopting performance modes which were becoming, at the same time, secular in their basic professionalism and commercialism. By the end of the thirteenth century, Sarugaku had successfully unified drama, dance, music and song into a composite form, performed by professional companies under the protection of a temple for mutual profit, and freely borrowing from its rivals — notably the secularized Dengaku which indeed preceded it in the next significant step: court patronage. In the fourteenth century there are records of "Dengaku madness, a passion on which court aristocrats lavished fortunes."[129]

None of these early forms was specifically Zen in its affiliation but, historically, it was Zen — known in Japan since the seventh century but flourishing from the twelfth century onwards — which provided Japan with its distinctively aesthetic Buddhism, conceiving of aesthetic pursuits as a means (*upāya*) of ego-loss: Lin-chi thus writes that "when one is entranced by the beauty and wonder of the world, it is no longer possible to be aware of oneself".[130] Zen, like Ch'an before it, added little new to Buddhism in the way of philosophy: Zen could and did build on the philosophical foundations laid by the Six Sects in the Nara period, and notably on Hua-Yen

---

128.   One must mention also Shugen Noh — developed in the Muromachi by itinerant monks to disseminate Shugendo — a fusion of Shinto mountain worship with Buddhism (cf. Inoura, *op. cit.*, pp. 10, 77).

129.   Hall and Takeshi, *op. cit.*, p. 185; cf. Inoura, *op. cit.*, pp. 71, 72.

130.   Cf. Matsunaga, *op. cit.* (1976), p. 210.

from which it took the key notions that every object is coterminous with the All, and every instant contains all time. Philosophically, Zen emphasizes impermanence; as Dogen would write:

> Existence is not placed within the framework of time, but existence itself is time.[131]

This time is, however, conceived as discontinuous:

> Dogen comprehended reality as a discontinuous stream of 'dharma-moments', each of which constitutes pure 'being-time' itself as the 'absolute now';

however:

> Each absolute now or eternal present of pure being-time is said to contain all worlds of the past, present and future at once so as to establish the complete simultaneity of the three temporal periods within the total exertion of each particular dharma-moment.[132]

With Zen, in other words, Japanese Buddhism moved beyond a general melancholic sense of transience to focus on the singularity and particularity of every unique experience — the *tathatā* and Satori theories summarized above.

This emphasis on uniqueness, on the unpredictable, unrepeatable is the basis of all 'Japanese' arts — raku pottery, calligraphy, sumiyo painting, haiku — for Zen's belief in sudden illumination,"a fleeting glimpse of existence just as it really is,"[133] can best use art forms which are themselves dependent on immediate inspiration and unrepeatable execution. Suzuki writes:

> The philosophy of intuition takes time at its full value. It permits of no ossification, as it were, of each moment. It takes hold of each moment as it is born from *Sunyata*.

---

131. Cf. Matsunaga, *op. cit.* (1976), p. 252.

132. Odin, *op. cit.*, p. 11.

133. Cook, *op. cit.*, p. 230.

Momentariness is therefore characteristic of this philosophy.[134]

The connections are — again — performative: Dogen wrote about "playing joyfully" in *samādhi*, and referred to enlightenment itself as "joyous play".[135] Hee-Jin Kim comments:

It (Enlightenment) is the activity of *homo ludens* par excellence.[136]

Play, Temporality, immediate Experience, Singularity, Particularity: all this is fundamentally a performative aesthetic. Lin-chi already compared the experience of an individual completely immersed in the objective world as equivalent to 'watching a play'.[137]

The marriage of Zen and Noh was, therefore, probably inevitable: towards the end of the fourteenth century, some Sarugaku actors found themselves confronted by a new audience and new patrons; notable among these was Zeami himself and the Shogun, Yoshimitsu.

How Zeami (1363-1443) and his father Kannami (1333-84) came under the patronage of the Shogun when the boy was 12 and the Shogun 17 makes a drama in its own right.[138] Zeami is described in contemporary reports as very beautiful and himself compared to a blossom;[139] whatever the reason — Yoshimitsu's passion for novelty, his homosexuality, his aesthetic sensitivity — the result was that Zeami was transported into a cultural atmosphere which was already intensely coloured by Zen aesthetics. Their relationship caused a scandal — less because of their homosexuality which was

---

134.   Dutt, *op. cit.*, pp. 175, 185, 186.

135.   Kim, *op. cit.*, p. 52.

136.   *Ibid.*, p. 60.

137.   Matsunaga, *op. cit.*, (1976), p. 210.

138.   There is indeed a play on Zeami's life: Yamazaki Masakazu's *Mask and Sword*.

139.   Hare, T.B., *Zeami's Style. The Noh Plays of Zeami Motokiyo*, Stanford U.P., 1986, p.17.

widespread among the court and Samurai class than because actors were considered unfit for the refined culture of the court, being classed as little better than beggars.[140] Partly to counter this, such actors (and other artists who rose from the lower classes) became 'Zen monks': experts in renga, tea-parties, painting, art and decoration as well as the theatre, they were enrolled in the Ji sect of Buddhism and changed their names by adding the suffix '-ami' (from Amida Buddha).[141] Kannami is sometimes referred to as a 'Shinto priest' since his company was attached to the Kasuga shrine in Nara; Zeami as a 'Zen monk' but it is clear that mere entry into the lay priesthood or attachment to a temple did not necessarily signal any religious conversion. It is true that Zeami became more than just a formal adherent of Zen but that came later: before that he had already recognized the professional and commercial need to adapt Sarugaku to the tastes of the new elite. This new elite were the Samurai whose leader was the Shogun, notably Yoshimitsu whose reign was distinguished by a general and intense patronage of the arts, for the Muromachi was an age of political intrigue, sectarian rivalry, civil disorder and violence but somehow also a great age of art:

> an age in which a brilliant culture was somewhat mysteriously supported on the weakest of political foundations and throughout long periods of incessant warfare.[142]

This art was consciously opposed to the classical aesthetics of the Emperor's court, and all of it was inspired by Zen. It is arguable that it was here that the foundations of a first truly national Japanese culture were laid,[143] for what distinguishes the artistic pursuits of

---

140. Hare, T.B., *op. cit.*, p. 16. There was a widespread belief that the Kamakura Shogunate had been destroyed from within by its "vulgar passion for Dengaku and dog-fighting" (Hall and Takeshi, *op. cit.*, p. 185.)

141. Hall and Takeshi, *op. cit.*, p. 186.

142. *Ibid.*, p. 5.

143. Hall and Takeshi, *op. cit.*, p. 293.

this period was a general cross-fertilization between popular and elitist forms on the one hand and between the various religious sects on the other: the Golden Pavilion was Zen-inspired but shows also Pure Land and Amidist influences in style; monochrome ink painting offered a synthesis of Confucianism, Taoism and Buddhism.[144]

Zen, however, dominated to such a degree that it must be described as the 'umbrella': it was Zen which supplied an aesthetic which enabled the new warrior elite to establish itself as the cultural equal of the Emperor's court until we find them "hosting poetry salons at their mansions and building pavilions in the Zen style in their residential compounds for purposes of meditation or entertainment".[145]

This hegemonic influence of Zen on Samurai culture can be dated from the thirteenth century: Zen received a privileged status in the Joei Code of 1232 and when Yoshimitsu took power in 1367 he founded Zen monasteries (including the Shokokuji and the Kamakura Gozan), encouraged Zen-inspired landscape painting, gardening, and himself practised zazen under a Zen master, Gido Shushin. Yoshimasa continued the patronage, encouraging ink painting, the tea ceremony, flower arranging and Zen-inspired architecture: the hegemony of Zen in the Muromachi has been compared to that of the Catholic Church in medieval France, virtually a state religion with Zen monks in charge of international trade with China and internal trade in patronage too.[146]

And the question must be asked: how can one explain that a religion of compassion and peace became the dominating cultural force for a warrior elite? Yoshimitsu's rules of conduct showed the way; Anesaki writes:

---

144.   Hall and Takeshi, *op. cit.*, pp. 16, 22.

145.   *Ibid.*, p. 7

146.   Cf. Colbath, A., *The Japanese Noh Drama and its relation to Zen Buddhism*, Ph.D. Diss., Western Reserve University, Cleveland, 1962, p. 73f.

The chief aim was to control the crude mind and life of the warriors by propriety of behaviour and observance, then to open a way to higher spiritual training. The rules of monastic life as practised by the Zen monks were taken as models, the ideal of calmness and the principles of spiritual exercise being applied to the arts of fencing, archery, and even to dancing. Through those codes of honour, the ideal of serenity and composure permeated the life of the warriors, and later, during the reign of peace, penetrated into the life of the common people through the example of the upper classes.[147]

Zen's anti-intellectualism was clearly a major attraction in this merging of ethos within which the Zen cult of 'spontaneity', of total commitment combined with self-control appealed especially to a warrior's instincts; as Storry writes:

A vital part in Zen training was directed to the release of a man's *honsho*, or 'true character'. This was a process not so much of building up as of stripping down, of sloughing of every outer element, until virtually a state of *Mu*, 'emptiness', 'void', 'no being', was attained.[148]

The relationship was specific: Zen directly revolutionized Japanese martial arts, above all swordsmanship and archery: its doctrine of 'munen' or 'mushin' (no mind, no thought) providing a 'religious' basis for military training, tuning a fighter's reflexes to the point where action becomes automatic through an internalization of technique. This was also Zeami's approach to training in the theatre, the secret in fact of 'hana': the connection was made by the great Takuan who in describing how the art of swordsmanship relates to the 'empty mind' of meditation adds:

This 'empty-minded-ness' applies to all activities we may perform, such as dancing, as it does to swordplay. The

---

147. Anesaki, M., *History of Japanese Religion,* Tokyo, 1963, p. 223; cf. Ch'en, *op. cit.,* (1968), pp. 185-86.

148. Storry, *op. cit.,* p. 48.

dancer takes up the fan and begins to stamp his feet. If he
has any idea at all of displaying his art well, he ceases to be
a good dancer, for his mind 'stops' with every movement he
goes through. In all things, it is important to forget your
'mind' and become one with the work at hand.[149]

The samurai were not only warriors nor did Zen influence only their
professional activities; they were the new rulers of Japan, upstarts
in a land where the court had been the centre of the aesthetic graces
since the Heian and whose members were expected to perform — on
a musical instrument and in poetry contests. This dominance of the
aesthetic is worth emphasizing; Storry writes:

every gentleman and lady was an amateur performer in
one or more of the arts. . . . Learning, speculative religion,
questions of social morality, were held to be subsidiary to
the more important values attached to excellence in poetry
and calligraphy.[150]

Matsunaga comments:

Today many believe that the samurai approached Zen for
spirituality, if the truth be known their spirituality was
generally of a superficial nature as they were uneducated,
yet they admired the cultural sophistication of Zen.[151]

Dutt writes:

it has to be considered that the most cultured among the
Japanese belonged to this class. They were warriors by
profession, not shrinking from its incidental cruelties, but
they were at the same time inheritors of Japanese culture,
— aesthetes by taste and temperament.[152]

---

149.   Quoted in Suzuki, D.T., *Zen and Japanese Culture,* Princeton U.P.,
        1959, p. 114.
150.   Storry, *op. cit.*, p. 19.
151.   Matsunaga, *op. cit.* (1976), p. 230.
152.   Dutt, *op. cit.*, p. 175.

What Zen brought to the Samurai was, then, a practice in composure and self-discipline, withdrawal from the passions and emotions, and a general cultivation of spontaneity-within-technique, all of which it indoctrinated less by moral or spiritual training than by artistic pursuits. Noh's 'Zen connection' lies here — no less than a conscious decision taken by Zeami and his father to adapt their art form too to these same tastes.

The most obvious way to achieve this was, of course, by dramatizing the samurai life itself and for this are many examples: of the five groups of Noh plays, the second are shura-mono — 'warrior plays' — while there are also examples in the fifth group about the divine origin of the art of war and sword-making, and many other plays which teach the virtues of obedience, self-control, patriotism, loyalty and self-sacrifice: *Fujito, Hachi no Ki, Manju, Kakekiyo.* What one finds here, however, is not just a playwright who reflects the interests and concerns of his audience but one whose plays directly tackle the latent contradictions in their code and provide guidance for their resolution. This guidance is no less than an aesthetic mediation based on Zen principles, notably affirmation of the world combined with an intense awareness of its transience and evanescence — a combination which the theatre as the most transient and yet sensual of art-forms is uniquely able to provide.[153] For the samurai ethos was fraught with tensions — between its code of death and its creed of mercy, its sudden access to material wealth and its creed of abnegation: Noh does not shirk these tensions — *Atsemori* presents a famous warrior, Kumagae no Naozane who, overcome by remorse at having killed the young Taira no Atsumori, becomes a priest. *Ebira* sharpens the tension, presenting the ghost of a warrior who tells of the torments to which all warriors are doomed in the after-life — the theme of *Tsunemasa* and *Shunzei Tadanori* too. The latter was written by Naito Tozaemon

---

153. Noh plays frequently include quotations from Buddhist hymns, poems, *sūtras*; there are references to *karma* too but two themes predominate: the pain of attachment and the evanescence of life: cf Waley, *op. cit.*, pp. 82, 84, 123, 150, 173, 209.

but the others were all written and performed by Zeami to his samurai audience.

One solution is provided by *Tamura* in which an old warrior tells of the divine assistance he received, and reinterprets war as the driving out of demons, though of more poignant relevance are two other warrior-plays: *Tadanori* in which the hero, when he re-appears, regrets more the anonymous publication of a poem he wrote than his death, and *Tsunemasa* in which the warrior plays the lute he loved so well. Both were clearly conceived for an audience which was coming to value artistic pursuits even more than military prowess, but their plots also point to the deeper, formal message which Noh had for its samurai audience: in aesthetic culture one can find a 'this-worldly' experience of transient beauty which does not divert from but in fact leads to a 'that-wordly' peace of mind. *Tamura* is a good example: it is about a general of the Gempei period who returns as a ghost to the Sensui-ji temple which he had erected to Kwannon in gratitude for his victory. This synthesis of Bushido and Buddhism is effected through the plot but the vehicle is its imagery:

> See! The garden of the God
> Is filled with snow!
> In dazzling white
> Buried are clouds and mist,
> Buried are clouds and mist.
> Try as I may, no branches can I see.[154]

This first surge towards the 'white light' is interrupted by the monk, by dialogue: the youth tells the story of the shrine, and the monk, inspired, sits down under a cherry tree and invokes the *Lotus sūtra* which, it is believed, can conjure up a vision of Buddha in pure light. The moon rises and shines on the white cherry blossoms, and the moon — which appears in some 90 per cent of all Noh plays — is not, as in the West, a symbol of fickleness but symbolizes the ability of the human mind to be flooded in Universal Reality. The monk sings:

---

154.   *The Noh Drama, Ten Plays from the Japanese*, Tuttle, Tokyo, 1955, p. 25f.

This is Spring's rapturous hour,
Which banishes all other thoughts,

a theme then taken up by the chorus:

The cherry blossoms of the Jishu Gongen!
What a breath-taking sight!
The moon-rays pierce the branches,
Evening breezes tempt the blossoms,
Filling the air with snowy petals
And ravishing the heart!
In the pale moonlight,
Cherry trees everywhere are in their glory
The very sky seems drunk
With the flowers' beauty.[155]

The mood has thus been transferred from person to person and now to the whole of space; the boy vanishes — into the white light:

Throwing wide its moon-blanched portals,
He glides across the hall
And vanishes into the sanctuary.[156]

What Zeami has done here is a remarkable achievement of synthesis: he has taken the this-worldly beauty of cherry blossom, associated it with the Buddhist theme of transience, related it to the sensual-spiritual symbol of the moon, used both to shift the focus from this-worldly beauty to the that-worldly white light of enlightenment and grafted the whole onto the famous legend of a famous warrior. As such he has simultaneously resolved the contradictions of a 'military-Buddhist' ideology, blended a warrior cult with indulgence in sensuous beauty and given it a transcendent purpose and direction, and synthesized a this-worldly cult of evanescent beauty with a that-worldly mysticism of the white light of satori.

Zeami could scarcely have done this without Zen, and it is scarcely conceivable that his audience would have received it other

---

155. Eadem.
156. *Ibid.*, p. 30f.

than through Zen. There are, indeed, other plays which are actually polemical in their championship of Zen: *Sotoba Komachi*, for example, in which the famous beauty upholds Zen against two priests of the Shingon sect, or *Kayoi Komachi*; these are, however, exceptional: any critic can point to other — and more — plays with overt references to the *Lotus sūtra*, Pure Land, Amidism, or Shinto.[157] Historically the Muromachi saw in fact an outbreak of sectarian rivalry in which Shinto turned against Buddhism, and the various Buddhist sects engaged in intense competition and even open, armed warfare — for economic more than doctrinal reasons. It would therefore be easy on textual evidence alone to conclude that the Zen connection applies only to certain plays. Texts — language — are, however, never the Zen method; to be Zen at all, Noh could never place its reliance on texts, and the more ambitious section of the argument must now be taken up, namely to demonstrate that Zen's connection to Noh lies not only in the writings of its founder and major theorist, Zeami, nor simply in the historical coincidence of the rise of Zen and Noh in the Muromachi and their common appeal and contribution to the samurai ethos, but that it dictated the performance technique too; indeed, that it is primarily through its technique that Noh remains profoundly Zen. As Zeami wrote: "Hana is in the mind, the seed is technique."[158]

Noh Performance

Zen influence on the martial arts provides a first point of connection: in swordmanship and archery [also Judo, Aikido], spontaneity is simultaneously controlled and released through the mastery of technique, the key being the achievement of a state of 'no-mind'. The case can be extended to Noh: what Zen taught the samurai about spontaneous action within a framework of internalized technique, about 'direct pointing', the exclusion of incidentals and the practice of concentrated energy: these are the foundations of Noh acting too. Kyuran of the Komparu school actually adapted the

---

157. Cf. Renondeau, G., *Le Bouddhisme dans le No*, Tokyo, 1950.
158. *Kadensho, op. cit.*, p. 52.

martial arts to Noh training in the sixteenth century, and A.C. Scott has published a provocative sketch of this relation, identifying the Zen characteristics of Noh acting in the reduction of gesture to its essence, the priority of sound over sense in its language, its cultivation of the 'vacuum' of stillness and, above all, in the whole foundation of the method:

> Technical skills must be absorbed so that the mind may dispense with retarding details.[159]

Suzuki writes similarly in *Zen and Japanese Culture* about *myo:*

> It is a certain artistic quality perceivable not only in works of art but in anything in Nature or life. The sword in the hands of a swordsman attains this quality when it is not a display of mere technical skill patiently learned under the tutorship of a good master. For *myo* is something original and creative. . . . The hands may move according to the technique given out to every student, but there is a certain spontaneity and personal creativity when the technique, conceptualized and universalized, is handled by the master hand.[160]

In other words: Hana . . . .

Any of the warrior Noh plays quoted above supplies an example: when one *reads the play* one finds good propaganda for Bushido intermingled with Zen imagery, but when one *sees the play in performance* one recognizes that beneath the plot and the moral theme, there is an experience of 'frozen moments' in which concentrated energy is seized and released. . . . such a description runs into the danger of subjectivity or mere noise: it begs a comprehensive analysis of Noh performance conventions. For the 'flower' can occur only in performance but, convincing though the evidence of Noh's intimate connection to Zen in the Muromachi may

---

159. Scott, A.C., "Reflections on the Aesthetic Background of the Performing Arts of East Asia", *Asian Music*, Vol. VI, nos. 1 and 2, 1975, p. 213.

160. Suzuki, *op. cit.*, (1959), p. 142f.

be, we have no way of knowing what an audience's actual experience was six hundred years ago. Much — too much — has been made of the continuity of the form: while it is true that some performers today can trace their lineage directly back to Zeami, and all claim absolute fidelity to his principles, the performance conventions of Noh have changed and quite radically.[161] Its present form dates from the Tokugawa when Noh underwent a comprehensive process of standardization, classification and formalization to become the 'seances' they are now.[162] If it is true that Zen has influenced not just the plots and imagery but the very structure and technique of Noh, then what must be undertaken is an attempt at a structural analysis of Noh as a performance system.

A performance begins at the 'rainbow curtain' — vertical strips of coloured brocade hanging in the doorway of a small, roofed gateway at the entrance to the 'hashigakari' — the bridge leading to the main stage. This curtain may be of Shinto origin: it is in the five 'auspicious' colours, and similar curtains are often hung below the crossbeams of Shinto torii and shrines.[163] The bridge itself may also be derived from Shinto shrines or it may be Buddhist. . . .[164] Together, curtain, gateway and *hashigakari* represent a clear 'crossing over' — a passage from one realm to another, and the

---

161.   In Zeami's own times, Noh was frequently performed at shrine and temple festivals in the atmosphere of a fair; also in river-beds where there were audiences of thousands (cf. Waley, *op. cit.*, p. 38); the hashigakari as we know it dates from the sixteenth century as does the Yoro pine (cf. footnote 164 below and Nakamura, *op. cit.*, p. 210); Zeami knew the chorus but saw it as an unwelcome innovation (Waley, *op. cit.*, p. 30).

162.   Cf. Nakamura, *op. cit.*, p. 135.

163.   Cf. Ono., *op. cit.*, p. 64.

164.   The earliest known reference to the hashigakari is from 1349 and it mentions two, curved bridges; the bridge as we know it today is described in the *Sarugaku dangi* of 1430 but as joining the back of the stage: there are diagrams in Ernst, E.R., *The Kabuki Theatre* (University of Hawaii Press, 1956) and in Waley, *op. cit.*, which indicate that the present arrangement whereby the bridge joins the stage at an angle of about 120 degrees dates from 1615.

nature of this transition, this 'limen', is also indicated, for the *hashigakari* is marked by three real pine trees planted at equal distances along its length but in diminishing size: the largest is closest to the stage, exaggerating the distance of the curtain — a technique probably derived from Zen landscape painting, "the creation of artificial depth through overt foreshortening, thereby simulating the effects of distance on our visual sense".[165] But what these three natural pines lead the eye towards is a huge *aesthetic* pine painted on the rear wall of the main stage: every Noh stage has this painting on the rear wall; it is the only decor of every play and indicates therefore that we too are crossing over from a natural world to one of aesthetic beauty and stylization.

The main stage is a cube — about nineteen feet square, made of cypress. It and the *hashigakari* are separated from the audience by a gravel strip about five feet wide, usually of white pebbles like a Zen garden (at the Itsukushima shrine, the sea flows between audience and stage). This division may have derived from early shrine performances when it was necessary to keep the audience from trespassing on the stage; it is now no longer necessary for this purpose any more than the magnificent Shinto roof is necessary for climatic purposes since the whole stage is built inside a concrete building, but this strip of gravel and that roof do serve an important purpose in sharply distinguishing the 'aesthetic' realm from the 'real' (for the pines grow in the gravel strip) and the roof remains necessary, for it completes the 'cube'. Modern spectators sometimes complain that the pillars supporting the roof block sight lines but while the technical explanation is that the actors need the pillars to orient themselves behind their masks, anyone who has attended a Noh performance on a proscenium arch or thrust stage knows what happens when the cube is reduced to a square: a proscenium arch (lacking defined depth) and a thrust stage (lacking both the vertically and horizontally defined space which the cube provides) fail to lock the eye in the necessary way. The cube provides a *contained* space, sharply differentiated in all directions from the

---

165.   Hoover, *op. cit.*, p. 89.

auditorium and its 'reality'. Lights can be and are left on in the Noh auditorium because there is no danger that the eye can escape its entrapment in a cube of alternative reality.

The journey from the curtain, along the bridge, past the three natural pines is made first by the musicians who set up their stools at the focal point directly in front of the aesthetic pine. Noh music is extremely hard to write about, but music is more central to Noh than text: it accompanies the songs and chanting, provides instrumental preludes and interludes and accompanies the dance.[166] There is a flute, three types of drum and also the musicians' 'cries' — again possibly of Shinto but also possibly of Zen origin:[167] they and the music itself establish the pace and build the architecture of the piece from the very beginning, carving time into a rhythmic structure within which the 'flower moment' can occur.[168]

In this they are aided by the chorus, who enter next: eight to ten men in 'anonymous' formal black kimonos with crests, *hakama* and a fan. They sit stage left throughout the whole performance, their only movement being to take up the fan when they sing and then replace it when they fall silent. They represent no character or group of people; instead they pick up a theme supplied by one of the main characters and develop it. They can describe actions on and off stage and, most interestingly, voice the thoughts of the *shite* (main performer), now inside, now outside his mind. This unique technique — called 'interlacing dialogue' — is described by Wells:

> One formula often employed divides a passage into three successive parts, commenced by two actors and concluded by the chorus; one person appears to understand another so fully that he speaks for him; two characters thinking alike speak not together but pronounce two parts of the same sentence; frequently the chorus or one of the characters

---

166.   On Noh music: Cf. Hoff/Flindt, *op. cit.*, and Tamba, Akira, *La Structure Musicale du No*, Paris, 1974 for detail.
167.   Cf. Ono, *op. cit.*, p. 65; Tamba, *op. cit.*, p. 228.
168.   Cf. Tamba, *op. cit.*, p. 209.

> utters the thoughts of another person who for the time
> being turns dancer; or the chorus voices the thoughts
> which the actor entertains but for some reason does not
> himself express.[169]

Wells argues that this serves to 'point' the message but it does far more than that: what it creates is an experience of mind-transference or transcendence: two or more voices, physically distinct, share one thought, one mind, radically shattering any sense of an individual, private 'self'. This chorus, in other words, can transcend the polarity of object and subject, the limitations of time and space and even the 'bubble' of the self.

They sing in a deep, resonant bass produced in the pharynx[170] but just as impressive is their immobility, their stillness ('What is Zen?' 'Just sit'). In this they are complemented by the first 'character' who enters — the *waki*.

The *waki* sometimes has attendants or companions but essentially he is always alone. Often a priest or monk, always a traveller, it is he who takes the audience into 'the other world', for after his opening couplet he introduces himself and then tells us where he is going and for what purpose. He then moves to 'his' pillar (stage left front) where he too sits — mostly immobile — for the rest of the play. Though he has a name and even a part, the *waki* is less a character than an agent: at first a guide, then a catalyst for the *shite* to appear, then our proxy on stage, asking the *shite* the sorts of questions we might wish to put and then, like us, sitting to one side and listening, watching (sometimes praying, meditating).

His opening travelogue already contains passages of 'lyrical geography'; Noh has no sets or scenery, only an occasional, schematic prop. Realistic props and elaborate scenery imply a material reality of which the stage is a copy whereas Noh's favourite text is the *Lotus Sutra* which teaches that all matter is, in essence, one spirit. A Noh

---

169. Wells, H.W. *The Classical Drama of the Orient*, New York, 1965, p. 162.
170. This is held to evoke a deep inner peace and has been compared to Zen meditation by Tamba (*op. cit.*, p. 49).

audience has to create props and sets in their mind — through the exercise of their aesthetic imagination and aided by the imagery of the *waki's* descriptions. The delusion of 'material reality' is not reproduced, instead we are all encouraged to penetrate beyond. This too is based on Zen aesthetics, for the arrangement of the stage itself in one corner of the auditorium and the distorted perspective of the *hashigakari* make it impossible for a spectator to adopt anything other than an oblique perspective. This is in conformity with the Zen principle of asymmetry as practised in its painting and gardening too: the spectator in all cases has to complete the act, provide the 'three-tenths' which Zeami had insisted the artist must never do for them.[171]

All this is preparation: architecture and decor have established that there are two 'realms' — one natural, the other aesthetic; musicians and *waki* have crossed over and, along with the chorus, have begun to activate the audience's complementary activity; all eyes now turn to the rainbow curtain.

The *shite* stretches the gap to its limit, Zeami already having given very precise instructions about how the *shite* must find exactly the right moment to enter.[172] The curtain parts; Nakamura writes:

> The appearance of the *shite* has been described as similar to a famous painting by the Chinese artist Liang K'ai depicting the descent of Sakyamuni from the mountain immediately after his enlightenment. The comparison is appropriate because the proper state of mind for the *shite* is the total emptying of all thoughts and feelings from the mind and complete concentration like the state required for Buddhist enlightenment.[173]

The *shite* is masked. Much has been made of the mystique of the 'mirror room ritual' — a special room where the *shite* goes to 'greet'

---

171.   Cf. Sieffert, *op. cit.*, p. 115.
172.   Cf. Rimer/Masakazu, *op. cit.*, p. 18.
173.   Nakamura, *op. cit.*, p. 214.

and then tie on his mask. It is part of Noh lore that it is here the actor leaves his 'self' behind and 'merges' with the mask. It is this sort of mystique which has damaged much more than assisted arguments about Noh's Zen-connection; Zeami would have been horrified by such talk, for what he taught was not some trance-like identification, but rather that the actor, behind the mask, project any 'self' he may have out into the audience and see himself as they see him — with an 'objective eye'. What he sees is what any spectator sees: not a mask or a face but both, for the mask does not fit. One can see the jowls and the chin and the neck — not (as some 'Zennists' claim) because Japanese once had smaller faces, but because this 'doubling' is clearly intentional: the mask is tied on with an inch-wide strip of brocade which lies and dangles *over* the wig and not, as would be possible if one wished to disguise it, under the wig. There is no attempt to hide the fact that this is a mask on a face, an actor wearing and working a mask. This mask itself is not a 'character', only a type: different *shites* select different masks according to their interpretation of the role,[174] and usually the mask is changed between the first and second part.[175] Noh actors do not engage in any kind of Stanislavskian 'affective memory' or research the background of their 'character': there is no loss of some 'self' in some 'character': such practices belong in other cultures with other psychologies, other metaphysics and other aesthetics.

The mask is itself a work of art, often too precious to be used in rehearsal, and the dialectic of mask and face reinforces that of natural pine and aesthetic pine — with the difference that the *shite* now plays with this dialectic, for the mask begins to change expression as the *shite* carefully raises and lowers and turns his head, catching the light from the inside of the roof, radically altering the mask's expression until it appears as if it more than the face behind it is the living thing.

This 'objectification' of self is reinforced by the convention of

---

174. Waley, *op. cit.*, p. 308.
175. Cf. Kunio Komparu, *The Noh Theater. Principles and Perspectives,* Tokyo and New York, 1983, p. 297.

voiced stage directions which invariably shift the delivery from first to third person, confirming what the chorus is also doing — breaking any remaining 'bubble' of any remaining 'self'. This technique often occurs at moments of climax and tension when the *shite* suddenly talks about 'himself' in the third person, describing his actions as if his spirit had left his body. . . .

The effect of Part One may be summarized: everything conspires to juxtapose two realities — a natural and an aesthetic — to transfer the audience's attention away from the former to the latter and, simultaneously, to break the bubble of the self, fracturing it into two and then objectifying any remaining subjectivity. All the most naturally and individually expressive parts of the human body are ruthlessly suppressed — face, eyes, even body shape.[176] Time, space and subject are all transcended as natural perceptions are transferred to an aesthetic realm which, in accordance with Zen, is expressly identified with a transcendence of subjectivity.

Although there are some Noh plays with only one act, the convention of a two-part structure was established already by Zeami and his father. What it means is that, regardless of particular details of plot, dialogue and character, the audience now anticipates a further radical shift when the *shite* will return in a second mask. For he is never what he at first seems to be, appearing in the first part only as what he has become and what he remains *to all appearances*. When he re-appears in the second part, in a different mask and costume, he reappears as what he was and what *in truth* he still is. This challenge to notions of 'self' is more than an exercise in Buddhist psychology; to a large extent it emphasizes the basic Noh soteriological theme: characters obsessed by emotions, passions, attachments, desires, ambitions, loves, memories will never escape *karma* and enter *nirvāṇa*. But this basic plot-line is not the only thing the change of mask serves: it also *reverses* time and, in the process, *freezes* it. A passage from *Tobuku* illustrates this shift:

---

176. The costume does not really fit, the padding disguising body shape: it is draped over the body and it too is changed between Parts One and Two.

Chorus: Listening to this ancient tale,
I will believe all round me here
Unchanged remains,
As in the spring days now long past.
I alone feel like a stranger here-
Maiden: Not you alone perhaps
Of whom, indeed, should you enquire
Concerning past things
Save only me?
Though I am no longer of this world,
Fleeting as a dew-drop on the wayside grass,
I still dwell within this flowering tree.[177]

'Real' time has been turned, in Part One, into some kind of 'aesthetic past time'[178] which is now, in Part Two, condensed into a moment of *suspended* time, one in which the *shite* is locked by his attachment and which he may now transcend through the intercession of the *waki's* prayers or by the Buddha's grace. For as the quotation above illustrates, time is suspended by the equation of eternity with an instant: a moment is both infinitely contracted and infinitely expanded simultaneously — the moment known to Hua-yen metaphysics and recorded in the 'Flower Sutra':

in this spiritual world of enlightenment there are no time divisions such as past, present and future, for they have contracted themselves into a single moment of the present where life quivers in its true sense.[179]

The same applies to space: the normal dimensions of natural perception are totally upset within the cube where vast distances can be covered by a few stylized steps, and, again, we are transported first into an 'aesthetic space' and then, in Part Two, into what one can only call a 'spaceless space' or what Arnott calls "a void beyond

---

177. Quoted from *The Noh Drama, op. cit.*, p. 83.
178. The costumes are eclectic and there is no real attempt to place the events in any precise historical context.
179. Suzuki, *op. cit.*, Vol. 3, p. 79.

time and space".[180] And this is not all: this plot-time/space — which stresses the Buddhist soteriological theme — is now translated into performance terms, for it is now, if at all, that the 'frozen moments' occur, the moments of 'no action' described and so highly prized by Zeami as supreme hana moments.

The musicians have been preparing for this: they follow the *shite's* pace, for it is he who has decided where he is going to place his particular flower moment this particular day. There are no rehearsals in Noh, only a 'walk through' usually on the morning of the performance, when the *shite, waki* and musicians first meet (for they are trained separately). This is, of course, the climax but unlike climaxes in most other performance modes, it is achieved in Noh not by the progressive escalation of sound and movement but the opposite: sound creates moments of intense silence, movement moments of concentrated stillness. This process accords with the radically different Zen notion of time, namely, fragmentation and discontinuity — core structural principles of Noh. Kunio Komparu has written eloquently about the significance of the concept of 'Ma' (meaning space but also interval, gap) in Noh and it is clear to any spectator: each gesture is a self-contained sculptured pose:

> the basis of Noh dance lies in stopping each movement just at the moment when the muscles are tensed. Certainly, the movement patterns concentrate dramatic power in moments of stillness . . . we must conclude here that the times of action in Noh exist for the sake of the times of stillness, and that the stance and carriage are the bases not of movement but of the acquisition of the technique of nonmovement.[181]

Similarly, each phrase of the music is a self-contained 'cell': just as the movement organizes *space* into units of ever more concentrated stillness, so too the music carves *time* into cells of ever more intense silence. Komparu writes:

> the body of the music is synthesized of silences that are

---

180.   Arnott, *op. cit.*, p. 102.

181.   Komparu, *op. cit.*, p. 216.

themselves framed by a pattern of rhythm woven of a minimum of percussion sounds . . . the interesting part is what is not played; the body of the music exists in the negative, blank spaces generated by the actual sounds.[182]

This is not far-fetched: performers are evaluated on their ability to hold the audience's concentration not when they are moving but when they collapse into frozen poses — which may last four or five minutes and which Zeami already used as his standard of excellence:

> in the hands of a peerless master Sarugaku will move the heart when not only representation, but song, dance, mimic and rapid action are all eliminated, emotion as it were springing out of quiescence. This is called 'frozen dance'.[183]

These are the moments of 'no-action' which Zeami expressly noted require from the performer entrance into a state of 'no-mind': Nose — a leading Japanese scholar of Zeami — comments:

> The influence of Zen Buddhism is particularly apparent. . . . The "mindlessness" which transcends mind, the moments of "no-action" which excite greater interest than those of action, the mind which controls all the powers — all these are familiar ideas of Zen, and show to how great an extent Zeami's aesthetic principles relied on the Zen teachings.[184]

This applies particularly to the *shite*, but the *waki* and the chorus too have already adopted such frozen poses and they, if anyone, are audience proxies or perhaps more accurately audience guides.[185] The *shite's* movements have been a series of still-lives in which he draws in energy, concentrates it, shapes it, holds it, rests in it, inhabiting for an eternal instant some 'timeless time and spaceless space': no-time, no-space, no-mind. . . .

---

182. Komparu, *op. cit.*, pp. 74, 168.
183. Waley, *op. cit.*, p. 44.
184. *Sources of Japanese Tradition, op. cit.*, p. 291.
185. Cf. Raz, J., *Audience and Actors,* Leiden (Brill), 1983, p. 132.

And then it is over.

Conclusion

Noh texts are sometimes read, prized and chanted as 'literature' just as Noh masks are often exhibited in galleries as 'art', but Noh is performance. Noh scripts are called 'utai-bon' — the word means chant-book just as the word *shite* means the 'doer': he is a performer not an actor — he dances, chants, sings more than speaks the lines of a quasi-person. The need to analyze Noh as performance has been recognized increasingly by researchers[186] and, given the essential ephemerality of performance, this is of course a complex operation. But it is precisely the *problems* of Performance — its temporality, particularity, singularity, ambiguity — which make it so Zen. Like a Zen instructor seeking to open a pupil's mind to the uniqueness of the ordinary, Zeami's writings are theories of how performers can and must individualize, personalize and particularize, not standardize what they do. The reason for his choice of the 'flower' metaphor may have been religious but could just as easily have been professional, for a performance of *any* play is like a flower in the sense that both are reproductions of a known, given form and yet each is somehow unique. All spectators know that the performance they are seeing is of a work which has been performed before and will be performed again but in a way which is nevertheless always different. This is a source of great anxiety for performers who appear torn between the stark choice between technical perfection and unique inspiration. Zeami decided he wanted both: the unique spontaneity of natural grace and presence but on the basis of technique. One of his last works, the *Kyui Shidai*, has been variously interpreted as a Zen document and as a training manual for professionals; if one follows its nine rungs one notes that Zeami guides his performers from their natural ability ('the squirrel')

---

186.   Cf. Frank Hoff and Willi Flindt's English version of Yokomichi Mario's analysis of Noh (*op. cit.*) where they stress that Noh must be treated "as a performance event not as a genre of literature" (p. 212) as does Monica Bethe and Karen Brazell's work: *No as Performance* (Cornell U.P., 1978) and *Dance in the No Theatre* (Cornell U.P., 1982).

through their enthusiasm, ambition, and competitiveness ('the tiger') to craftsmanship ('the hammer') — a first realization of the need to harness natural talent and ambition through technique. This they learn through mastery of conventions ('the Path') and practice in versatility and precision ('clouds in the mountains') — which is where most performers stop. Zeami sought to take them further — to creative variation ('the mountains are crimson'), a stage where the skillful, competent performer now colours the conventions with his personal creative genius. This, in turn, is the doorway to the highest three stages: 'snow in a silver bowl' (namely concentration; focus on achieving one startling moment) then on to the 'barren mountain peak' (unique, ambiguous, complete in itself) and finally to a brand new, unique experience where the 'sun shines at midnight', a moment beyond comparison and reproduction, an area where no-one has ever been before (and which Zeami himself doubted hardly anyone ever gets to).[187]

This late document reveals clearly that Zeami's ambition was to settle neither for spontaneous genius nor technical perfection but to locate the former in the latter. And so it remains: there is no general training in Noh: every class is practice in a particular dance or song or segment of a play. It is a rigorous discipline: every position, every gesture, pose, action is fixed: it cannot be altered as such but it also cannot be merely reproduced; it must be given that personal, 'mezurashiki' touch. There is only one way to express sorrow or catch the moon's reflection in the water but, after it has been mastered, it must be made to work. Akira Matsui, a Noh actor who was adopted into a family and is therefore less reticent than most about explaining secrets to foreigners, tells how he had worked for months mastering one particular gesture — that of catching the moon's reflection in the water — until he and his master, Roppeita, were both satisfied and he was allowed to perform. On the afternoon of the performance, during the 'walk-through', he performed the gesture, only to hear his master guffaw from the auditorium: "What? You want to show the moon's reflection

---

187. Cf. M.J. Nearman, "Zeami's Kyui", in *Monumenta Nipponica*, Vol. 33, 1978, pp. 299-332.

doing that?" Roppeita hammed up the gesture, then added: "but tonight, you must do just and only that but we must see you really catch the moon's reflection as if it had never been done that way before. . . ."[188]

Noh theorists and performers and spectators all know that the secret of performance and its special magic lie in the unpredictable; Komparu writes about the lack of rehearsals:

> they do not rehearse together precisely because there is no guarantee that what is produced in joint rehearsals can be reproduced on the day of the performance. In other words, what is valued in Noh is the kind of beauty generated by the spontaneous and unpredictable harmonization of a combination of performers who come together to produce a play only once.[189]

For the final remarkable fact is that Noh plays are performed by Noh performers only once: there are no runs. An actor may train for anything between ten and fifty years (some plays, such as *Sagi*, may be performed only by boys under twelve or men over 68); there is only one rehearsal which is more properly a 'talk-through' without costume or mask, and then he will perform it once. There are exceptions to this general rule, especially today when the renaissance of Noh and its sponsorship by patron-societies have led to a demand for certain popular Noh plays and performers to repeat their shows but the principle remains: Noh performances are once-off.[190] It takes little imagination to appreciate what a performer

---

188. Told to the author personally.

189. Komparu, *op. cit.*, p. 165f.

190. Consultation of the records of the Kanze school in early 1981 revealed that there are 350 qualified shites in the Tokyo school alone; the Kanze gives just over 100 performances a year, each averaging two to three plays: the statistics are therefore obvious: even with patronage societies supporting actors, most shites can survive only by giving classes to amateurs: each will perform an average of three times a year. Put differently: each shite will perform some 90 plays in their 30-year career and therefore only very exceptionally repeat the same play twice.

therefore brings to his performance: the intensity of Noh derives in the end not least from an arrangement which replaces the pressure on a Western actor to recreate each night 'the illusion of the first time' by the quite different pressure of knowing that it is always the first time and probably the last time too!

We may now return to Sieffert's denunciation of the 'Zennistes' which he had concluded with the words:

> j'admettrai volontiers néanmoins que le Nô est un art liturgique, si l'on veut bien reconnaître que l'esthétique est un phénomène religieux.[191]

Westerners have no religious framework within which to place such aesthetic moments; Japanese do: Noh, one can conclude, is a professional theatre without any sacrifice of its Zen ambitions and *vice versa*. Its Zen has been sought in the overtly religious plays and their message, in the samurai and Buddhist culture of the Muromachi, and in Zeami's and Zenchiku's theories but perhaps it lies really where no-one expected to find it — in its professionalism. Just as a Zen satori occurs most authentically in the primary experience of something entirely ordinary and repetitive, so too one can conclude: there is no contradiction between the professionalism of Noh and its Zen-connection when both are realized to be a common practice in selfless discipline aimed at a single moment of 'break-through', the moment of the flower.

There is a fascinating passage in the *Yugaku shudo fuken*, where Zeami quotes the *Heart of Wisdom Sutra*: "Form is no other than Emptiness, Emptiness no other than Form," adding:

> In the case of the *no*, once the stages of the seedling, the first flowering, and the true ripening have occurred, and the actor has reached the stage of Perfect Fluency in his performance, he will truly have reached the level where

---

191.   Sieffert, *op. cit.*, p. 165.

'Form is no other than Emptiness' [When the actor's unconscious intensity of mind produces spontaneously all effects of performance that can consciously be recognized]."[192]

'Hana' moments are frequently 'empty', moments when 'nothing happens', sometimes it is at such a moment that the character is released from bondage and achieves entry to *nirvāṇa*; a trained spectator may well achieve simultaneously a 'small satori' and then leave, just as the Zen monk returns to the world, affirming it —as a source of such peak experiences.

---

192.   Rimer/ Masakazu, *op. cit.*, pp. 115f. and cf. 118f.

Bibliography

Adikaram, E.W., *Early History of Buddhism in Ceylon*, Colombo, 1953.

Ames, Michael, "Buddha and the Dancing Goblins: A Theory of Magic and Religion", *American Anthropologist*, Vol. 66 (1), Feb. 1964.

Anesaki, M., *History of Japanese Religion,* Tokyo, 1963.

Arnold, P., *Le Théâtre japonais,* Paris, 1957.

Arnott, P.D., *The Theatres of Japan*, London, 1969.

Aśvaghoṣa, *The Buddhacarita or Acts of Buddha*, Oriental Books Reprint, 1972.

Aung, Shwe Zan, "An Introductory Essay to the Compendium of Buddhist Philosophy", *Compendium of Philosophy,* Pali Text Society, O.U.P., London, 1929.

Barish, Jonas A., *The Antitheatrical Prejudice*, Berkeley, University of California Press, 1981.

Bell, S., *Reading, Writing, and Rewriting the Prostitute Body,* Indiana U.P., 1994.

Bernbaum, Edwin M., "The Way of Symbols: The Use of Symbols in Tibetan Mysticism", *The Journal of Transpersonal Psychology,* Vol. 6., no 2, 1974.

Bethe, Monica and Brazell, Karen, *No as Performance,* Cornell U.P., 1978.

Bethe, Monica and Brazell, Karen, *Dance in the No Theatre*, Cornell U.P., 1982.

Beyer, Stephan, *The Cult of Tara. Magic and Ritual in Tibet,* University of California Press, 1973.

Blacker, Carmen, *The Catalpa Bow. A Study of Shamanistic Practices in Japan,* London, 1975.

Blofeld, John, *The Tantric Mysticism of Tibet,* New York, 1970.

Brook, Peter, *There are no Secrets,* London, 1993.

Buddhadasa Bhikku, *Heart-Wood from the Bo Tree,* Suan Mok, 1935.

Calinescu, M. and Fokkema, D., *Exploring Postmodernism,* Amsterdam and Philadelphia, 1987.

Cantwell, Cathy, "The Dance of the Guru's Eight Aspects", *The Tibet Journal,* Vol. 20, no. 4, 1995, pp. 47-63.

Carrithers, Michael, *The Forest Monks of Sri Lanka,* Oxford University Press, Delhi, 1983.

Ch'en, Kenneth K.S., *Buddhism in China. A Historical Survey,* Princeton U. P., 1964.

———, *Buddhism, the Light of Asia,* Baron's educational series, 1968.

———, *The Chinese Transformation of Buddhism,* Princeton, 1973.

Chandra, Pratap, *Metaphysics of Perpetual Change,* Bombay, New Delhi, 1978.

Chang, Garma C.C., *The Buddhist Teaching of Totality. The Philosophy of Hwa Yen Buddhism,* Penn State U.P., 1971.

Cleary, Thomas, *Entry Into The Inconceivable. An Introduction to Hua-Yen Buddhism,* University of Hawaii Press, 1982.

Colbath, A., *The Japanese Noh drama and its relation to Zen,* Ph.D. thesis, Western Reserve University, 1962.

Cole, T., and Chinoy, H.K. (eds.), *Actors on Acting,* London, 1949.

Collins, Steven, *Selfless Persons,* Cambridge U.P., 1982.

Connor, Steven, *Postmodern Culture: An Introduction to Theories of the Contemporary,* Oxford, 1989.

Conze, Edward, *Buddhist Thought in India,* University of Michigan Press, Ann Arbor, 1973.

———, *The Perfection of Wisdom in 8000 Lines,* Bolinas, California, 1973.

Corrigan, R.W., "The Search for New Endings: The Theatre in Search of a Fix, Part III", *Theatre Journal,* Vol. 36, no. 2, 1984, p. 160.

———, *The World of the Theatre,* Glenview, Illinois, 1979.

Covell, J.E.H.C., *Zen Gleanings,* Idyllwild, Cal., 1973.

Dalai Lama, *The Opening of the Wisdom-Eye,* Theosophical Publishing House, Wheaton, Illinois, 1972.

Dasgupta, Shashibhusun, *Obscure Religious Cults,* Calcutta, 1976.

Dayal, Har, *The Bodhisattva Doctrine in Buddhist Sanskrit Literature,* Motilal Banarsidass, Delhi, 1970.

de Marinis, Marco, *The Semiotics of Performance,* Indiana U.P., 1993.

de Nebesky-Wojkowitz, Rene, *Tibetan Religious Dances,* Paris, 1976.

———, *Oracles and Demons of Tibet,* Kathmandu, 1993.

de Silva, K.M., *A History of Sri Lanka,* O.U.P., 1981.

de Silva, Lily, "Sense Experience of the Liberated Being as reflected in early Buddhism", *Buddhist Philosophy and Culture,* ed. by D.J. Kalupahana and W.G. Weeraratne, Colombo, 1987.

Driessens, Georges (ed.), *The Preliminary Practices of Tibetan Buddhism,* Washington, 1974.

Duncan, Marion H., *Harvest Festival Dramas of Tibet,* Hong Kong, 1955.

Dutt, Sukumar, *Buddhism in East Asia,* New Delhi, 1966.

Ernst, E.R., *The Kabuki Theatre,* University of Hawaii Press, 1956.

Evans-Wentz, W.Y., *Tibetan Yoga and Secret Doctrines,* Oxford University Press, 1958.

Fantin, Mario, *Mani rimdu Nepal,* New Delhi, 1976.

Feral, J., "Performance and Theatricality: The Subject Demystified", *Modern Drama,* Vol. XXV, no. 1, 1982.

Fürer- Haimendorf, Christoph von, *The Sherpas of Nepal,* New Delhi, 1968.

Geiger, Wilhelm, *Culture of Ceylon in Medieval Times,*Wiesbaden, 1960.

George, D.E.R., *India: Three Ritual Dance-Dramas,* Cambridge, 1986.

———, "Performance as Paradigm: the Example of Bali", *Modern Drama,* 35, 1992.

———, "On Ambiguity", *Theatre Research International,* Vol. 14, no.1.

Godakumbura, C.E., *The Cult of the Kohomba,* R.A.S., 1946.

Gombrich, Richard F., *Theravada Buddhism,* London, 1988.

Goonatilleka, M.H., "Sanni Yakuma: its mythical dimensions and religious interaction", *Ananda. Papers on Buddhism and Indology,* ed. by Y. Karunadasa, Colombo, 1990.

Govinda, Lama Anagarika, *Foundations of Tibetan Mysticism,* Bombay, 1977.

Govinda, *The Way of the White Clouds,* Shambhala, Berkeley, California, 1970.

Gray, S., "About Three Places in Rhode Island", *TDR, The Drama Review,* Vol. 23, no. 1, 1979.

Gregory, Peter N. (ed.), *Sudden and Gradual. Approaches to Enlightenment in Chinese Thought,* University of Hawaii Press, Honolulu, 1987.

Gudmunsen, Chris, *Wittgenstein and Buddhism*, MacMillan, London, 1977.

Guenther, Herbert V., *Buddhist Philosophy In Theory and Practice,* Penguin Books, London, 1971.

Gundert, W., *Der Schintoismus im japanischen No-Drama,* Tokyo, 1925.

Hall, J.W. and Takeshi, T., *Japan in the Muromachi Age,* University of California Press, 1977.

Hardison,O.B., *Christian rite and Christian drama in the Middle Ages,* Johns Hopkins Press, 1965.

Hare, T.B., *Zeami's Style. The Noh Plays of Zeami Motokiyo,* Stanford U.P., 1986.

Harvey, D., *The Condition of Postmodernity: An Enquiry into the Origins of Cultural Change,* Oxford, 1989.

Heuvel, Michael Vanden, *Performing Drama / Dramatizing Performance. Alternative Theater and the Dramatic Text,* University of Michigan Press, Ann Arbor, 1991.

Hoff, R. and Flindt, W., "The Life Structure of Noh", *Concerned Theatre Japan,* Vol. II, nos. 3 and 4.

Hoover, Thomas, *Zen Culture,* London, 1988.

Hume, David, *A Treatise on Human Nature,* ed. by L.A. Selby-Bigge, Oxford, 1888.

Inoura, Yoshinobu, *A History of Japanese Theater,* Japan Cultural Society, 1971.

Iyer, P. Sarvesvara, "Puranic Saivism in Ceylon during the Polunnaruva Period", *Proceedings of the First Conference — Seminar of Tamil Studies,* K.L., 1968, Vol. 1.

Jayasuriya, W.J., *The Psychology and Philosophy of Buddhism. An Introduction to the Abhidhamma,* Colombo, 1963.

Jerstad, Luther G., *Mani-rimdu,* University of Washington Press, 1976.

Johansson, Rune E.A., *The Dynamic Psychology of Early Buddhism,* Curzon Press, Oxford, 1979.

———, *The Psychology of Nirvana,* London, 1969.

Kalupahana, David J., *Causality: The Central Philosophy of Buddhism,* University Press of Hawaii, Honolulu, 1975.

Kalupahana, David J., *The Mulamadhyamakakarika of Nagarjuna,* Motilal Banarsidass, New Delhi, 1991.

Kant, Immanuel, *Prolegomena to Any Future Metaphysics,* Indianapolis, 1950.

Kanze Hideo, "Noh Business", *Concerned Theatre Japan,* Vol. 1, no. 4, 1971.

Kapferer, Bruce, *A Celebration of Demons,* Indiana U.P., Bloomington, 1983.

———, "First Class to Maradana. Secular Drama in Sinhalese Healing Rites", *Secular Ritual,* ed. by Sally Falk and Barbara Myerhoff, Assen, Netherlands, 1977.

Katz, Nathan (ed.), *Buddhist and Western Philosophy,* New Delhi, 1981.

Kaufmann, Walter (ed.), *The Portable Nietzsche,* Penguin Books, 1976.

Kaye, N., *Postmodernism and Performance,* London, 1994.

Kidder, J. Edward, *Early Buddhist Japan,* London, 1972.

Kim Hee-Jin, *Dogen Kigen Mystical Realist,* University of Arizona Press, Tucson, 1987.

Kindermann, H. (ed.), *Fernöstliches Theater,* Stuttgart, 1966.

Kirby, E.T., *Ur-Drama,* N.Y.U. Press, 1975.

Kite, Bill and Childs, Geoff *Myths, Mountains and Mandalas,* Tengpoche Trust, 1988.

Kiyota, Minoru (ed.), *Mahayana Buddhist Meditation. Theory and Practice,* University of Hawaii Press, 1978.

Klein, Anne Carolyn, *Meeting the Great Bliss Queen,* Beacon Press, Boston, 1995.

Kohn, Richard, "Destroyer of Illusion", produced by Franz-Christoph Giercke and distributed by Sky Walker Productions, 1989.

Kohn, Richard J., *Mani Rimdu. Text and Tradition in a Tibetan ritual,* Ph.D. dissertation, University of Wisconsin, Madison, 1988.

Komparu, Kunio, *The Noh Theater. Principles and Perspectives,* Tokyo and New York, 1983.

Kornfield, Jack, *Living Buddhist Masters,* Unity Press, Santa Cruz, 1977.

Ku, Hung-ting, *The influence of Zen on Noh plays in Japan,* Singapore, 1976.

Kushwaha, M.S. (ed.), *Indian Poetics and Western Thought*, Lucknow, 1988.

Lankavatara Sutra, tr. by D.T. Suzuki, Routledge, London, 1952.

Laughlin, Charles D. Jr., McManus, John and d'Aquili, Eugene G., "Mature Contemplation", *Zygon. Journal of Religion and Science*, Vol. 28. No. 2, London, 1967.

Luckmann, Thomas, *Phenomenology and Sociology*, Penguin, 1978.

Lyman, S.M. and Scott, M.B., *The Drama of Social Reality*, Oxford U.P., 1975.

Makulloluwa, W.B., *Dances of Sri Lanka*, Colombo, N.D.

Mair, Victor H., *T'ang Transformation Texts*, Harvard U.P., 1989.

Malalgoda, Kitsiri, *Buddhism in Sinhalese Society 1750-1900*, University of California Press, 1976.

Marko, Ann, "Cham: Ritual as Myth in a Ladakhi Gompa", in *Tantra and Popular Religion in Tibet*, ed. by G. Samuel, H. Gregor and E. Stutchbury, New Delhi, 1994.

Marranca, Bonnie, *Theatrewritings,* Performing Arts Journal Publications, New York, 1984.

Masson J.L. and Patwardhan, M.V., *Santarasa and Abhinavagupta's Philosophy of Aesthetics*, Poona, 1969.

Matsunaga, Alicia, *The Buddhist Philosophy of Assimilation*, Tokyo, 1969.

Matsunaga, Daigan and Alicia, *Foundations of Japanese Buddhism*, Los Angeles and Tokyo, 1974-76.

McGovern, W.M., *A Manual of Buddhist Philosophy*, Chinese Materials Center, San Francisco, 1977.

Mishra, Hari Ram, *The Theory of Rasa in Sanskrit Drama*, Bhopal, 1964.

Molamure, Arthur H.E., "Aspects of the Kohomba Kankariya", *Ceylon Journal of Historical and Social Studies*, Peradeniya, January 1958.

Mookerjee, Satkari, *The Buddhist Philosophy of Universal Flux*, Motilal Banarsidass, New Delhi, 1975.

Moore, C.A. (ed.), *The Status of the Individual in East and West*, University of Hawaii Press, Honolulu, 1968.

Mudiyanse, Nandasena, *Mahayana Monuments in Ceylon*, Gunasena and Co., Colombo, 1967.

Nakamura, Y., *Noh. The Classical Theatre*, New York and Tokyo, 1971.

Nandi, T., *The Origin and Development of the Theory of Rasa and Dhvani in Sanskrit Poetics*, Ahmedabad, 1973.

Nash, M. (ed.), *Anthropological Studies in Theravada Buddhism*, Cultural Report Series, no. 13, Yale U.P., 1966.

Nearman, M.J., "Zeami's Kyui", in *Monumenta Nipponica*, V. 33, 1978.

Norbu, Namyang, *Zlos-Gar Performing Traditions of Tibet*, Dharamasala, 1986.

O'Flaherty, W.D., *Karma and Rebirth in Classical Indian Tradition*, University of California Press, 1980.

O'Neill, P.G., *Early No Drama*, Westport, Conn, 1958.

Odin, Steve, *Process Metaphysics and Hua-Yen Buddhism*, State University of New York Press, Albany, 1982.

Ono, *Shinto. The Kami Way*, Tokyo, 1962.

Ortolani, B., "Zeami's Aesthetics of the No and Audience Participation", *Educational Theatre Journal*, Vol. 24, no. 2, May, 1972.

Paranavitana, S., "Mahayanism in Ceylon", *Ceylon Journal of Science*, Vol. 2, Pt. 1, 1928.

———., *The Story of Sigiri*, Colombo, 1972.

Park, Sung Bae, *Buddhist Faith and Sudden Enlightenment*, State University of New York Press, 1983.

Paul, Robert A., *The Sherpas of Nepal in the Tibetan Cultural Context*, Delhi, 1989.

Pavis, P., "The Classical Heritage of Modern Drama: The Case of Postmodern Theatre", *Modern Drama*, Vol. XXIX, no. 1, 1986.

Peters, S.J., "Modern to Postmodern Acting and Directing: An Historical Perspective", Ph. D. Diss., Texas Tech, 1986.

Phelan, P., *Unmarked. The Politics of Performance*, London and New York, 1993.

Pontbriand, C., "The eye finds no fixed point on which to rest . . .", *Modern Drama*, Vol. 25, no. 1, 1982.

Prasad, H.S., *Essays on Time in Buddhism*, Delhi, 1991.

Prebish, Charles S. (ed.), *Buddhism. A Modern Perspective*, Penn State University, 1975.

Pye, Michael, *Skilful Means: A Concept in Mahayana Buddhism*, London, 1978.

Raghavan, M. D., *Sinhala Natum. Dances of the Sinhalese*, Colombo, 1967.

Rahula, Walpola, *History of Buddhism in Ceylon*, Colombo, 1966.

Raz, J., *Audience and Actors,* Leiden (Brill)., 1983.

Renondeau, G., *Le Bouddhisme dans le No*, Tokyo, 1950.

Ross, Joanna, *Lhamo. Opera from the Roof of the World*, Paljor Publications, New Delhi, 1995.

Samuel, G., Gregor H. and Stutchbury, E. (eds.), *Religion in Tibet*, New Delhi, 1994.

Sangharakshita Bhikshu, *The Three Jewels: An Introduction to Buddhism*, London, 1967.

Sarathchandra, E.R., *The Folk Drama of Ceylon*, Colombo, 2nd edn, 1966.

Saunders, E. Dale, *Buddhism in Japan*, University of Pennsylvania Press, 1964.

Schechner, Richard, *The End of Humanism*, New York, 1984.

———, *Between Theater and Anthropology*, University of Pennsylvania Press, 1985.

———, *Performance Theory*, London, 1988.

———, *The Future of Ritual*, London and new York, 1993.

Schmitt, Natalie Crohn, "Theorizing about Performance: Why Now?", *National Theater Quarterly*, 7, no. 23, 1990.

Schrempf, Mona, *Der sakrale Maskentanz der Tibeter am Beispiel des Yak Sang 'Cham im Kloster Dzongkar Choede*, M.A. Dissertation, Berlin, 1990.

Scott, A.C., "Reflections on the Aesthetic Background of the Performing Arts of East Asia", *Asian Music*, Vol. VI, nos. 1 and 2, 1975

Seami, *Kadensho*, Tokyo, 1968.

Seneviratna, A., "Kandyan Dance", in *Sangeet Natak*, 32, 1974, pp. 5-25.

———, "Kohomba Kankariya", in *Senarat Paranavitana Commemoration Volume*, Leiden, 1978, pp. 204-14.

Shimazaki, Chifumi, *The Noh, Vol. I. God Noh*, Tokyo, 1972.

Shively, D. H., "Buddhahood for the Nonsentient: a theme in No plays", *Harvard Journal of Asiatic Studies*, Vol. 20, June, 1957, pp. 135-61.

Sieffert, R., *La tradition secrète du Nô*, Paris, 1960.

Smith, A.C.H., *Orghast at Persepolis*, NewYork, 1972.

Snellgrove, D.L., *Buddhist Himalaya*, Oxford, 1957.

Sogen, Yamakami, *Systems of Buddhistic Thought*, Chinese Materials Centre, San Francisco, 1976.

Sopa, Geshe Lhundrup and Hopkins, Jeffrey, *Practice and Theory of Tibetan Buddhism*, Grove Press, New York, 1976.

Sources of Japanese Traditions, ed. by Tsunoda, de Bary and Keene, Columbia U.P., 1958.

Spae, J.J., *Shinto Man*, Tokyo, 1972.

Stanislavski, K., *Building a Character*, Methuen, London, 1979.

Stcherbatsky, T.I., *The Central Conception of Buddhism*, London, Royal Asiatic Society, 1928.

Stcherbatsky, Th., *The Conception of Buddhist Nirvana*, New York, 1973.

Stevenson, Leslie, *The Metaphysics of Experience*, Oxford, 1982.

Storry, R., *The Way of the Samurai*, London, 1978.

Suzuki, D. T., *Essays in Zen Buddhism*, London, 1949-53.

———, *Zen and Japanese Culture*, Princeton U. P., 1959.

Tamba, Akira, *La Structure Musicale du No*, Paris, 1974.

Tatz, Mark, *Difficult Beginnings, Three Works On the Bodhisattva Path*, Shambhala, Boston and London, 1983.

The Noh Drama, Ten Plays from the Japanese, Tuttle, Tokyo, 1955.

Thornhill, Arthur H. III, *Six Circles, One Dewdrop. The Religio-Aesthetic World of Komparu Zenchiku*, Princeton University Press, 1993.

Trungpa, Chögyam, *Journey Without Goal. The Tantric Wisdom of the Buddha*, Shambhala, Boston and London, 1985.

Tsung, Kok Cheng, *Meditation as Performance*, unpublished Honours thesis, Murdoch University, Western Australia, 1995.

Tucci, G., *Tibetan Painted Scrolls*, Rome, 1949.

———, *Minor Buddhist Texts,* Rome, 1956.

———, *The Religions of Tibet*, University of California Press, Berkeley and Los Angeles, 1980.

Varela, Francisco, J. Evan Thompson and Eleanor Rosch, *The Embodied Mind*, M. I. T. Press, Cambridge, Mass., 1991.

Vyas, C.S., *Buddhist Theory of Perception*, Navrang, New Delhi, 1991.

Waddell, L. A., *The Buddhism of Tibet or Lamaism,* 2nd edn, Heffer and Sons, Cambridge, 1971 (first published 1894).

Waley, Arthur, *The No plays of Japan,* New York, 1957.

Wayman, Alex, *Calming the Mind and Discerning the Real. Buddhist Meditation and the Middle Way*, New York, 1978.

Welbon, Guy Richard, *The Buddhist Nirvana and Its Western Interpreters*, University of Chicago Press, 1968.

Wells, H.W., *The Classical Drama of the Orient*, New York, 1965.

Wijesekera, Nandadeva, *Deities and Demons Magic and Masks*, Part I, Colombo, 1987.

Zangbu, Ngawang Tenzin, *Stories and Customs of the Sherpas*, Khumbu Cultural Conservation Committee, Kathmandu, 1988.

Zeami, *On the Art of the No Drama: The Major Treatises of Zeami*, ed. by Thomas Rimer and Yamazaki Masakuza, Princeton U.P., 1984.

Zürcher, E., *The Buddhist Conquest of China*, Leiden (E.J. Brill), 1972.

Index